THIS BOOK
BELONGS TO

....

....

Table of Contents

Mark Boucher - Short-Term Trading Course 01. Money Management.doc	3
Mark Boucher - Short-Term Trading Course 02. Relative Strength.doc	29
Mark Boucher - Short-Term Trading Course 03. Characteristics of Runaway Markets.doc	47
Mark Boucher - Short-Term Trading Course 04. Liquidity Cycles.doc	75
Mark Boucher - Short-Term Trading Course 05. Top Market Indicators.doc	94
Mark Boucher - Short-Term Trading Course 06. Market Selection.doc	131
Mark Boucher - Short-Term Trading Course 07. Best Short-Term & Long-Term Patterns.doc	160
Mark Boucher - Short-Term Trading Course 08. Market Timing Models.doc	185
Mark Boucher - Short-Term Trading Course 09. The Foundations of Trading Success.doc	198
Mark Boucher - Short-Term Trading Course 10. Putting It All Together.doc	210

Week 1: Money Management

How much do you know about Money Management?

As we begin the course, I thought it would be fun and informative to start this week's topic with a **short quiz**. The purpose of this is to help you to evaluate your strengths and weaknesses so that you know exactly what issues you have to concentrate the most on. Are you ready? Let's go!

Begin the quiz

1. It's important to use a stop-loss the vast majority of the time. But there are certain market conditions under which you should not use a stop-loss. Which of the following are they:

   a) Immediately after I've entered a trade

   b) A highly volatile market

   c) Runaway markets

   d) All of the above

   e) None of the above

The correct answer is: e) None of the above.

You should use stop-losses no matter what.

Find out why in Rules 1, 2, 4, 5, and 6.

2. If I made a series of bad trades and my account losses 70% of its value, I have to show a return of how much before I get back to break-even?

   a) 45%

   b) 70%

   c) 140%

   d) 230%

The correct answer is: d) 230%

Large losses can have a devastating affect on your recovery ability. That's why it's important to never have them in the first place.

Find out more about this in Rules 1, 2, 4, 5, and 6.

3. True or False: If a trading strategy has earned an average annual return of 120%, it's average maximum drawdown is irrelevant because no matter how large it is, the strategy will always make up for it.

The correct answer is: False.

Drawdown is always important and can affect your profit potential dramatically no matter what the "average total return" is.

Find out more about this in Rules 1, 2, and 3.

4. The world's most successful traders do which of the following most often:

    a) **Buy at market bottoms and sell at market tops**

    b) **Trade in the direction of trends of the strongest or weakest markets**

The correct answer is: b). The world's most successful traders trade in the direction of trends in the strongest or weakest markets.

Find out more about this in Rules 12, 13, 16, and 17.

Next Question

5. True or False: A stock's fundamentals (or business outlook) are irrelevant to short-term traders. That is, a short-term trader should only look at technical factors when deciding whether or not to take a trade, not a company's balance sheet

The answer is False.

Find out more about this in Money Management Rule 3, Trade With Fuel on Your Side

6. If you want to improve your results as a trader, your main goal should be which one of the following:

   a) To understand the markets

   b) To develop a set of mechanical trading rules, which back-tested over a period of years, produces maximum returns

   c) To read articles in trading publications to find trading systems that meet your minimum profit objectives

It is most important to understand the markets so that no matter what happens, you'll know what trading strategies work and which don't work. Find out more about this in Money Management Rule 3.

Next Question

7. Take a look at the following table:

Year	Trader A Annual Returns(%)	Trader B Annual Returns (%)
1	21	18
2	35	18
3	20	18
4	-26	18
5	32	18
6	12	18
7	42	18
8	-16	18
9	31	18
10	56	18

Trader A: Average Annual Return = 20.7%
Trader B: Average Annual Return = 18%

Which trader made the most money by the 10th year?

   a) Trader A

b) Trader B

Trader B made more money. Find out why in Money Management Rule 2.

That's it for the questions. I hope you found this quiz enjoyable. Now let's get started and learn more about Money Management.

Enter the Course

Week 1: Money Management: The Real Holy Grail

Fellow Traders:

A key component to successful trading is **proper money management.**

Traders, in general, spend far too much time and effort trying to find magical systems or methodologies that produce high returns, rather than increasing their understanding of the markets and using astute money management to apply what they learn.

I agree with Stanley Kroll who once said:

> **"It is better to have a mediocre system and good money management than an excellent system and poor money management."**

In this first week of our 10-week course, I'm going to teach you **everything** I've learned about the discipline of money management in the past 17 years of trading and fund management. You'll not only review some familiar rules, but also learn about some powerful principles that go way beyond just cutting your losses short and letting your profits run. Even though these principles can make you a lot of money, I doubt that you'll hear very many fund managers or system vendors talking about them in their ads because they know that the public is drawn toward glitzy performance numbers--not risk control.

But, if you want to know the real truth about what it takes to be a successful trader, be assured that I won't pull any punches.

Now let's get started. The first three rules are what I consider to be the most important. Without them, everything falls apart. I consider them to be the very foundation my success as a trader.

The first one is:

Rule 1: Minimize Losses!

As simple as it sounds, **failure to keep losses small is the #1 reason why most traders blow out early in the game**. That almost happened to me, in fact.

When I first started trading, I bought call options on gold stocks right before the big explosion in Gold prices in 1979. In less than a year I made 500% on my money. I thought I knew everything. But then my real education started.

In 1981, I got caught short Orange Juice during a series of limit-up moves that lasted more than a week. By the time I exited, I had lost nearly half of my account. It was at this point that I realized the importance of limiting my losses.

Very few traders understand the mathematics of losses and risk. But I believe that just understanding the following concept can turn a losing trader into a winning one because it can help you to focus on doing the right things and turn you away from the wrong things.

Here is the concept that I strongly suggest you chew on for awhile:

- **When you lose money in trading, you wind up having less capital to work with. Therefore, to make back what you lost you have to earn a substantially higher percentage return than what you lost.**

Example: If you make a series of bad trades and your account drops 70% in value, you will not get back to your break-even point until you have made over 230% on your remaining money!

That doesn't sound fair does it? You'd think that if your account dropped 70%, you'd be at the break-even point again when you've made 70%. Sorry, but this is not reality. A trader who loses 20% or more must show a return of 30% to make up for the loss. It can take a year or more for even the best traders I know to produce such a return.

This is one of the principles that keeps many losing traders from digging themselves out of the hole they've dug for themselves. They lose a big chunk of money and, even if their skill improves, they are not able to recover unless they add more money to their trading account--usually from their hard-earned paychecks or credit cards.

As I studied the qualities of successful traders, the concept of weighing risk and reward hit home. Trading performance meant more to me than just shooting for big gains; it meant looking closely at the risks I was willing to take to make those gains.

Indeed, as I studied the qualities that the most successful traders have in common, **I noticed that most strived to keep their draw-downs to around 20% to 30% or less.**

When you trade, you always have to be conscious of the dangers of suffering big losses. You not only lose the money, but you also have the potential to be knocked out of the game permanently. Realizing this will produce a fear in you that I assure you will be quite healthy. That fear will help you to remember to keep your position sizes small and to apply trailing stops religiously.

Winning traders minimize losses.

Rule 2: Consistency is the Key

For most individual traders and investors, the single most important criteria for judging the performance of a trading methodology is total return. Consequently, when you look at ads selling trading systems and methodologies, you see a lot of wild claims of 80%, 100%, or even 300% average annual rate of return.

It's ironic that in talking to the vast majority of traders who've made their millions through trading, **total return is the very last number they look at** when judging the viability of a trading strategy. What matters more to this elite class of trader is risk, maximum draw-down, the duration of draw-downs, volatility, and a wide assortment of other risk-oriented benchmarks. Only when all their risk criteria is met do they consider total return.

The typical trader might wonder if these traders are just overly cautious and conservative. But that is simply not the case. As a whole, they are just as fanatical about the accumulation of wealth and financial freedom as anyone else who trades.

What has caused these traders to shift their focus to this winning strategy is that they've worked through the numbers. Doing so, they find:

- **Total return is only a valid measure of performance when risk is taken into consideration.**

I credit my success as a money manager to my voracious study and practice of this concept. Let me show you a simple example that you may find surprising. Even though I use investment funds in my example, this concept I'm illustrating is directly applicable to all traders no matter how short-term their orientation is:

1. Over the past 30 years, investment **Fund A has returned 12 percent annually on average**, has a strategy that is not dependent on any particular market doing well, and has had a **5 percent worst-case historical drawdown.**
2. Over the past 30 years, investment **Fund B has returned 17 percent annually on average**, has had performance highly correlated with U.S. stock indexes, and has had a **15 percent worst-cast historical drawdown** (both investments are vastly superior to the S & P).

Which fund would you invest in?

Most traders and investors would be most attracted to Fund B, which showed greater total returns over the 30 year period. In justifying this they'd say: "I have no problem accepting a worst-case 15 percent hit because I'll come out ahead in the end. The extra protection in the Fund A doesn't help me that much.

Now--check this out. Most professional traders who **understand the math** would select Fund A. With the lower maximum drawdown, they would simply concentrate more fire power in Fund A by buying it on margin (putting 50 percent down). Doing this they were earn a 19 percent annual return after margin costs and sustain only a 10 percent expected drawdown risk, compared with a 17 percent return on Fund B with a 15 percent expected risk.

But there's even more to it.

The Smoke and Mirrors Behind Average Annual Returns

Whenever any trader, trading system vendor, or money manager brags about their performance in terms of Annual Average Return, they are--whether or not they know it--engaging in smoke and mirrors.

What is concealed in this statistic is the harm that is wreaked upon capital growth by drawdowns and losing streaks. In Rule #1, "Minimize Losses," we talked about how the difficulty of making up for a large trading loss is seemingly disproportionate to the magnitude of the error that caused the loss in the first place. That factors greatly into how much money you wind up making.

The real truth behind how much money you make is to be found in "Compounded Annual Return." That is, calculate your annual return by adding every gain and subtracting every loss that occurs during the course of a year. This is illustrated in the following table:

Let's consider the following table:

Year	Volatile Returns Annual Returns(%)	Principal	Dependable Gains Annual	Principal

			Return (%)	
1	21	1,210,000	18	1,180,000
2	35	1,6333,500	18	1,392,400
3	20	1,960,200	18	1,643,030
4	-26	1,450,500	18	1,938,780
5	32	1,914,720	18	2,287,760
6	12	1,347,450	18	2,699,560
7	42	3,045,170	18	3,185,480
8	-16	2,557,950	18	3,750,887
9	31	3,350,910	18	4,435,460
10	56	5,233,000	18	5,233,850

Average Annual Return = 20.7%   **Average Annual Return = 18%**

Compound Annual Return = 17.98%   **Compound Annual Rate = 18%**

As you can see, the fund that makes a steady 18% per year actually makes you more money than the one that posts spectacular gains eight out of ten years. The damage caused by the two losing years is quite evident.

Again, this example is applicable whether you are a day trader or a long-term investor.

The vast majority of trading strategies that boast spectacular gains, also take great risks. This means greater drawdowns and more volatile performance. To be successful as a trader, you must ignore the flashy statistics and work through the numbers. Evaluate your strategy by calculating on paper where your total trading equity would hypothetically be for every trade over a period of several years.

You will find that it is far, far better to use strategies that earn steady and consistent returns year after year after year. You will inevitably find that the annual returns of these strategies are far less spectacular than those that are widely advertised, but the math makes it clear that you are far more likely to be laughing your way to the bank this way.

Oh yes, you'll sleep better at night now. For successful traders, **consistency is the key.**

Rule 3: Understanding the Markets is Much More Important Than Methodology

Many traders are fixated on finding the Holy Grail, that is, a mechanical trading system or methodology which generates large and consistent profits with no discretionary judgment on the part of the trader.

Most traders who read this will deny they are looking for the Holy Grail, stating that they'd be happy with a mechanical system offering only a 60% win to loss ratio as opposed to the 80% to 90% that is claimed in many ads--as long as the system makes them a millionaire within a year to two.

I would, without hesitation, say that anybody in search of an enduringly profitable trading system that makes all your trading decisions for you is in search of the Holy Grail. In other words, such a money making machine simply does not exist.

But wait, you may say--"aren't all the highly successful traders in the world using some kind of unique methodology or system? Why can't I simply use the same exact approach they are and become just as successful?"

The answer is this: **The markets are always changing. All trading strategies go through seasons of winning and losing.** The key to long-term success is to understand the markets well enough so that you know how to adjust or switch strategies or even develop new ones in response to changing market conditions. Focus on systems and you may make money for awhile, but eventually you'll give it all back (and more). **Focus on true understanding and you will be well on the way to consistent trading success.**

What "Understanding" Is

You may wonder what I mean by "understanding." "Understanding" is the pot of gold that comes through your skills as a trader and on your ability to consistently find ways to limit your risks while participating in opportunities that have much more reward than the risk you are taking. It is the ability to see a strategy as nothing more than a tool and see when it's applicable and when it's not.

In short, the pot of gold does not lie in some system outside of yourself; it lies in the set of skills and degree of understanding and insight that you build within.

A True Story to Illustrate My Point

The **Master Trader** strives for understanding. The **Novice Trader** searches in vain for magical systems.

In closing this section, let me share a true story with you that will graphically illustrate my point:

In the mid-eighties, I met two traders who had attended a seminar by a very well known and reputable trader. These two traders did not know each other, but coincidentally, they both learned and applied the same system.

The first trader was the **Novice Trader**.

He began to trade the system in 1986 and was shocked at how much money he made. He was anxious to commit more capital to it, but wanted my opinion first. I back-tested the system and found that it had an identical performance to what was claimed in the seminar. However, I explained to this trader that I had three serious reservations. First, there was no stop-loss protection. Secondly, even though the system showed phenomenal gains in its four years of testing, that was not a sufficient time frame in which to evaluate the system properly. Third, the system was tested during a bull market. I didn't think it would perform well during a bear market.

To address these concerns, I suggested that the trader employ stop-losses and trend filters. This would have cut the total hypothetical profits during the four year testing period and hence, likely reduce future profits. The trader, however, did not heed my advice and left my office intending to continue trading the system "as is."

This trader's confidence in the system continued to build over the next several months as he made a fortune by racking up steady and consistent profits month after month. ***On October 17, 1987, the day of the great market crash, this trader was completely wiped out.***

A few months later after the crash, I was talking to another trader. This trader was one I'd call a **Master Trader.**

I found out that he had attended the same seminar spoken about above and that he had been exploiting the same strategy as the Novice Trader, but in contrast, he'd been successful using it, despite the 1987 crash.

I noticed that this trader had not taken the system's signals on October 27, nor during the entire October-November 1987 period. He explained to me anyone with a true understanding of the markets would not be applying the system during that period. He thought the system was good at identifying opportunities, but he'd only exploit them if he could limit risk with a stop-loss and in an upward trending market. That was not the case during that period.

The Novice Trader focused on the "system" and not "understanding the markets." In so doing, he assumed that the system was infallible and he was not able to anticipate the market environment that would usher in the system's inevitable season of loss. *The Novice Trader wanted to find a fishing hole where the fish were always biting.*

The Master Trader was simply looking for ideas that help him increase his understanding. He didn't consider what he learned at the seminar to be a "system", but rather, it was knowledge that he could use to find more low-risk, high reward opportunities. There was no way he would use it without fully understanding it so that he'd know the conditions under which it applied best and when it might not apply. The Master Trader was looking for another way to find a fishing hole where the fish might be biting for a while.

Winning traders seek to understand the markets and not to find magical systems.

Now let's move on to my more general money management rules.

Rule 4: Always use Open Protective Stops (OPS)

An Open Protective Stop (OPS) is an open order to exit a long or short position should prices move against you to a specified price. OPS's act as insurance against an unusually large loss, though the actual fill price may be less favorable where fast moving markets squeeze liquidity or when, in futures, limit moves cease market trading before the OPS is executed.

Before you enter any order, always determine the maximum risk you want to take. I call this Theoretical Risk. Theoretical risk is the distance between your entry price and your OPS. As shown in Figure 1, if you get into a stock at 10 and place an OPS at 8, your theoretical risk is (10-8) = 2 points. Winning traders know it's important to not only use OPS's but also, position them so that the theoretical risk is kept at 2 percent of capital or less. For example, if you have a $1,000,000 account, you should only risk $20,000 per trade in a theoretical risk.

The use of OPS goes hand-in-hand with overall trading strategies. Therefore, I will delve into more detail about OPS techniques in Week 7 in which I discuss specific patterns I use and how to trade them.

Figure 1:

1) Initial Open Protective Stop (OPS). I placed it here because it is at a level of recent major support.

2) The initial buy order was placed after an upside breakout from a trading range.

Source: Quote.com QCharts

Rule 5: Always Use Trailing OPS's to Lock in Profits as a Trade Moves in Your Favor

A Trailing OPS is a method by which you shift a stop order to liquidate your position as price moves away from your original entry point. A Trailing OPS for a long position would follow the market up as it moves higher, so that if the market moves down from its highest level a certain amount, one would automatically take profits. As the price moves up, your stop order trails the market by moving up with it. A trailing OPS for a short position trails the market down by moving lower as prices make new lows.

After you've entered a position and price moves significantly in your favor, it will often consolidate and trade for a short while in a narrow trading range. If it breaks through that range, it's time to move your OPS to the next support level established by that consolidation. This way you are protecting profits as price moves up just as you were when you first entered the trade.

I will delve into more detail about OPS techniques in Week 7 in which I discuss specific patterns I use and how to trade them.

Rule 6: Always Let the Market's Own Price Action Determine Where An OPS is Placed

The trader should not just randomly select where an OPS is placed; that level should be determined by patterns that occur as the price action unfolds. Doing so requires a knowledge of basic chart patterns which I will discuss in Week 7. The main thing to remember here is that markets tend to trend in stair-step fashion. That is, they will move in a fast spurt, pause or consolidate, and then spurt again.

Each time the market resumes the trend from one of these consolidations, it establishes a new threshold which, as long as the trend continues, will not be penetrated. This threshold becomes a support level. For this reason, these levels make ideal points at which to move your trailing OPS's.

Figure 3:

1) Initial OPS.

2) Buy order executed here.

3) Trailing stop moved to this level once price has broken through previous resistance. Resistance levels, once penetrated, usually become support.

Rule 7: Use Creeping Commitment

Creeping Commitment is the process of increasing you position size as a trade moves in your favor.

Start with a small position and buy more as your trailing stop eliminates the risk to your initial capital. Let's say we bought a stock at 10 with an OPS at 8 and that stock makes a fast move to 14 where it makes a brief consolidation. The consolidation may prove to be another buy signal which may allow you to buy more stock. You can, at this point, increase the size of your position as long as your trailing stop is above your entry price so that there is no Theoretical Risk on the initial purchase.

In this manner, our **commitment to a trade creeps higher as price moves in our favor**.

Figure 4:

1) We bought into this stock.

2) Our initial stop was placed here.

3) Trailing stop was moved here once price touched the 14 level

4) While this could have been a potential point at which to buy more stock, we don't because our trailing stop at 3) is below our initial entry at 1).

5) Once price moves to new highs we move our trailing stop to 5).

6) We add to our position here (we buy more stock).

I'll explain points 7) through 9) in Rule 8.

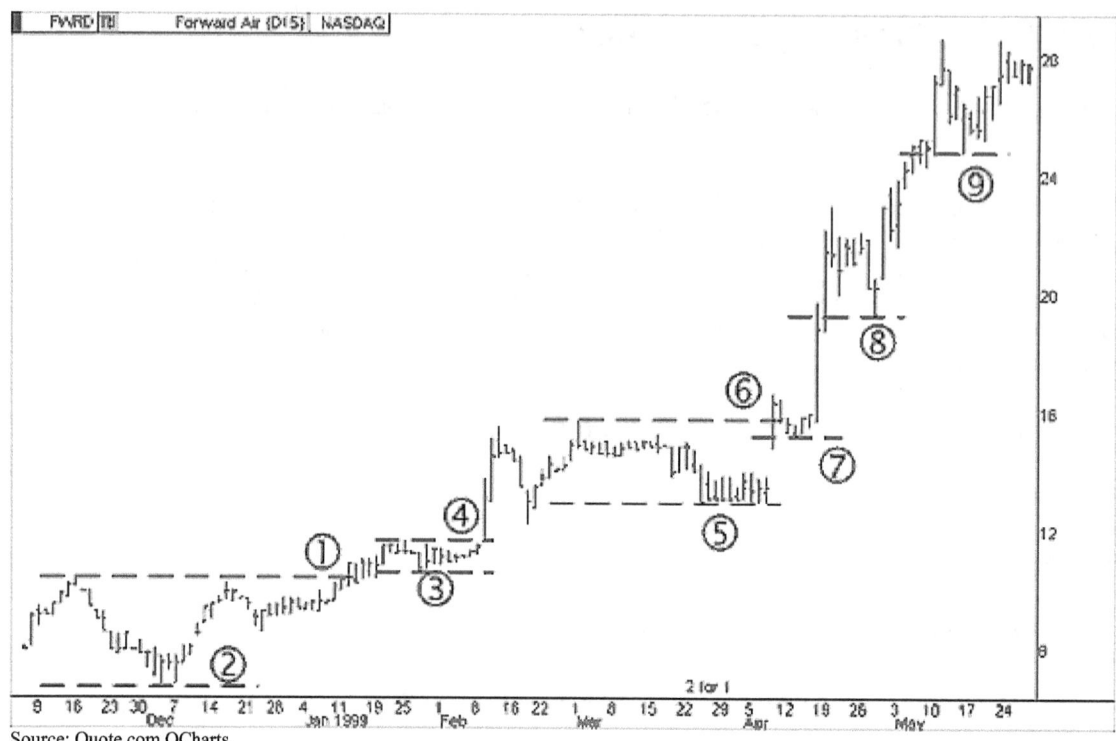

Source: Quote.com QCharts

In Week 7, I will describe a number of criteria, which further refines the process of whether or not to increase your position size.

Rule 8: Let Your Profits Run

I advocate trading in runaway markets. In such instances, the stock or futures market you're positioned in will often continue moving much longer than you originally thought. Getting into these markets and then staying positioned in strong trends until I get stopped out is my bread and butter approach.

Figure 5

1) We bought into this stock.

2) Our initial stop was placed here.

3) Trailing stop was moved here once price touched the 14 level

4) While this could have been a potential point at which to buy more stock, we don't because the our trailing stop at 3) is below our initial entry at 1).

5) Once price moves to new highs we move our trailing stop to 5).

6) We add to our position here (we buy more stock).

7), 8), and 9) show each successive potential trailing stop point as directed by price action. In each instance, we move the trailing stop to the next level of demonstrated support or resistance. It is important to also consider tightening your stops. That is, move your stops closer to the current price action in order to lock in a better profit. This is a more conservative strategy that can be employed in more volatile markets.

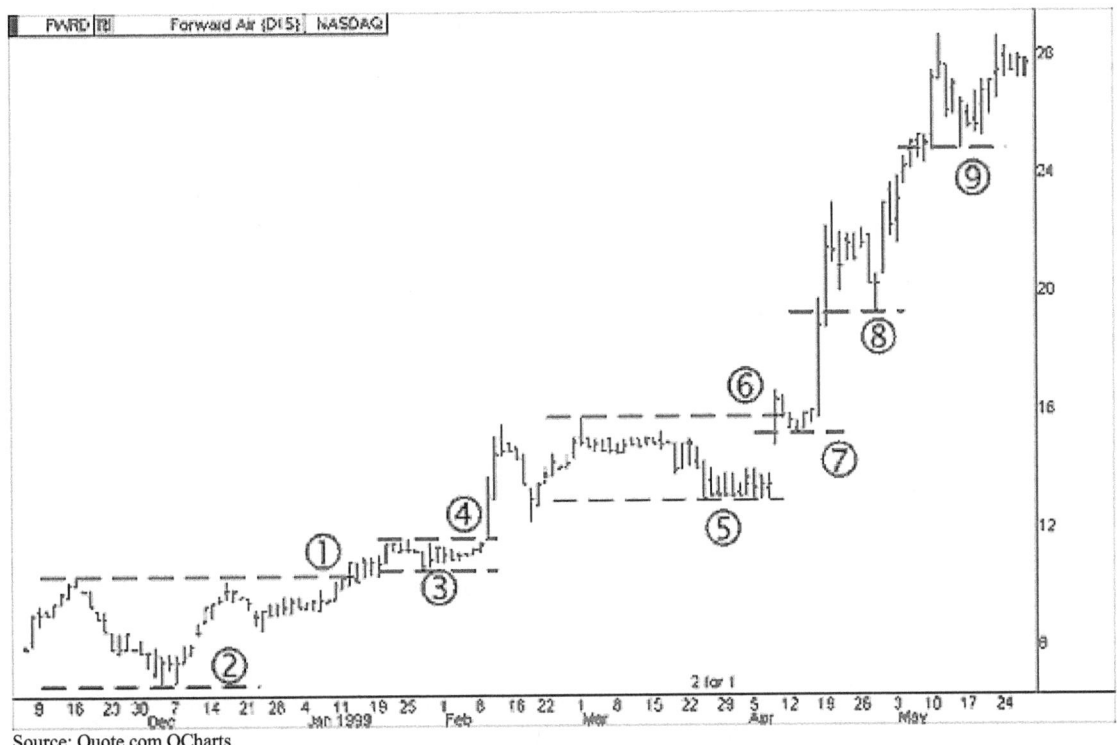

Source: Quote.com QCharts

Rule 9: When in Doubt, Stay Out or Get Out; Do Not Get Back in Until You are Sure About a Position

You should only enter a trade when all technical factors, patterns, valuation, and a host of other factors show strong profit potential in relation to risk. An essential activity of trading is "waiting on the sidelines." You should never crave the activity of trading for its own sake, but be happy to sit in cash or bonds until the right combination of risk/reward, reliability, and technicals shows up.

Figure 6

1) This was our original entry point.

2) Through the use of the series of trailing stops shown in previous charts, we are finally stopped out here. We sit on cash, patiently waiting for the next opportunity.

3) Several technical factors come into play which justify re-entering trade here. I will go into more detail about these specific factors in future weeks of the course.

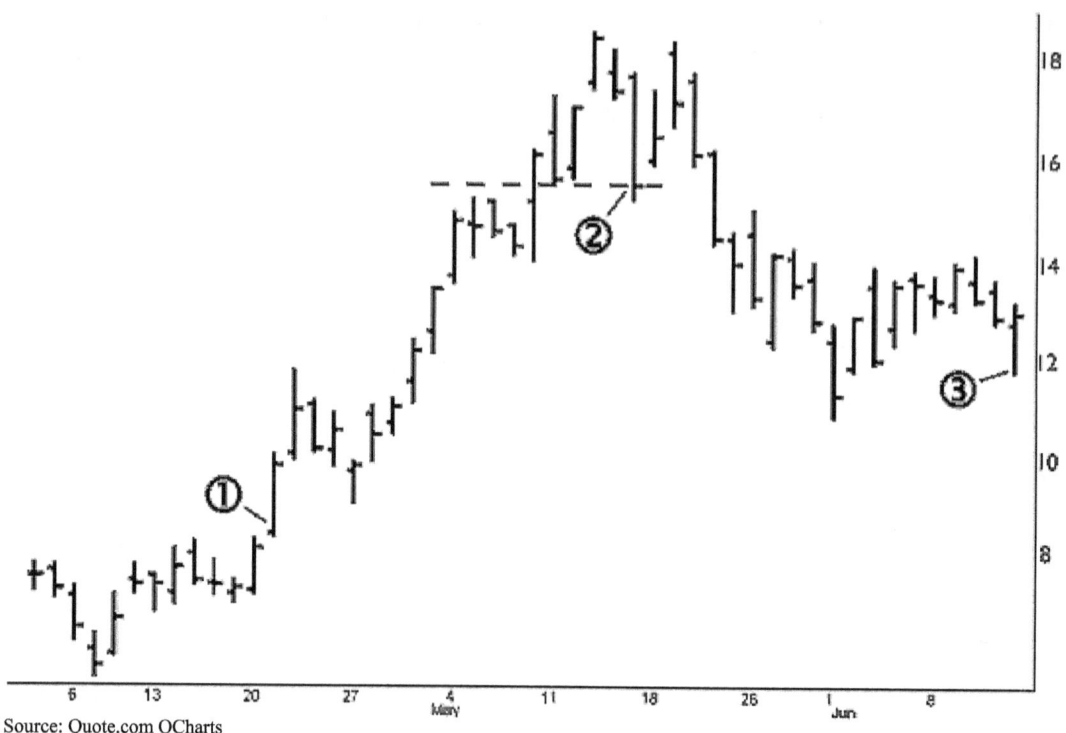

Source: Quote.com QCharts

Rule 10: Remember That Price Makes News, News Does Not Make Price

When you study market action over the course of several months and longer, you will see that it has an uncanny knack for reflecting future economic events and trends well before they become public. That is one of the reasons why trading and investing is so befuddling to most people. What is happening currently in the market usually seems way out of sync with traders' expectations.

Markets tend to "discount" current news. **That is, important and relevant news that is made public today is already reflected in the markets' current price action**. Studies performed by numerous market researchers tend to agree that the markets anticipate news by about 6 to 12 months.

Figure 7

When the news is bad and public pessimism is rampant, the market is usually bottoming out or about to explode to the upside. At the start of the explosive leg of the current bull market which began in December 1994, record unemployment and renewed recessionary fears were dominant in the headlines. Such worrisome headlines followed the market up for nearly two years before the press and the public began to sense that an economic recovery was on the way. Today in 1999, everyone acknowledges that we are living in a time of an economic boom largely fueled by the growth of the high tech sector. Somehow, the market seemed to know about this before everyone else.

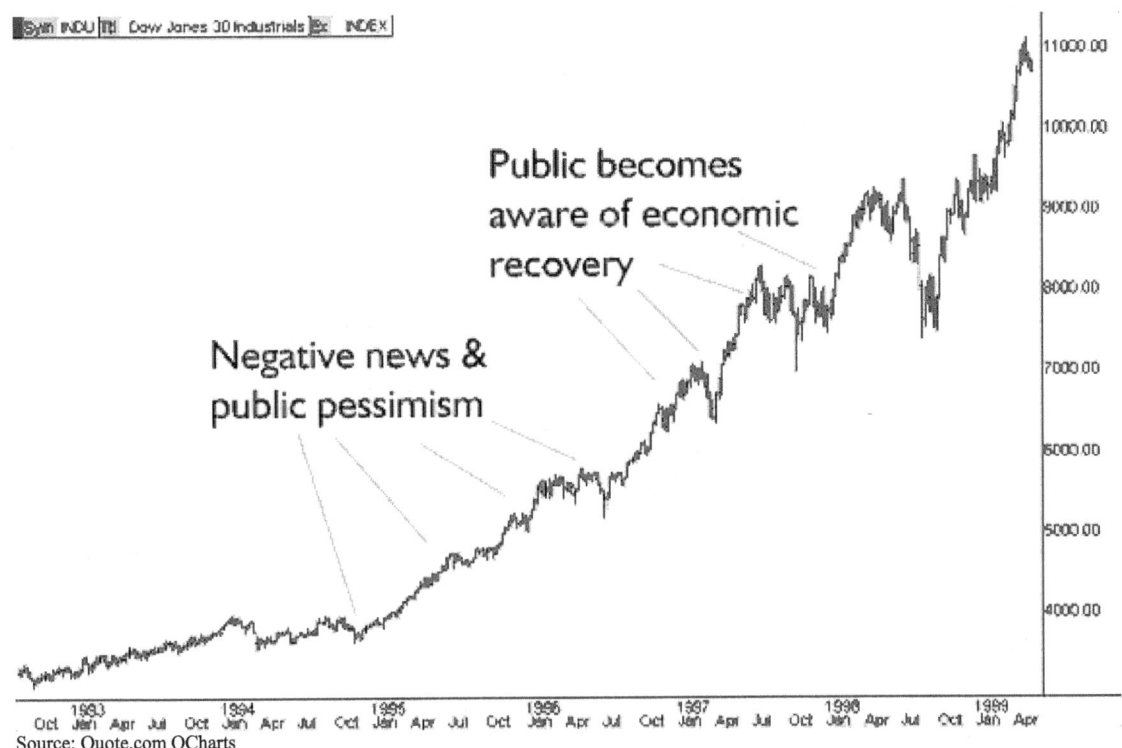
Source: Quote.com QCharts

Figure 8

Here's another example. On January 27, 1999, Compaq announced worldwide sales of $10.9 billion for the fourth quarter of 1998, an increase of 48 percent compared to sales reported for the fourth quarter of 1997. As you can see in Figure 8, Compaq began to sell off just about when this fantastic news was released. Over the course of the next three months that the stock sustained continued losses, all the news surrounding the company's performance continued to be good. Finally, on April 21, 1999, the company issued a warning stating that its 1st Quarter earnings would be substantially lower than expected. Clearly, if you look at the price action of the stock and compare it against the timing of news that is made public, you can clearly see the point I'm making. The price action of the stock takes news into account well before the news is made public. Once the news is widely known, the market has already discounted it.

Source: Quote.com QCharts

Rule 11: Scrutinize How Markets React to Good and Bad News

Given the fact that, as stated in Rule 10, price action precedes news, you would often expect good news to accompany market tops and bad news to accompany market bottoms. This is indeed the case. But, we can go one step further than just observing this fascinating phenomenon. We can actually use it as yet another tool in our trading arsenal.

Figure 9

When a market reacts negatively to good news, it is a confirmation that the good news has already been discounted by recent price action. It sends the message that the market is especially vulnerable to further downside movement. Reviewing the chart of Compaq once again, you can see this principle at work. In January, the good news about record earnings are released about Compaq. Yet the stock starts to sell off and continues to do so in spite of rising prices in the tech sector during the 1st quarter of 1999. This price pattern in combination with the news was telling you that Compaq was in trouble well before the announcement of disappointing 1st Quarter Results in Mid-April.

Figure 10

Similarly, when a market reacts positively to bad news, it is a confirmation that the bad news has already been factored into recent price behavior. The market is saying, "I already know this" and that there's a good potential that it'll be continuing to move up from that point. This is what happened with the U.S. Stock market as a whole in December 1994 as reflected by this chart of the Dow Jones Industrial Averages. Skepticism about the economy and the sustainability of the bull market continued well into the second year of the leg.

Source: Quote.com QCharts

Rule 12: Concentrate Most of Your Time and Effort on Market Selection

The foundation of my approach to trading is to spend most of my time **looking for strong markets I can buy and weak markets I can sell**. Only after I have narrowed down my list of candidates to these two extremes do I look for low-risk, high-reward patterns that justify an actual trade.

Most novice traders spend their time looking for mechanical trading systems or learning theories to predict major market tops or bottoms. Technical analysis offers many valuable tools that help you to anticipate future market action and I use some of them myself. **But the real key is to find the right markets to trade in the first place so that you already have the home court advantage when you apply your arsenal of trading tools**. This is where the bulk of profits come from.

Take a look at my Watch Lists on TRADINGMARKETS.COM. You'll see that my primary focus is the scan through thousands of stocks in search of a small handful that have the strongest combination of technical and fundamental factors. High relative strength assures that a stock has near-term technical strength while good earnings tell me there is good long-term foundation for higher prices in the stock.

These are the stocks whose powerful trends are most likely to continue. I am only interested in looking for trading opportunities in these stocks.

Rule 13: Remember that Trading is an Odds Game

You should never look at any trading system, indicator, or market analysis method as providing you with anything more than an **edge** in understanding what might happen in any given trade. The most brilliant trader in the world is dead meat if he holds many heavily margined long positions in stocks and the market crashes 1,000 points.

Always be prepared to be wrong. Being wrong is part of odds game and has to be factored into your overall strategy trading plan. Take your lumps and move on. Winning traders do not become depressed when they lose, nor do they become euphoric when they win. They just work through their numbers and structure their strategy so that when all the wins and losses are tallied, they come out way ahead.

One of the things that differentiates a great quarterback from a mediocre one is his ability to throw brilliantly immediately after getting sacked. The same goes for trading.

Remember, most of what happens in the markets is not predictable so it is foolhardy to trade on the basis of predictions. It is best to gain an understanding of all the technical factors that might affect a market's direction at any given moment and cautiously step into a market when a confluence of those factors occur at the same time. It is impossible to quantify all these factors such that they can be assimilated into a mechanical trading system. Thus, as stated in Rule 3, understanding the market is the key component to consistent success.

Rule 14: Constantly Devote Time and Effort to the Study of Market, Trading Techniques, and Economic History

Who would you prefer entrusting your triple bypass surgery to? An experienced surgeon who has spent many years gaining an understanding into the inner workings of the human body? Or someone who's reasonably intelligent, but who's merely following the steps outlined in a detailed instruction manual?

Okay then. **When your money is on the line you need to understand what's going on.** This is not what people want to hear and I know there's a big market out there for quick and easy solutions. But that's why most people don't make money trading the markets.

You need to separate yourself from the crowd and expose yourself to the many parallels between current and past market events. While the similarities are rarely identical, a grasp of market history opens your mind to the possible events that might happen in the present.

For example, you might better comprehend the current trends in the U.S. Stock Market by comparing how the markets behaved during the deflationary environment of the 1930s. On the shorter-term front, if you study the many variations in Flag Formations (one of my favorite patterns to be described in Week 7) you will be better trained to recognize them in the future.

Rule 15: Keep a Trading Journal and Review and Evaluate Your Past Decisions Periodically

All great traders I have talked to keep a trading journal.

In a trading journal you should write down what **thought process, technical evidence, or insights** that led you to make the trading decisions you make. Follow every trade to its ultimate completion and record what the net outcome was.

Periodically, (every week, month, or quarter), review the trades you've made for the most recent period. Be your own best critic and do your best to note any consistent errors or counterproductive tendencies you have so that you can take immediate corrective action.

Analyze the results of your trading techniques by looking for common patterns between losing trades and winning ones. Make every effort to **fine-tune your techniques**.

Take a careful psychological inventory as well. Are you following your trading strategy in a disciplined fashion? Did you blow it just because of some fleeting emotion which clouded your judgment? What can you do to avoid that temptation in the future?

Keeping a journal is one of the most important disciplines you can have because the best self-improvement book you could ever read is the one you write for yourself. **Those traders I know who have kept a journal religiously for years tend to be the consistent winners**

Rule 16: In Trading the Trend is Your Friend.

Master Traders know that trends are important no matter how short-term the orientation of their trading is. When trading within trends that are visible in the context of days, it is also important to be in sync with the next longer time frame by looking at a weekly or monthly bar chart.

In coming weeks, I will show you how to identify strongly trending trading candidates.

Figure 11

In the example below if you look at the daily bar chart alone, it's not that easy to tell what the overall trend is. Once you view it, however, in the context of the weekly bar chart, it becomes more clear how strong a trading candidate Dell might be from the standpoint of its trend.

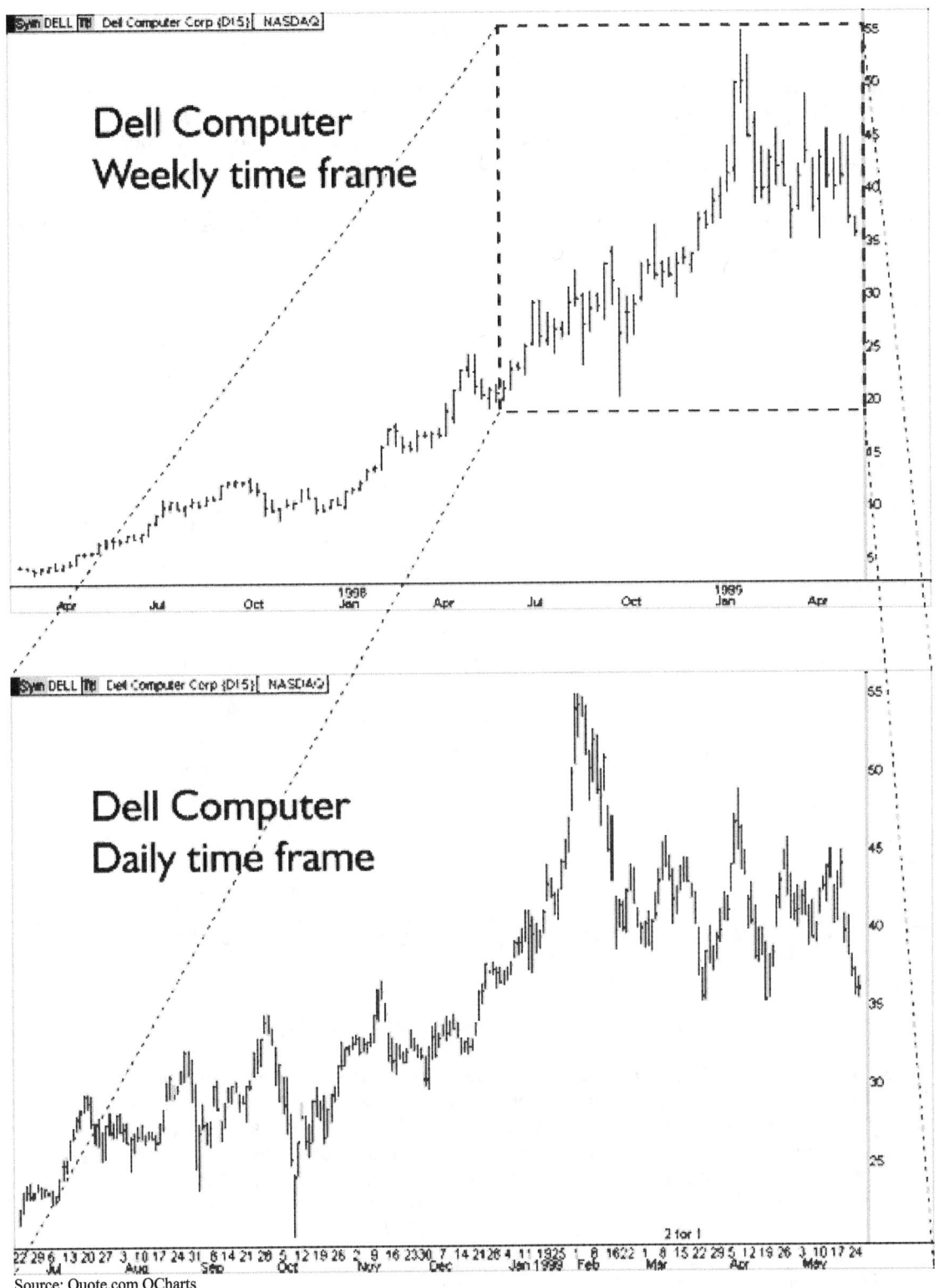

Source: Quote.com QCharts

Rule 17: Buy Strength and Sell Weakness

Professional traders know that market tops and bottoms cannot be predicted with consistent accuracy. They focus instead on determining where the strongest trends are. Upon finding markets with exceptional strength or weakness, they will look for opportunities to trade in sync with those trends by trading on pullbacks and consolidations.

Trends, coupled with other measures of technical strength will often make the difference between winning and losing,

Figure 12

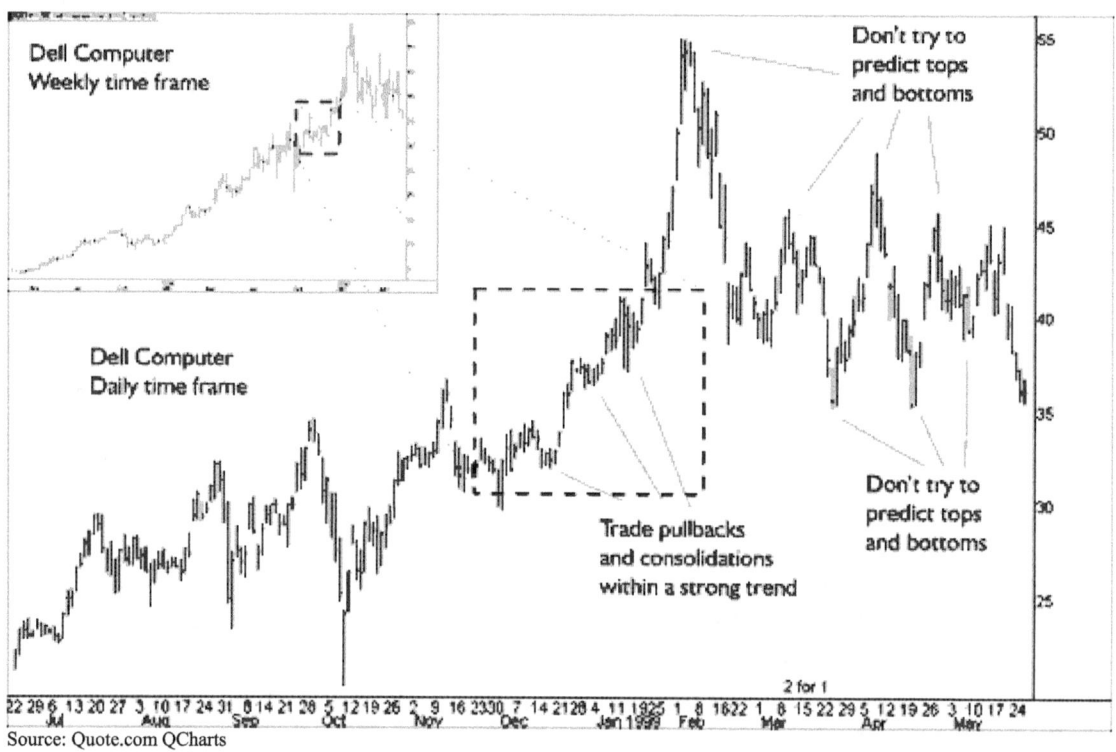

Source: Quote.com QCharts

Rule 18: Go Where the Oil is

J. Paul Getty once said, **"The best way to find oil is to go where other people are finding it."** When I trade, I'm always trying to ascertain what where the strongest trends and strongest potential is. I isolate the best trading opportunities a whole host of factors are all converging together. I never limit myself to one particular market because there is always there is always a rotation between what is hot and what is out of favor. Today Internet-related stocks are. Tomorrow it might well be oil stocks. Or it might be gold or currencies.

I always keep my trading sphere extended well beyond my immediate neighborhood to markets throughout the globe as well as different asset classes. I strive not to just trade with the strongest trends, but the strongest trends on the planet.

Rule 19: Trade with Fuel on Your Side

When stocks launch into strong sustained trends that last years, there are always strong companies with good earnings growth underlying them. You already know how important risk control is in my trade strategy, so it shouldn't surprise you that **I advocate only going long stocks whose underlying business outlook is favorable and shorting stocks whose business is in the dumps**. This applies even when other factors such as patterns, trends, and relative strength look good.

Rule 20: Put the Value-Added Wealth Equation on Your Side

Ultimately, the results you can see, feel, and touch are a manifestation of what's first realized in your inner world. Thus, to increase wealth, you must increase your skills, ability, intelligence, and specialized knowledge. You find will find yourself to be more balanced, adaptable, productive, and teachable. As you proceed through life's challenges you will do so more confidently and skillfully which, in turn, will lead to increased well-being and wealth.

Summary and Closing Remarks

Of all the topics in my 10 week summer trading course, I put Money Management first. The reason is that far too many traders focus on the rules and techniques, and not the framework in which they're applied. Yet, among all the traders I have ever talked to who've experienced consistent and enduring success, Money Management is the very foundation of their success.

If there really is a Holy Grail, Money Management is it. Let me summarize all my rules for you now.

The components of good Money Management are as follows:

Your number one goal should always be to Minimize Losses. When you understand risk and the permanent damage that large losses can cause to you trading account, you'll realize that Consistency is the Key. To become consistent in your trading, you have to do more than just learn mechanical rules, techniques, or purchase trading systems. Understanding the Markets is Much More Important Than Methodology.

Once you've laid the foundation of risk control and understanding, you will automatically see the importance of the right money management techniques. Some of these you've heard before, but you may have not fully comprehended their importance until now. Now it should be clear to you why it's important to Always use Open Protective Stops (OPS) and to Always Use Trailing OPS's to Lock in Profits as a Trade Moves in Your Favor. If you don't, you will inevitably suffer a devastating loss that you cannot recover from without adding money to your account. In addition, too many people place stops haphazardly. Instead you should Always Let the Market's Own Price Action Determine Where An OPS is Placed. There will be areas of support and resistance that provide ideal levels at which to place stops.

When you do your homework and buy into runaway markets, you're likely to get into trades which move strongly in your favor--and perhaps even farther than you initially imagine. In such cases, Use Creeping Commitment to add your position when the risk on your initial position is zero. In that way, you'll be following the old adage, Let Your Profits Run. But don't fall in love with any trade you're in. When in Doubt, Stay Out or Get Out; Do Not Get Back in Until You are Sure About a Position. Remember that there are always plenty of opportunities on the horizon. Focus on the search, not the money you theoretically might have made in sub-optimal trade.

Be careful how you interpret what you read in the paper or watch on CNBC. Price Makes News, News Does not Make Price. So once news comes out through any public venue it is likely to already have been discounted by the markets. In fact, news often means the opposite of how it appears on the surface so Scrutinize How Markets React to Good and Bad News.

To use a horse racing analogy, too many traders focus on trying to find the right betting system rather than finding the right horse. So in trading, you should always Concentrate Most of Your Time and Effort on Market Selection. Remember that Trading is an Odds Game and concentrating on market selection is one of the things that will tilt the odds in your favor. In addition, don't just look at trading through a microscope. Expand your view and Constantly Devote Time and Effort to the Study of Market, Trading Techniques, and Economic History.

One of the most important things you must start doing today, if you haven't already is: Keep a Trading Journal and Review and Evaluate Your Past Decisions Periodically. I realize that many traders start doing this, then it becomes a mundane, boring task and they fall out of the discipline. Well, don't always expect journal-keeping to be fun. Just do it!

You may have heard that the Trend is Your Friend. But traders think of this as being mainly for long term "buy and hold" investors. In reality, everyone I know who's successful, even day-traders, are looking for the strongest trends and entering them in the midst of small pullbacks or breakouts. When you do this, you will naturally Buy Strength and Sell Weakness. Do what J. Paul Getty did in order to accumulate his fortune: Go Where the Oil is. That is, trade where the strongest runaway trends are. When all is said and done and all the technicals are in place, you should still pay attention to the fundamentals. By doing this you'll be Trading With Fuel on Your Side.

Finally, invest in yourself. Create order in your inner world and it'll be manifested in the outer. Put the Value-Added Wealth Equation on Your Side.

In closing. . .

Over the next week, make a 100% effort to apply these rules to your trading. Reading about these things is good, but only actually using them in the real world will lead to mastery. Please make every effort to participate in our private **Boucher Trading Course Message Board** and share your insights with other traders.

Next week, we'll take an in-depth look at Relative Strength. Relative Strength is one of the most underrated, and yet proven technical tools available. Relative Strength is a very simple concept. Let's say we're talking about the stock market. It simply looks at the percentage change of a stock over a defined period and compares that change to all other stocks.

To me, using Relative Strength properly is sort of like betting on a horse race after the race is 3/4 of the way done. **You get to see who's out in front and bet on that horse.**

See you next Friday,

Mark

WEEK 2 : RELATIVE STRENGTH

This week I'll be discussing **Relative Strength**, one of my favorite indicators.

To start off, let me present you with a riddle to get your juices flowing and maybe challenge your belief system a bit. One day, two fictitious traders, who I'll call Mr. Timing and Mr. Selection, decide to engage in a trading contest. Each has their own speical talent:

- Mr. Timing is able to **buy an index fund just prior to every market rally of 10%** or more and exits right at the top just before the onset of the next decline.

- Mr. Selection **invests 100 percent of his funds in the top-performing sector fund each year**. He does not employ any market timing strategies whatsoever, so he is in the sector fund whether it is going up or down.

Who makes the most money?

Think about this before proceeding.

The Answer

I credit TradingMarkets.com members as being among the most intelligent traders on the planet. **Therefore, I bet most of you correctly answered that Mr. Selection made the most money.**

However, I am just as certain that traders as a whole would, incorrectly, consider Mr. Timing to be the winner. The trading public is just heavily biased in favor of market timing, as you can tell if you scrutinize the typical subject matter of popular trading books, advisory services, articles, seminars, Web sites and Internet chat groups. Everybody wants to predict market tops and bottoms.

But even if you are patting yourself on the back for answering that Mr. Selection was the big money winner, what will still be shocking is just **how badly he kicked Mr. Timing's behind**.

For the sake of argument, let's pretend that index funds and sector funds have actually existed for many decades. If we do this:

- From 1940 to 1973, Mr. Selection made **over 30 times** as much money as Mr. Timing.
- From 1980 to 1992, Mr. Selection's bottom line results still beats Mr. Timing's by **4 to 1**.

The results speak for themselves. <u>Focus on market selection, not market timing</u> to identify trading opportunities. To create your own market selection strategy, the best place to start is **Relative Strength,** and that is the subject for Week 2 of my trading course.

The Quest for the Most Reliable Indicator in the World

In the mid- to late-1980s, I was involved in a large research project with Stanford Ph.D., Tom Johnson and his graduate students. Our objective was very similar to what every trader is obsessed with today: We wanted to determine which tools actually made money in stocks, bonds, currencies, and futures.

I am pleased to report that we found what we were searching for.

We measured the performance of all indicators that had results we could easily measure. These included: PE's, P/S's, volume accumulation, volatility, trend-following tools, earnings models, earnings growth and momentum, growth rates of earnings, projected earnings growth, value compared to earnings growth, chart patterns, pace of fund accumulation of the stock, capitalization—you name it.

Of all the independent variables we tested, **Relative Strength (RS) was the most consistent, reliable, and robust. It single-handedly improved profit better than anything else we tested.**

Other researchers have since confirmed our work. Indeed, some money managers like Dan Sullivan have put these findings to practical use. His almost exclusive use of relative strength has enabled him to consistently outperform the S&P 500 on a risk-adjusted basis since the 1970s.

The bottom line is this: If you're looking for the most rigorous tool to help you pick the top-performing stocks. . .

>. . .Relative Strength is it.

Relative Strength and Its Many Flavors

There are many varieties of Relative Strength. **All of them basically look at the percentage change of a stock over a defined period and compare that change to all other stocks.** Once all stocks have been compared in this way, we can sort all of them in descending order from strongest to weakest. That is, stocks with the most positive changes will be ranked at the top of the list; stocks with the most negative changes will be ranked at the bottom of the list (please note; "relative strength" as used in this course does not refer to **RSI**, which is an oscillator that is used in an entirely different way).

RS, then, is a way of finding the biggest winners and losers of the recent past.

The Variations

- **Investor's Business Daily**: RS is calculated by taking the quarterly percent change of a stock, over the past four quarters. Double-weight, however, is given to the most recent quarter so that IBD's RS ranking places more importance on recent market behavior.

- **TradingMarkets.com**: We use the Investigator Relative Strength engine which calculates RS the same way as IBD.

- **Stock vs. S&P**: Another approach, which I use extensively, takes the percentage change of a stock and compares it to the percent change of the S&P 500 index. This calculation is called "normalized division" and is available on a number of charting programs. Doing this has an advantage over just following numerical rankings in that you can **graphically display a chart of the relative strength of a stock in comparison to the S & P**. What I like to do, as you'll see in the following pages, is identify patterns in both the relative strength chart and the stock's bar chart itself that are in sync with each other.

- **Short-term RS**: Shorter-term traders will be more interested in shorter-term RS numbers vs. the overall market. I use 5-day, 30-day, 60-day, and 90-day RS readings to help locate shorter-term trading opportunities. Longer-term investors will be more interested in smoothed versions of RS.

How I Use Relative Strength

There are many ways to use RS. Here's one of my favorite ways for short-term and intermediate-term trading.

- First, generate lists of stocks that are at the **strong and weak ends of the spectrum** according to their RS rankings. These **"Watch Lists"** can be found every trading day on my TradingMarkets.com content pages.

- Next, use RS (usually versus the S&P 500) to confirm that a stock is still accelerating upwards or downwards faster than the overall market. **If RS is moving up, then the stock is moving upwards faster than the overall market. If RS is moving down, then the stock is moving downwards faster than the overall market.** Also try to **confirm breakouts** to new highs or lows. This break out can occur prior to or simultaneously to the break out in price on the stock's bar chart.

On the following pages, I'll share with you how Relative Strength, when combined with pattern recognition (Week 7) and money management (Week 1) produces great short-term opportunities. All of these recent examples from our daily Watch List on TradingMarkets.com involve break outs from consolidations. An RS chart is then used to determine just how strongly or weakly the stock is moving in comparison to the S & P 500.

Example 1: IBM: Up 80% in 7 Months

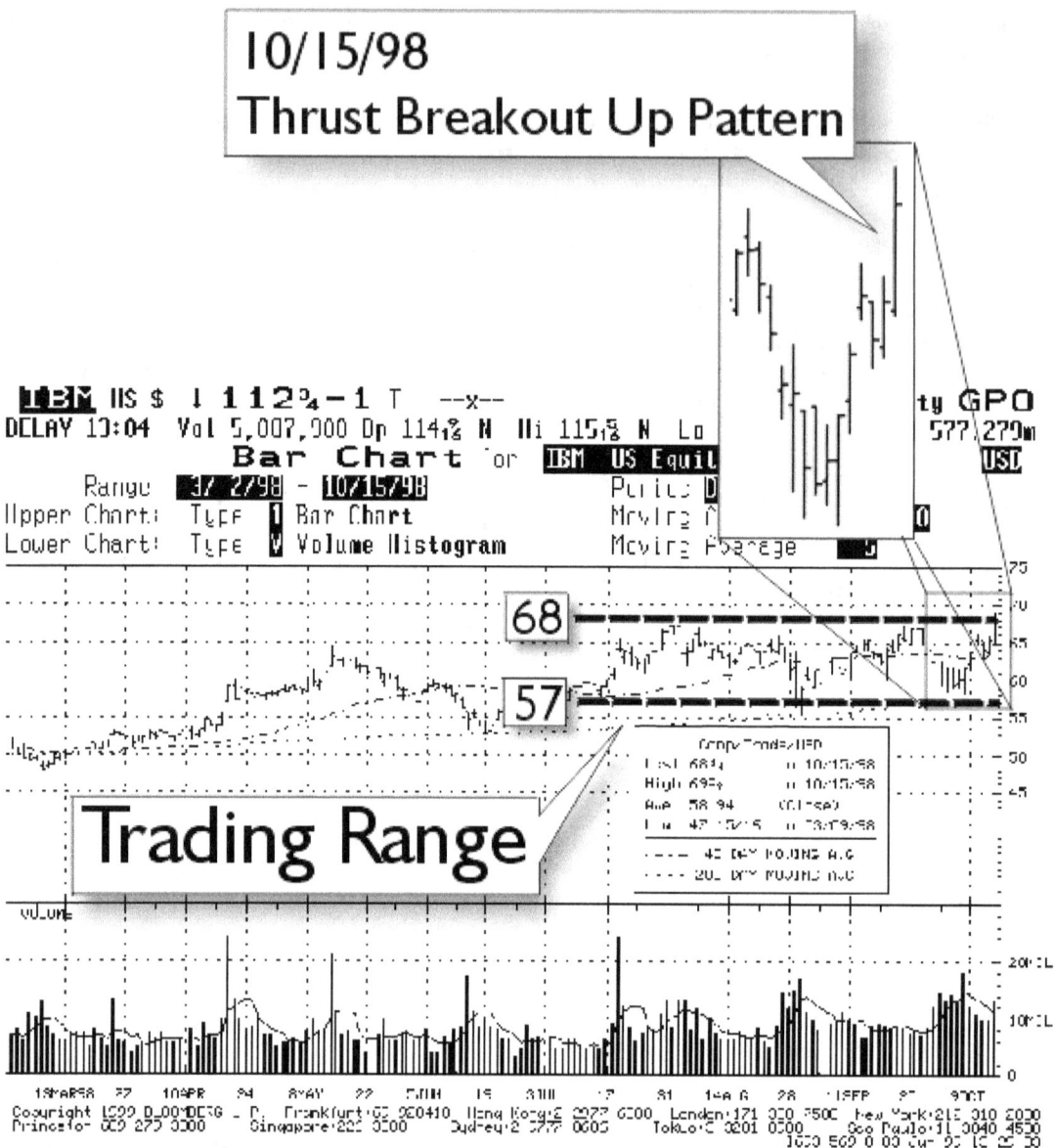

The first example is IBM. While the S&P 500 declined from mid-July 1998 to October 8, 1998, IBM stock bucked the downtrend and remained in a broad trading range between about 57 and 68. While the S&P 500 made a lower low on October 8, IBM bottomed in the high 50's, above the low of its first low made in early September near 57.

On October 15, the S&P 500 moved up sharply and began to show signs of a bottom. On this same day IBM stock broke out to new highs as shown in **Figure 1**, breaking above a consolidation high on a solid Thrust Breakout Up.

Figure 2

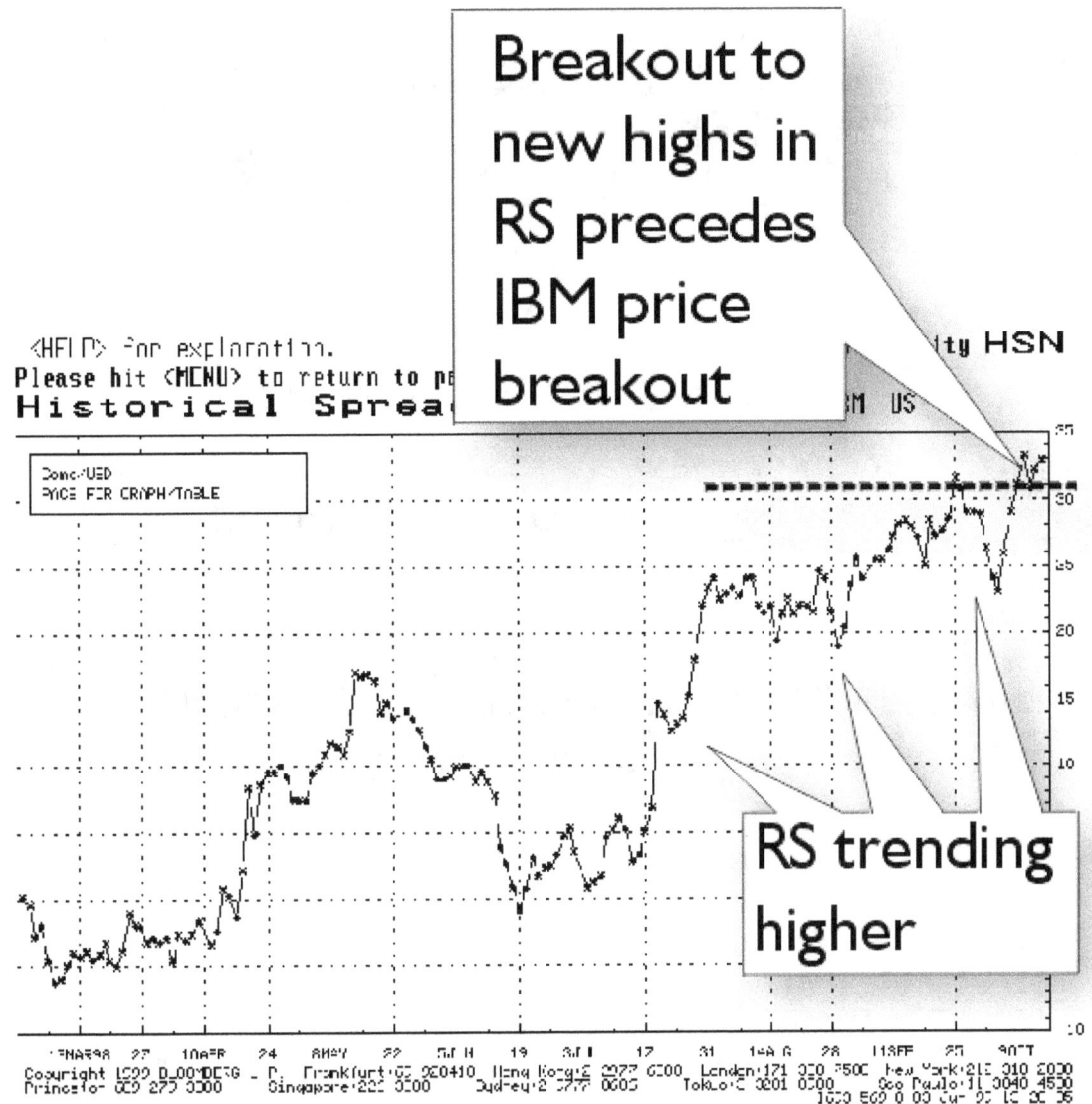

From the break out on 10/15/98 at 68.25, IBM ran up sharply and continued to show strong relative strength right up to its high of 123 in mid-May 1999, a **gain of over 80% in seven months (Figure 3).**

Figure 3

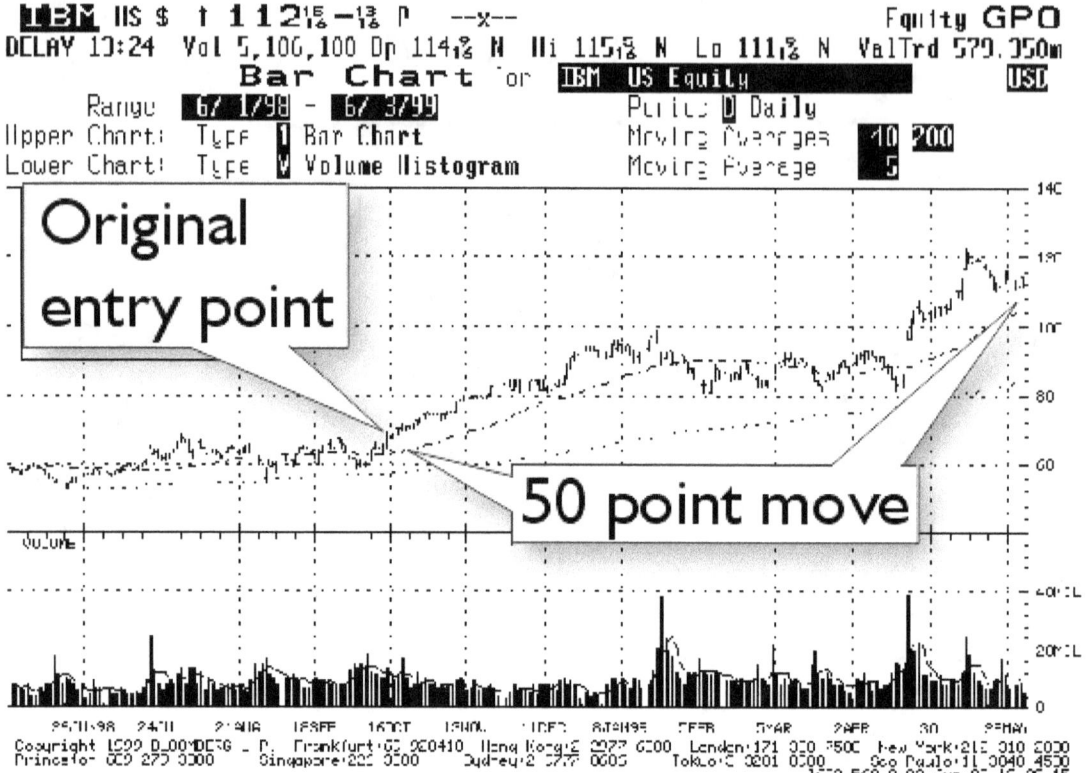

JAKK Takes Off

Another recent example from our Watch List was JAKK, which broke out above a flag-type consolidation on 3/18/99 at 18 7/8 on a lap and thrust (**Figure 4**).

Figure 4

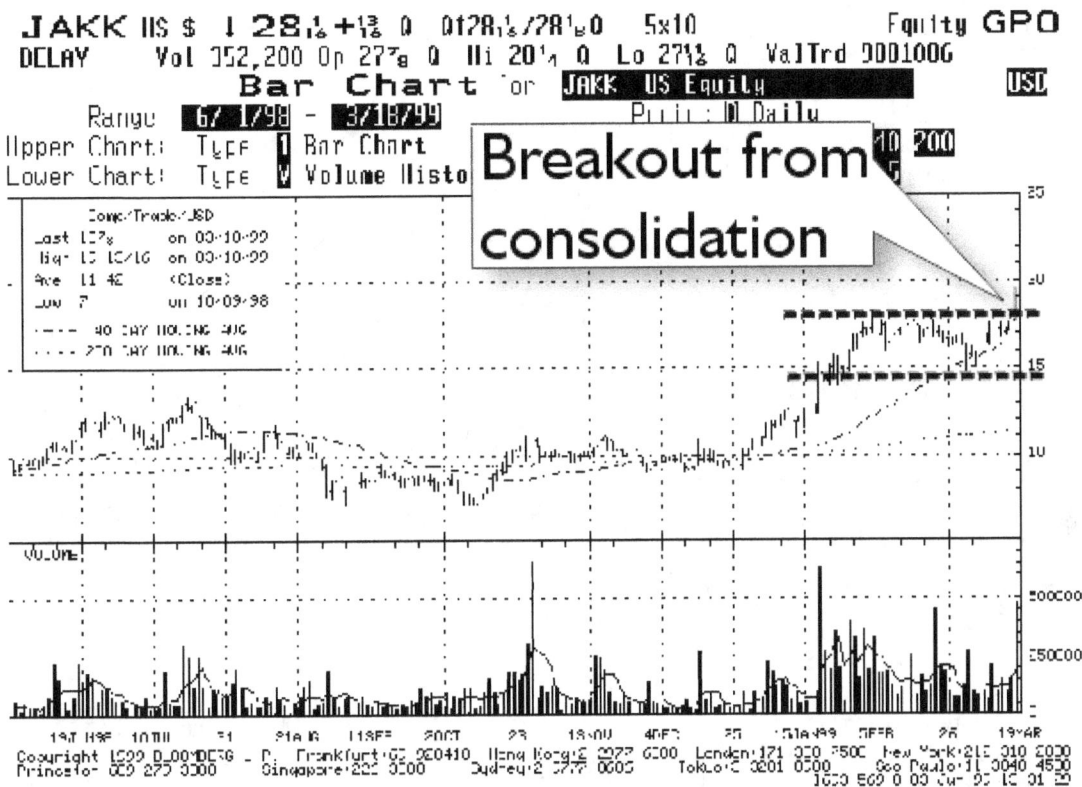

In addition, JAKK's normalized RS versus the S&P was exploding and broke out strongly to new highs just as the stock did on 3/18/99 (**Figure 5**). A trader buying at 18 7/8 could use a 15 5/8 OPS for a 4.25-point risk.

Figure 5

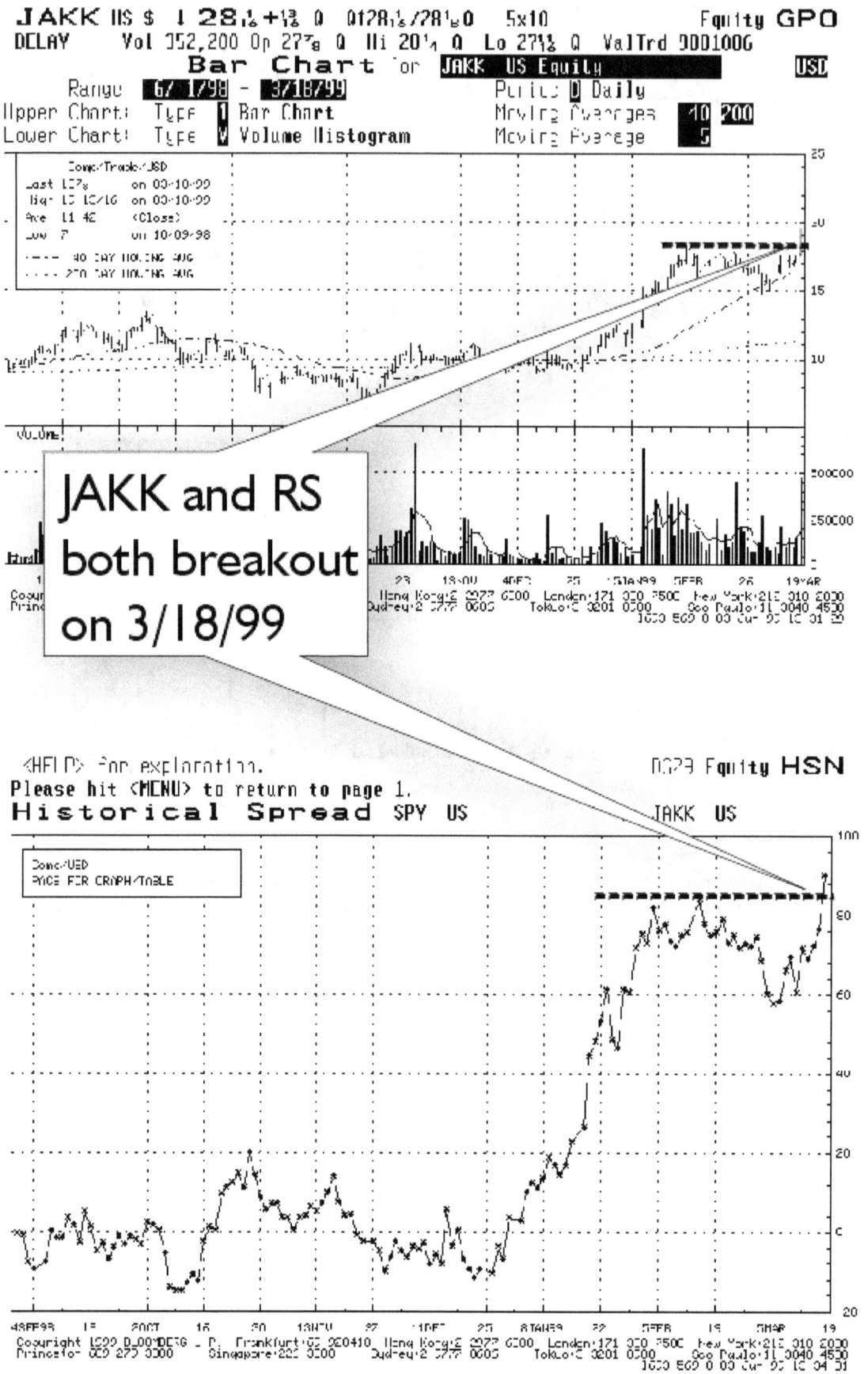

As **Figure 6** shows, JAKK has moved sharply to just over 28.5, more than two times initial risk in the last two months alone.

Figure 6

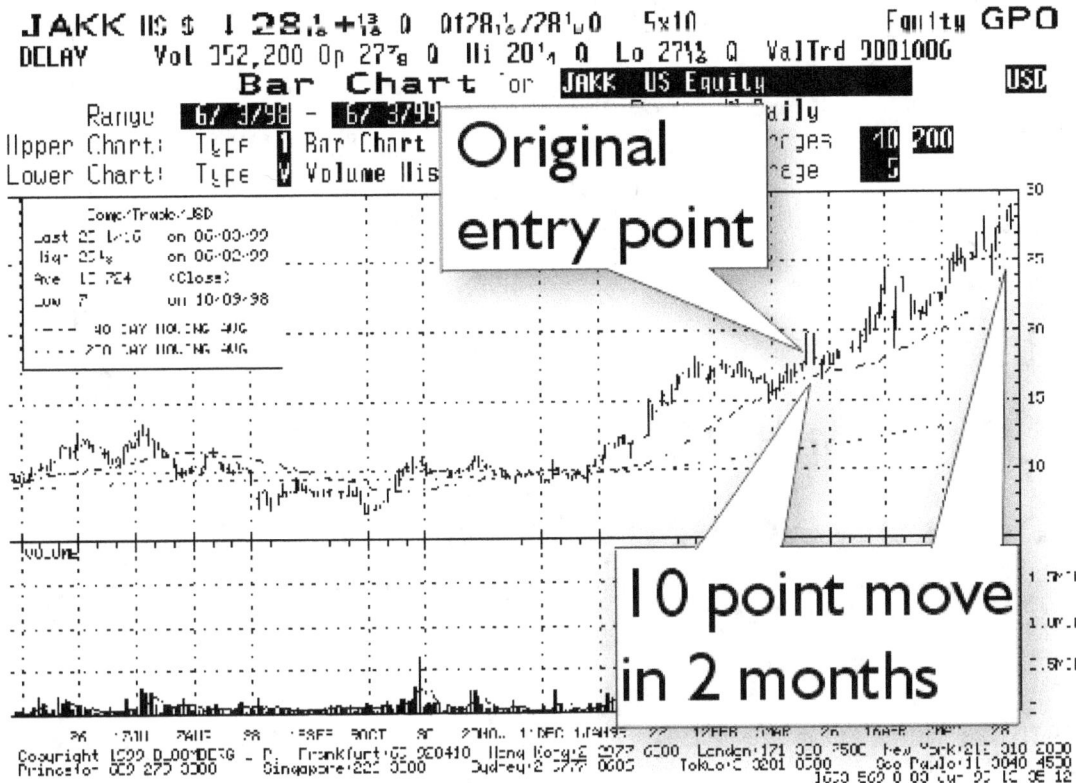

Example 3: Another Great Play: UNPH

Figure 7 shows a similar example for UNPH, another stock from our list that broke out late last year.

Figure 7

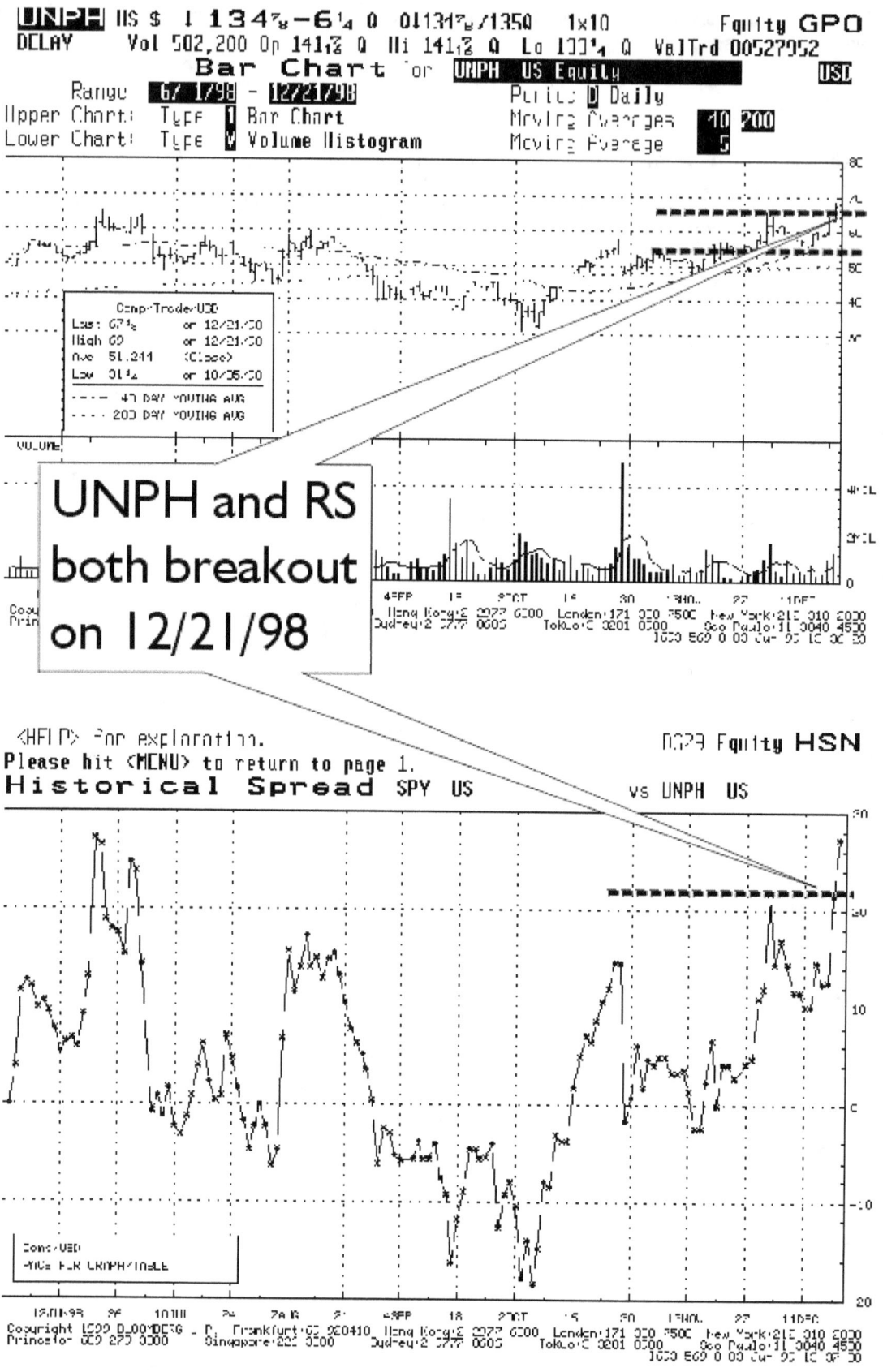

Here is the nice 70 point move that ensued.

Figure 8

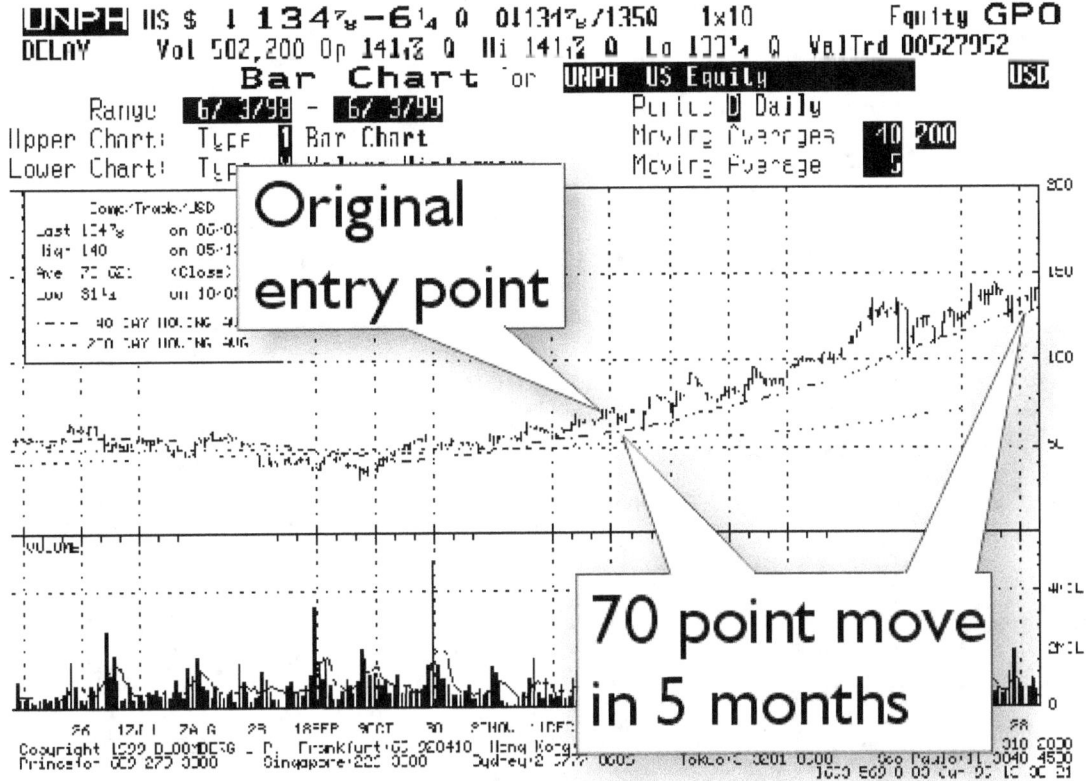

Example 4: Going Short on Disney (DIS)

Going Short on Disney (DIS)

RS is used in an opposite fashion for choosing short-sales. On 3/31/99 DIS stock broke down out of a descending triangle and below its 200-day moving average on strong volume on a Thrust Breakout Down **(Figure 9)**.

Figure 9 also clearly shows that DIS has a strongly declining trend in its RS versus the S&P going back more than nine months. DIS's RS versus the S&P broke to new lows on the same day that DIS broke down from its descending triangle. A trader could have shorted DIS on the descending triangle signal at 31.13 with a 37 OPS.

Figure 9

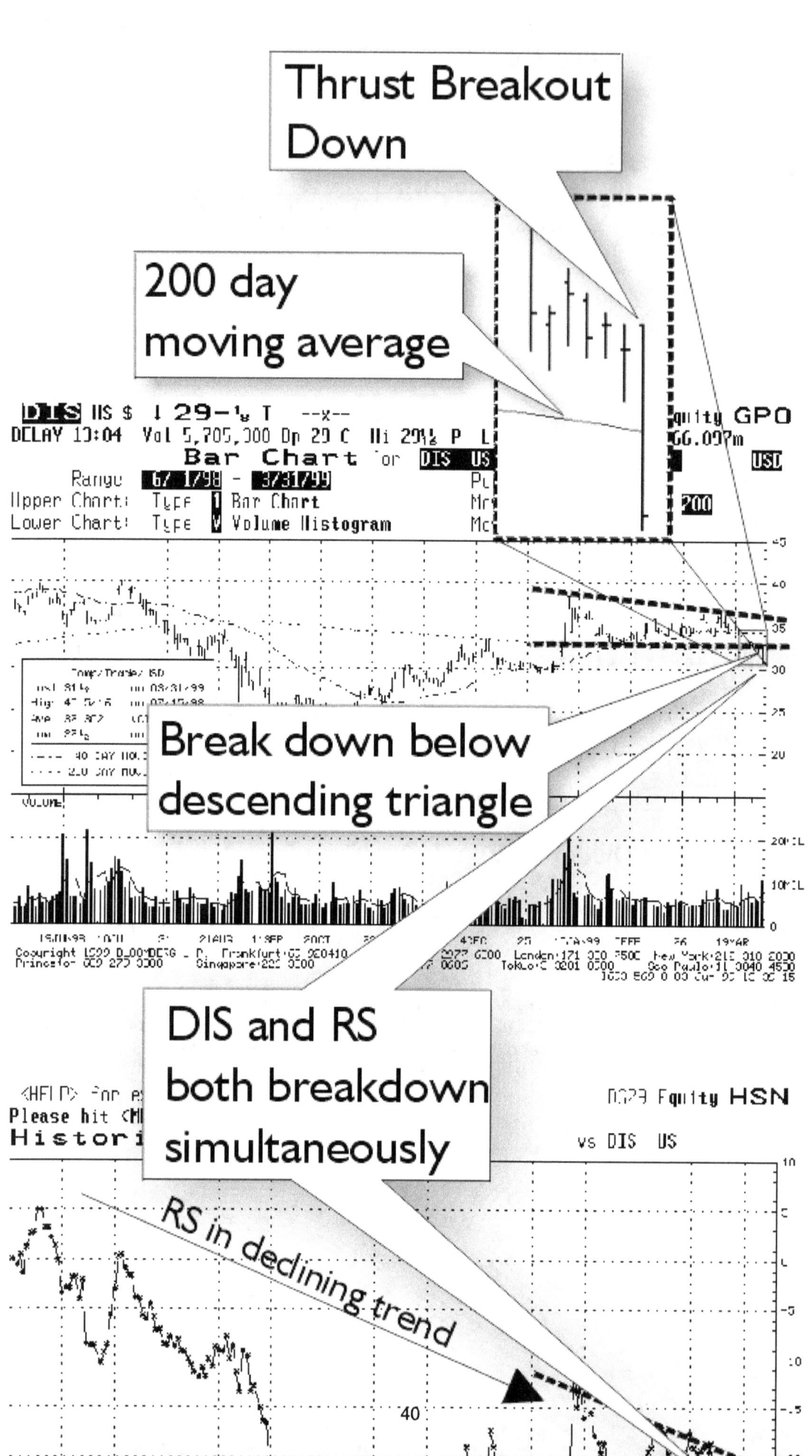

Currently **(Figure 10)**, the stock has broken down below 29 and is set to retest its Oct. 98 lows of 22.5ñduring a period of time when the S&P is up. DIS has now gone low enough that traders can move their stop to a break-even point.

Figure 10

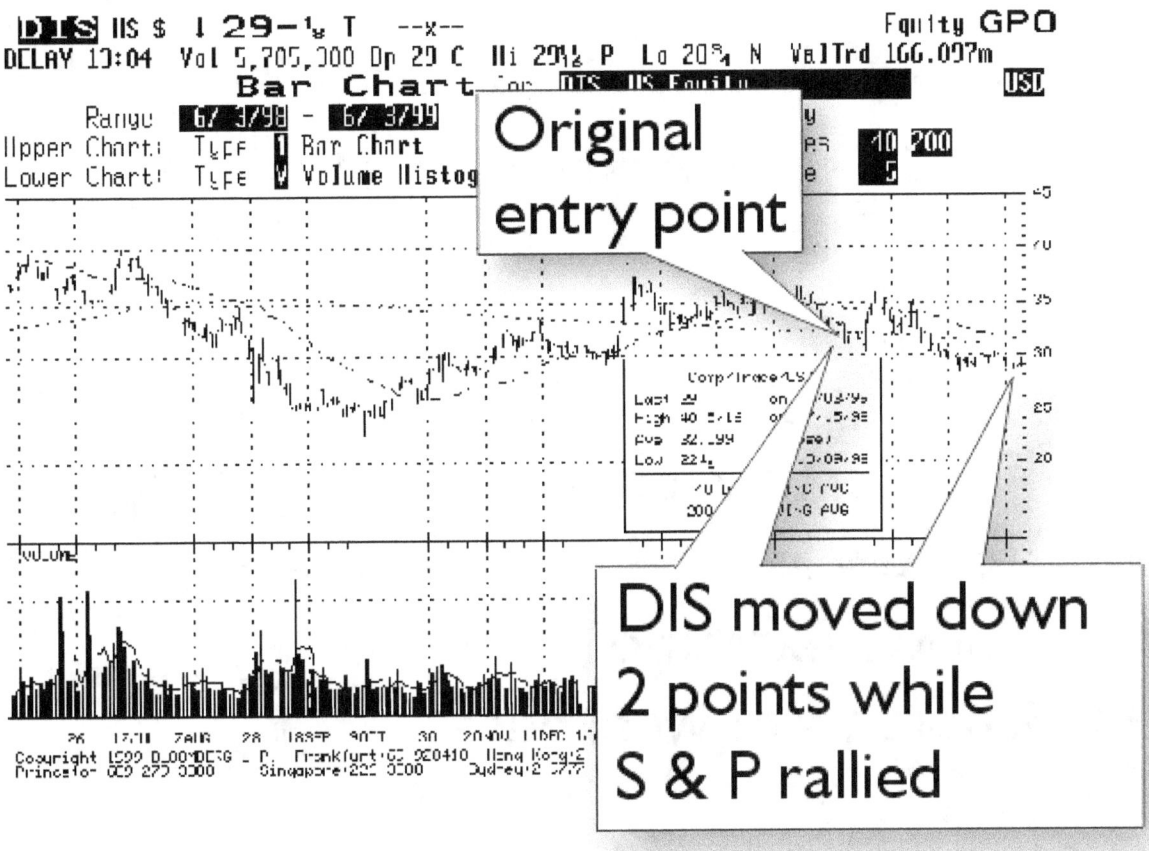

Example 5: TEN: Another Great Short Sale

TEN: Another Great Short Sale

Figure 11 shows a similar story for TEN, another great short sale over the past few months from the Watch List. TEN showed some of the weakest short-term RS in the market in mid-February at the time of a breakdown to new lows. The trend in RS versus the S&P was declining rapidly, and RS versus the S&P was consistently leading the stock to new lows.

Figure 11

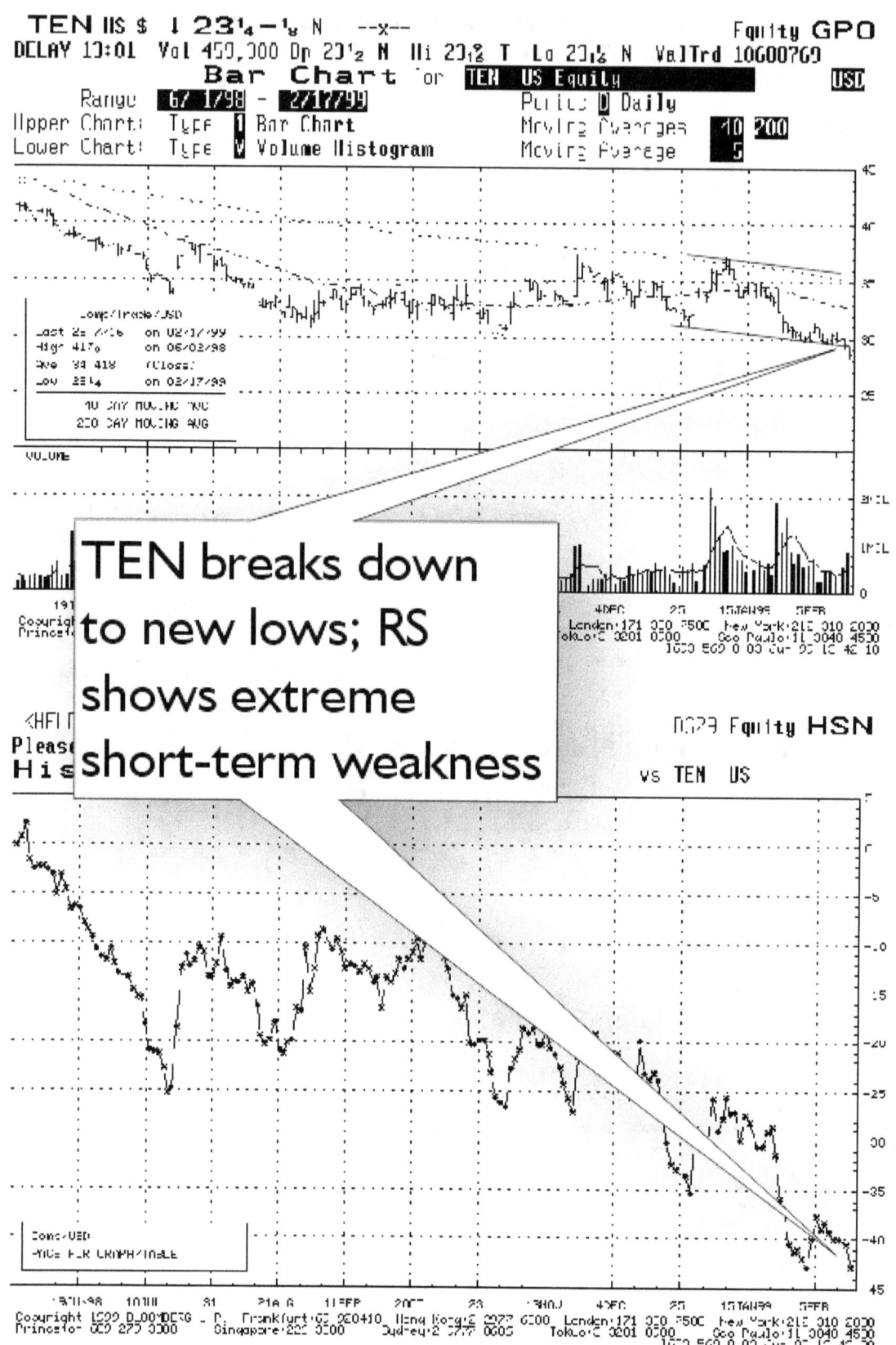

TEN breaks down to new lows; RS shows extreme short-term weakness

Traders who sold the breakout to new lows at 28 ½ now have around a 20% open profit and have moved their Trailing OPS's to 26, locking in a profitable trade which continues to move down sharply.

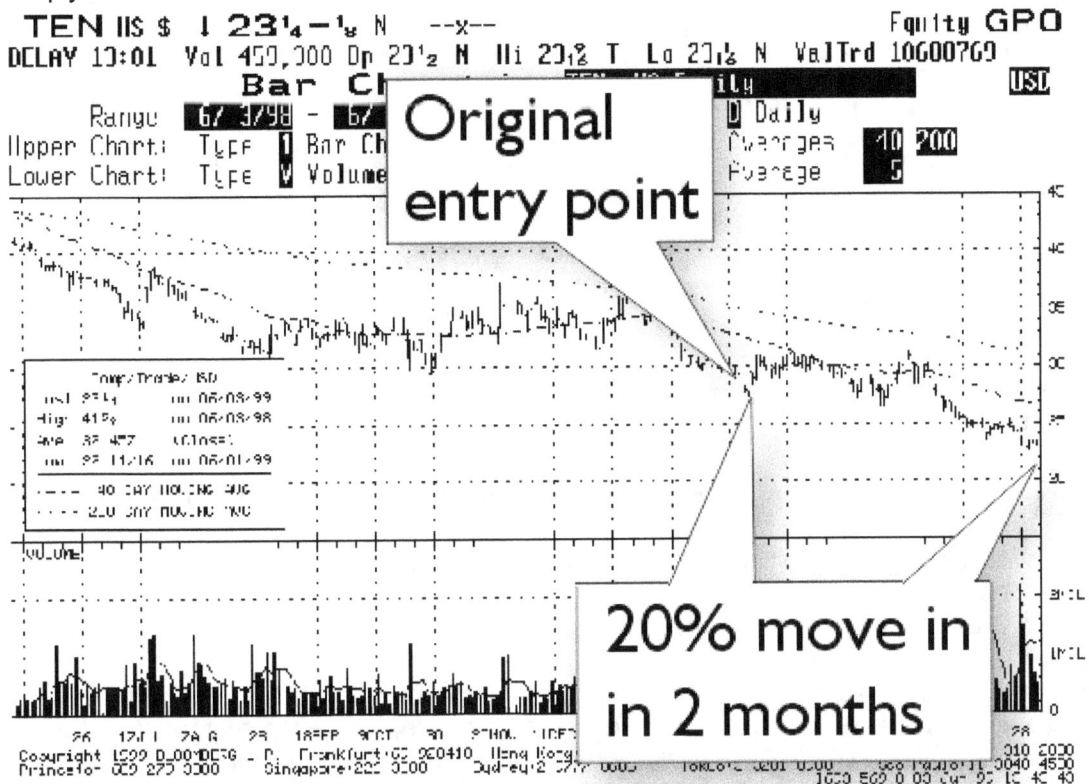

Watch the Watch Lists

The most statistically valid tool we have found for selecting stocks that outperform the market on either the upside or downside is Relative Strength.

In addition to methods shown in the previous examples, there are unique ways of exploiting RS readily available on TradingMarkets.com. There are two powerful Watchlists I use in my own trading that are also made available to TradingMarkets members. They are:

- Top Relative Strength and Earnings New Highs list (Top RS)
- Bottom Relative Strength and Earnings New Lows list (Bottom RS)

These two lists are very powerful and when combined with a broad understanding of the markets (Week 1), good money management (Week 1), and pattern recognition skills (Week 7). They can help you achieve trading results that are beyond the norm.

Mark Boucher's Trading Watch Lists

Short-term trading

- **Top Relative Strength and Earnings New Highs list** (Updated at 9:30 pm EST)
  - New High RS Industry Sector Concentration (Updated at 9:30 pm EST)
  - New High RS Group Concentration (Updated at 9:30 pm EST)
  - New High RS Sub-group Concentration (Updated at 9:30 pm EST)
- **Bottom Relative Strength and Earnings New Lows list** (Updated at 9:30 pm EST)
  - New Low RS Industry Sector Concentration (Updated at 9:30 pm EST)
  - New Low RS Group Concentration (Updated at 9:30 pm EST)
  - New Low RS Sub-group Concentration (Updated at 9:30 pm EST)

These stocks have the best technical and fundamental prospects to move significantly higher.

These stocks have the best technical and fundamental prospects to move significantly lower.

Let's use the Top RS list as our example, keeping in mind everything we discuss here applies equally to the Bottom RS list.

In the Top RS list, I have isolated stocks that meet 3 technical and fundamental criteria. They are:

- Technical: Ranked in the top 15%-20% of Relative Strength.
- Technical: Making new highs.
- Fundamental: Ranked in the top 15%-20% of Earnings.

The top ranking in Relative Strength assures us that the stock's behavior has recently been strong and that it is currently a leader relative to all stocks. The requirement that the stock be making new highs should be of particular interest to short-term traders because new highs frequently occur when stock is breaking out of a consolidation pattern.

Also, the fact that the stock has good earnings, tells us that the stock has the fuel (Money Management Rule 19) it needs to blast off into higher ground.

Clicking into the Top RS list, you'll get the following page:

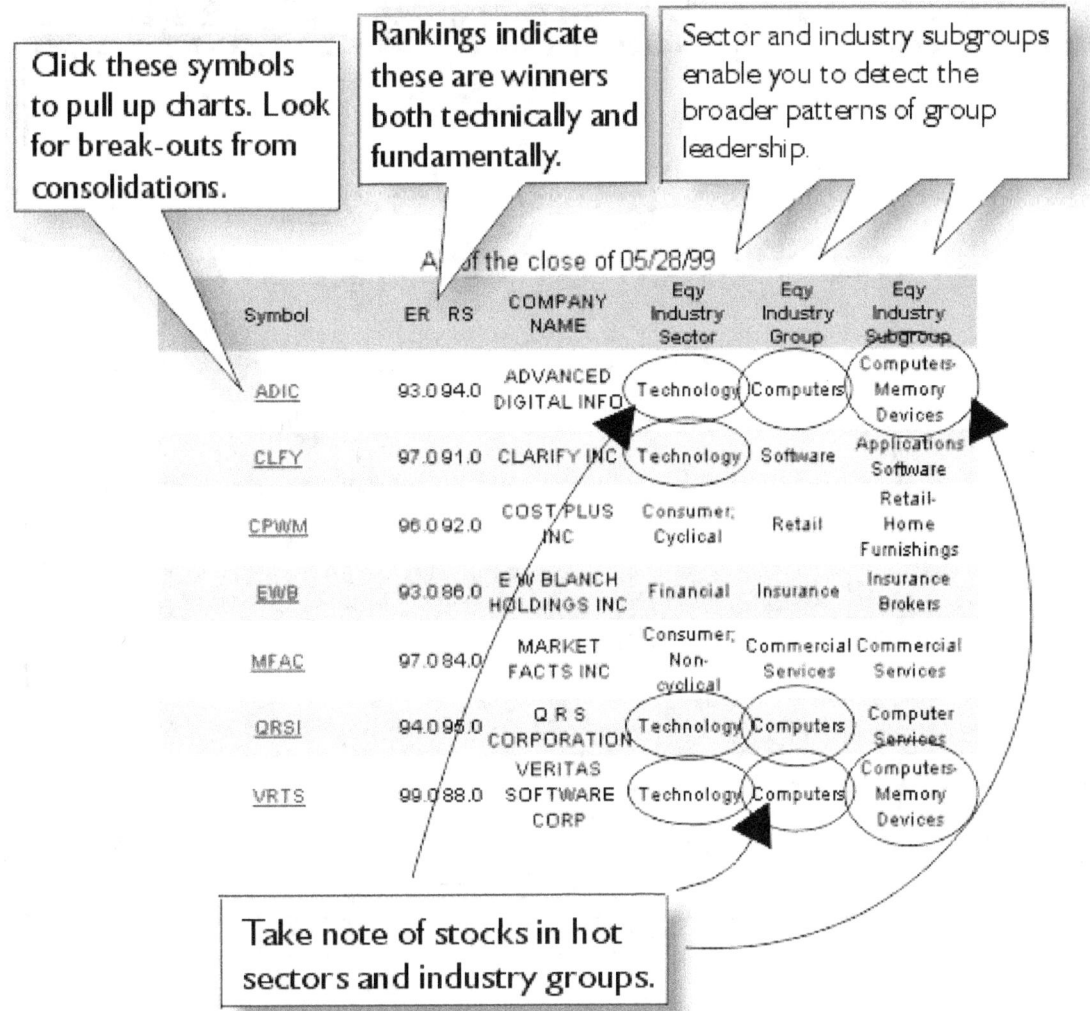

As you can see, besides relative strength and earnings rankings, the list includes information regarding Sectors and their respective Industry Subgroups. This is important because it helps you to see your list of super-strong stocks in the context of their industry groups. Since stocks within industry groups have a strong tendency to move in sympathy with each other, any stock appearing on this list which is also a part of a hot industry group has an additional positive factor weighing in its favor

So what commonalities do you see on the above list? I see a lot of technology and computers. But I also see two stocks, ADIC and VRTS, that belong to the same industry subgroup, Computers-Memory Devices. **As a trader, this would draw my attention.**

At this point, you can begin to see how Relative Strength fits into the trading equation. Relative Strength helped us to generate a list of powerful trading candidates. This narrowing of candidates saves us a tremendous amount of time and gives us an inherent edge on top of any other attractive indications we may see as we evaluate each stock on the list.

In fact, if you were to click on the chart for ADIC as of the date the above list was generated, you'd get the following. See the breakout? Theoretically, you'd buy at 2) and place your OPS at 1), given that all other technical factors are in place. **I will talk about just what these factors are in coming weeks.**

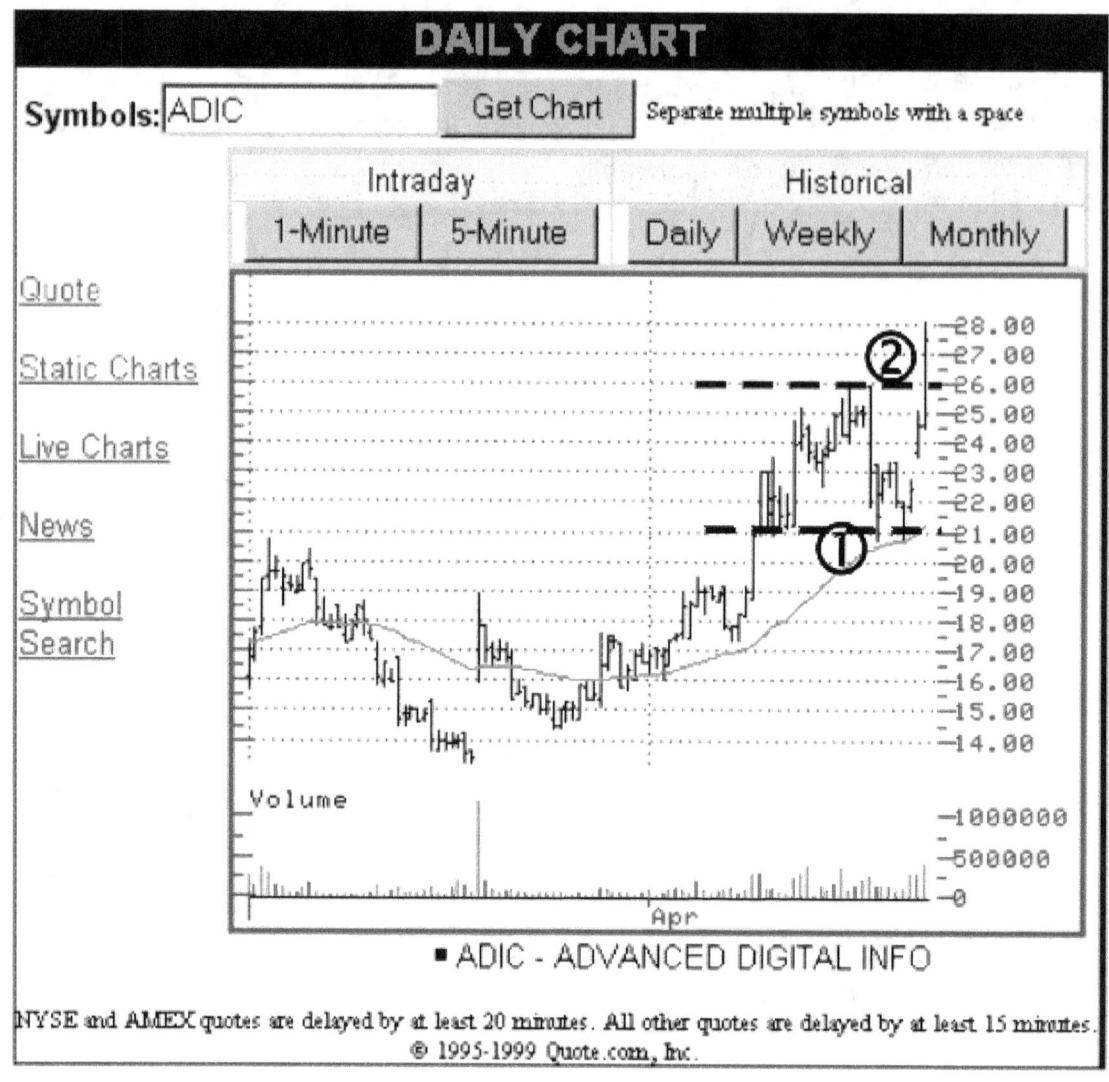

In Conclusion:

*Make no mistake about it. If I had to choose only one quantitative indicator to trade with, **I would definitely choose Relative Strength.*** Many successful money managers use this tool almost exclusively, and with it, they've beaten the market consistently for decades.

Investors and traders alike need to concentrate their research and time on the most reliable and consistent indicators. The most reliable and consistent of them all, is RS. Use it and and you'll see an increase in your trading results. Avoid it at your peril. It is simply one of the most powerful tools for improving trading performance.

Introduction to Week 3

To get started and to give you some perspective, let me first review Rule 8 from Week 1's money management rules:

Rule 8: Let Your Profits Run

> I advocate trading in runaway markets. In such instances, the stock or futures market you're positioned in will often continue moving much longer than you originally thought. Getting into these markets and then staying positioned in strong trends until I get stopped out is my bread and butter approach.

Runaway markets are important. This week, I'll give you a general overview of what a runaway market is and how to identify one. I will describe in great detail **the bar chart patterns** typical of runaway markets as well as the **characteristics that are common to the underlying companies themselves.**

Before we move on, let me give you some sense of how runaway markets fit with what we've learned so far.

Money management is the basis of my trading techniques. Any tool I actually use in my trading approach has to be proven and tested statistically over long time periods and many markets to **provide maximum returns with minimal risk.** Anyone can develop nifty indicators and trading systems to their heart's content, but unless they are founded on principles that **allow you keep as much of the money you make as possible**, they are worthless.

My money management rules dictate I select the **hottest markets** to trade in (market selection), as opposed to just trying to time my entries in run-of-the-mill markets. The hottest markets are, by nature, those with the highest relative strength (Week 2) and so strong that they seem to be **"out of control."** These are markets that are moving so **explosively in one direction** they seem to defy logic and reason. This is the characteristic we'll discuss this week.

Now, let's proceed.

Overview of Runaway Markets

Overview of Runaway Markets

There's an old saying in the markets:

> "In the financial world, there are many **meteors**, but few **fixed stars**."

What this means is **there are many stocks whose prices blast off into the stratosphere, reach extreme overvaluation and then plummet back into relative obscurity. On the other hand, there are few stocks that can sustain steady price growth for more than a decade.**

My research shows that **the very best opportunities** for both traders and investors are in both **Meteor or Fixed Star type stocks.** What is so exciting about this is that the techniques for identifying and trading these stocks are practical and easily understandable for the average trader. Let's look at their general characteristics.

Meteors

If you study the market using all the available data on U.S. stocks for this century, you will find at least one bull market each decade with enough power to produce many "meteors:" **Stocks that explode up 300% or more in a one- to three-year period.** These fad stocks exhibit the following generally characteristics:

1) Strong, consistent earnings

2) Explosive price moves

3) High relative strength

In the final third of their upward price movement, they will finally attract the notice of Wall Street analysts, only to get wildly overvalued and over-owned by institutions before **collapsing back into relative obscurity**. These are the meteors of the stock market.

Stars

Besides Meteors, **each decade also produces a small handful of Fixed Stars**. These stocks start off the same way as meteors and generally progress through the same explosive growth stages. But **unlike meteors, they do not become wildly overvalued.**

The key underlying factor that accounts for this difference is that they continue to sustain high, consistent earnings growth long after they cease to be a fad with the Wall Street crowd. Because of this, **these stocks do not collapse, but just continue to move upward, except at a slower rate and with more volatility than during their initial pre-popularity phase**.

In past years Meteors and Stars have sprung out of variety of industries that, at the time, observers thought were trends that would continue for many years. **Many of them turned out to be fads.** Consider the following list:

- Buggy makers and cigar stores;

- Aviation, oil, ice, and closed-end investment trust;

- Higher yielding utilities, no-debt financials with earnings;

- Uranium, bowling chains;

- Conglomerates, recreational vehicles;

- Nifty fifty, OTC growth, oil, gold stocks;

- Junk bonds, REITs, Japanese stocks, discount distributors of PC software, hardware, electronic supplies, pharmaceuticals;

- Medical, biotechnology, capital goods, software, telecommunications, communication software and hardware, health maintenance organizations (HMOs), financials, emerging markets and debt, Internet companies, cigar manufacturers.

The Best Way to Profit from Meteors and Fixed Stars

The wartime years of the 1940s being the exception, each decade has had its series of (mostly) Meteors and with a few Fixed Stars interspersed. **These are the runaway markets I and other savvy traders covet so highly.** The point that I want to make, however, is that **it is close to impossible to predict with any degree of consistency which stocks are going to be meteors and which are going to be fixed stars**; you only know after the fact.

Thus, even if you know how to position yourself in these hot, runaway markets, it is highly probable you will be holding mostly Meteors and just a few Fixed Stars. In other words, most of these stocks will be hot only until they fall out of favor. If you buy and hold them, you will not see anywhere near maximum profits. **The bottom line is that it's very important to trade Meteor stocks rather than invest in them.**

As traders, the most important thing is for us to **identify these markets at the earliest possible stage of their rise to fame.** We'll deal with that in the next section.

How I Identify Runaway Markets

Well, after a few years of staring at all those charts on my walls and ceiling, as well as the mountains of economic data I referred to earlier, **the patterns that are common to all runaway markets began to emerge.**

Just over 85% of the top stocks in the past 100 years displayed these patterns during the first third of the rise to "Wall Street Darling" status. In the following sections I will describe these patterns in detail.

Before I do, let make sure that you have some terms in your pattern vocabulary.

In the patterns I'll show you, it's important to understand the **specific components** of bars within a standard bar chart. Here are those components:

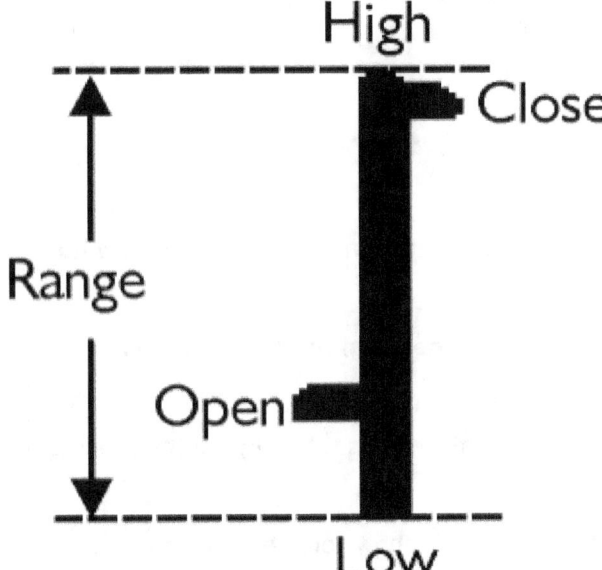

The **open, high, low, close and range** of adjacent bars can have specific relationships that **define important patterns**, as you'll see below.

TBBLBG

I use the acronym "TBBLBG" which stands for Thrust Breakout (TB), Breakaway Lap (BL), and Breakaway gap (BG). These are three small patterns that occur at the tail end of larger breakout patterns that I always see in runaway markets. These patterns are similar and interchangeable in the sense that it's not so important which one you see as long as one of them actually present. **Referring to them in one acronym has been more of a mental shorthand for me than anything else**

Here is what these patterns look like:

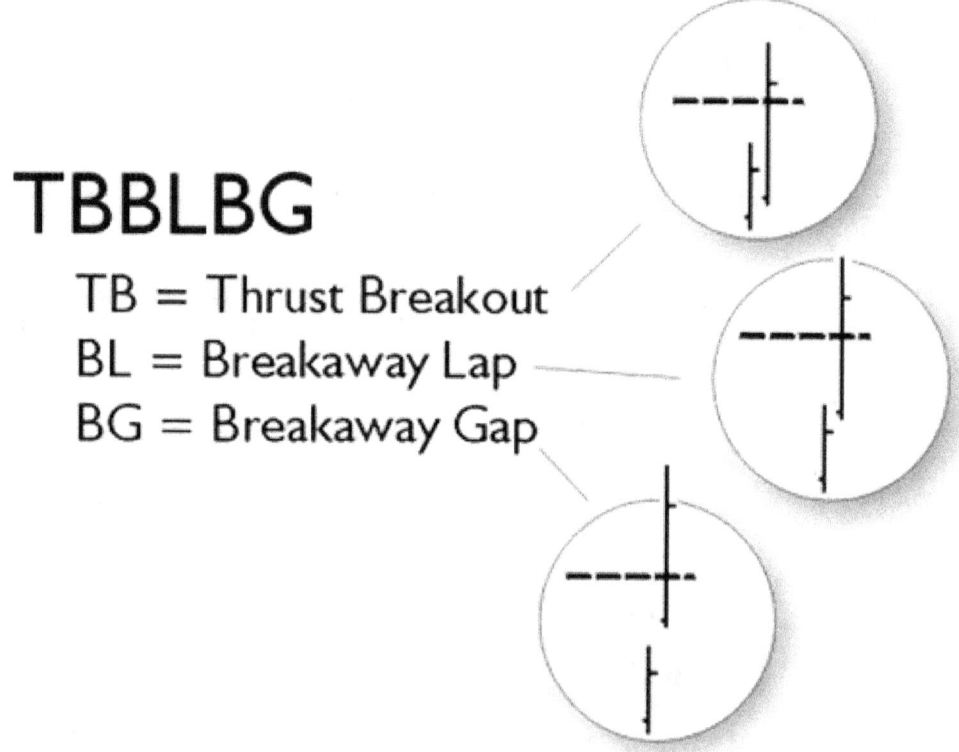

TBBLBG
TB = Thrust Breakout
BL = Breakaway Lap
BG = Breakaway Gap

Thrust Breakout (TB): The low of the Breakout Bar is higher than the low, but below the close of the preceding bar.

Breakaway Lap (BL): The low of the Breakout Bar is higher than the close, but below the high the preceding bar.

Breakaway Gap (BG): The low of the Breakout Bar is higher than the high of the preceding bar.

Now that you have some familiarity with the terminology, I will show you the patterns **that over 85% of the top stocks of the past 100 years have displayed.**

Runaway Market Pattern 1
Thrust Breakout Up

Runaway Market Pattern 1
Thrust Breakout Up

A **Thrust Breakout Up** is a move in which:

- Price breaks above resistance on a day whose range is two or more times the average range of the preceding 20 days;

- The volume is higher than the volume of the prior day;

- The close of the breakout bar is in the top one-third of the day's range.
- The low of the breakout bar is lower than the close of the previous day.

As with all the patterns I'm going to show you, this pattern **must occur within a fast moving trend** to be valid. In other words, the consolidation you see will be a pause within a larger trend.

Note:

In the preceding description, I have described the pattern in a way that makes sense to computer programmers. It is, in fact, the way I have it programmed on my computer.

However, much of the time, I do not rely on a computer and I just scan through charts, eyeballing the patterns as I see them. For all practical purposes, you can do the same, because there is a degree of "wiggle room" in these pattern definitions that allows for variation from the exact mathematical parameters. Those who are married to some systematized or mechanical approach won't like that statement, but hey--this has worked for me long before I had ready access to computers.

Developing the art of just recognizing what's there on a bar chart is something I hope you will take the time to practice over and over again. Use your computer as a tool, not a crutch.

Runaway Market Pattern 2
Thrust Breakout Down

During bear markets, you are going to want to find runaway markets that are plummeting to the downside.

A **Thrust Breakout Down** is a move in which:

- **Price breaks below support on a day in which the range is two or more times the average range of the preceding 20 days;**

- **The volume is higher than the volume of the prior day;**

- **The close of the breakout bar is in the bottom 1/3 of the day's range.**
- **The high of the breakout bar is higher than the close of the previous day.**

Here is what the pattern looks like:

Runaway Market Pattern 3
Breaklap Up

The next component of TBBLBG is the **Breaklap**.

A lap is a "hole" in trading between the previous day's close and the next day's action that doesn't meet the criteria of the traditional "gap."

In the pattern below, the **Breaklap Up**, the following occurs:

- **A move above <u>resistance</u> occurs in which the low of the day is higher than the previous day's close, but less than the previous day's high.**

Here's how it looks:

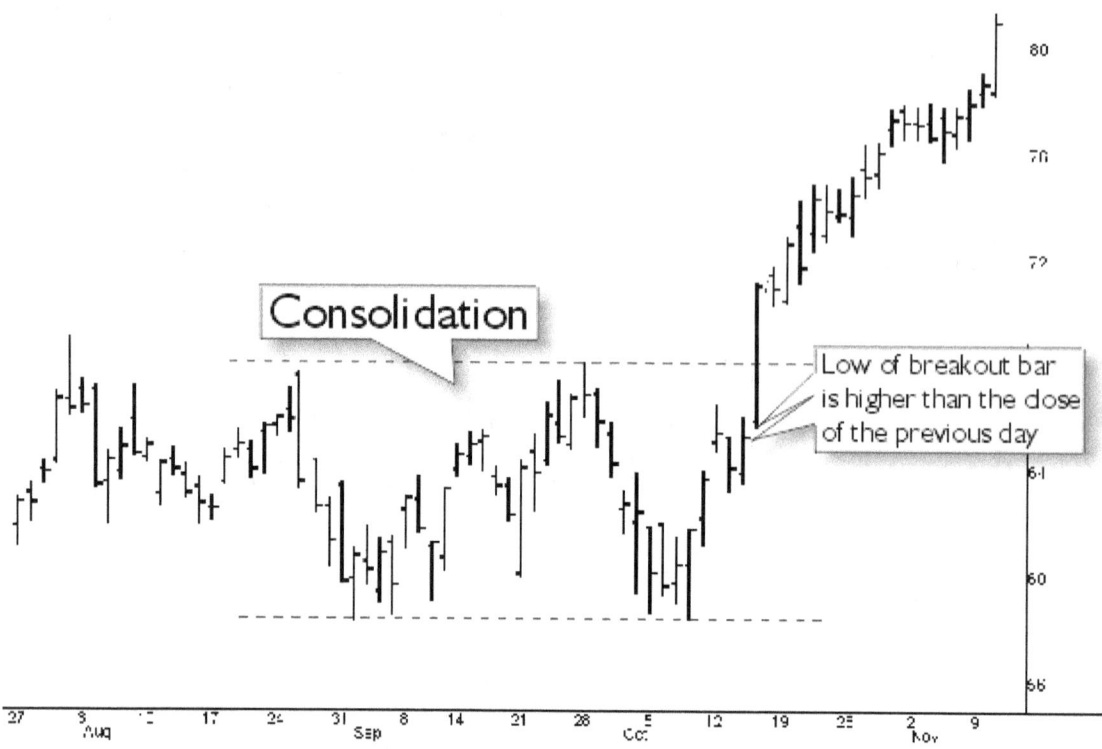

Notice that, unlike the Thrust Breakout-type pattern, there is **no constraint placed upon the range of the breakout bar or the volume for that day.**

Runaway Market Pattern 4
Breaklap Down

In the Breaklap Down:

- A move below support occurs in which the low of the day is lower than the close of the previous day, but higher than the previous day's low.

Runaway Market Pattern 5
Break Gap Up

Gaps are fairly familiar to most traders. In the **Break Gap Up**, price has penetrated through resistance such that:

- **The low of the breakout bar is higher than the high of the previous day. In effect there is just an empty space where no trading occurred on the bar chart.**

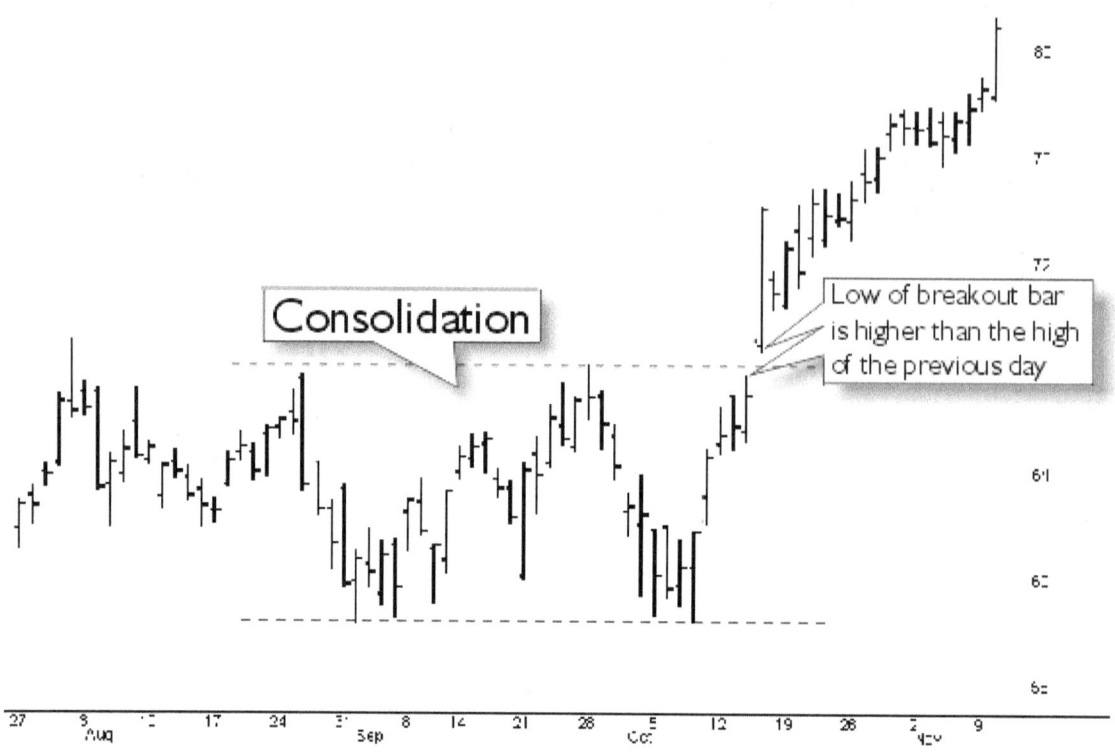

In runaway markets, gaps are common. Prices are moving so crazily that traders cannot help but pile on top of one another into a stock. This mechanism feeds on itself, driving prices higher in **powerful spurts**.

Novice traders are often afraid to trade these moves because they think a stock has suddenly become too expensive or that the move is somehow climatic in nature. In reality, in a runaway market, **Break Gap Ups** are often the beginning of huge moves that go far beyond your expectations.

Runaway Market Pattern 6
Break Gap Down

In the **Break Gap Down**:

- **The low of the breakout bar is higher than the high of the previous day. In effect, there just an empty space where no trading occurred on the bar chart.**

This pattern looks like this:

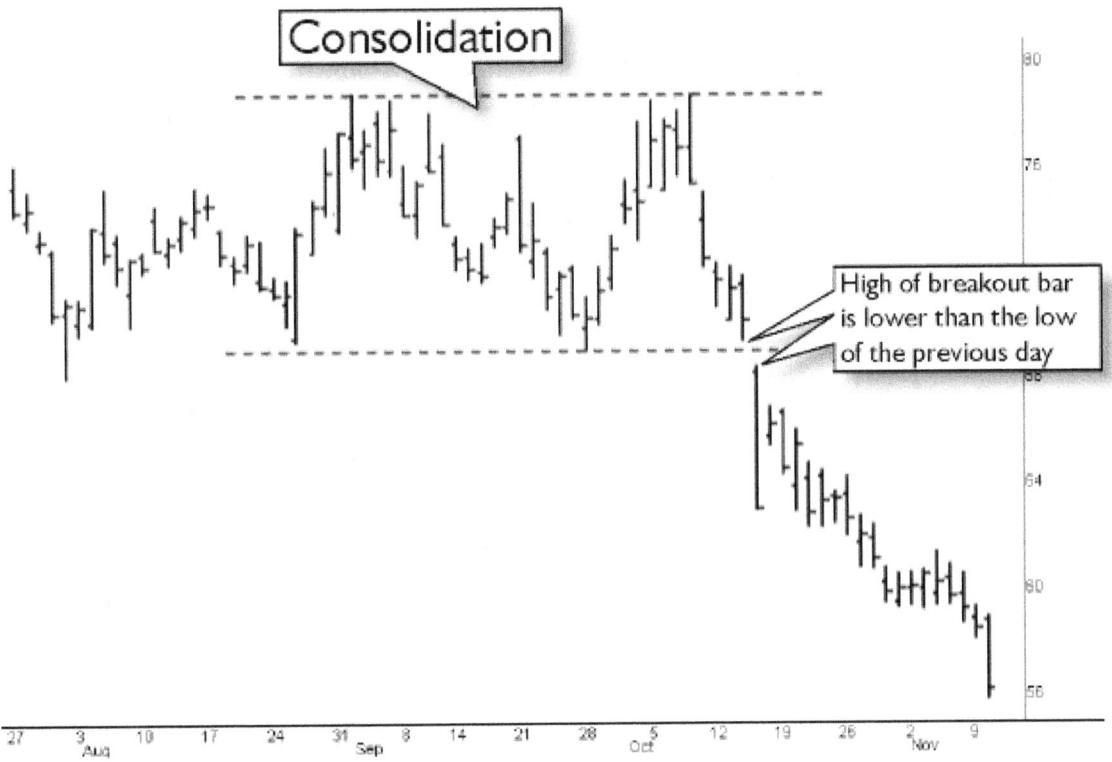

Now you've seen the basic patterns that have occurred in 85% of all the top stocks in the past century. But there is one more crucial ingredient:

What You'll See When TBBLBG's Occur in a Real Bar Chart

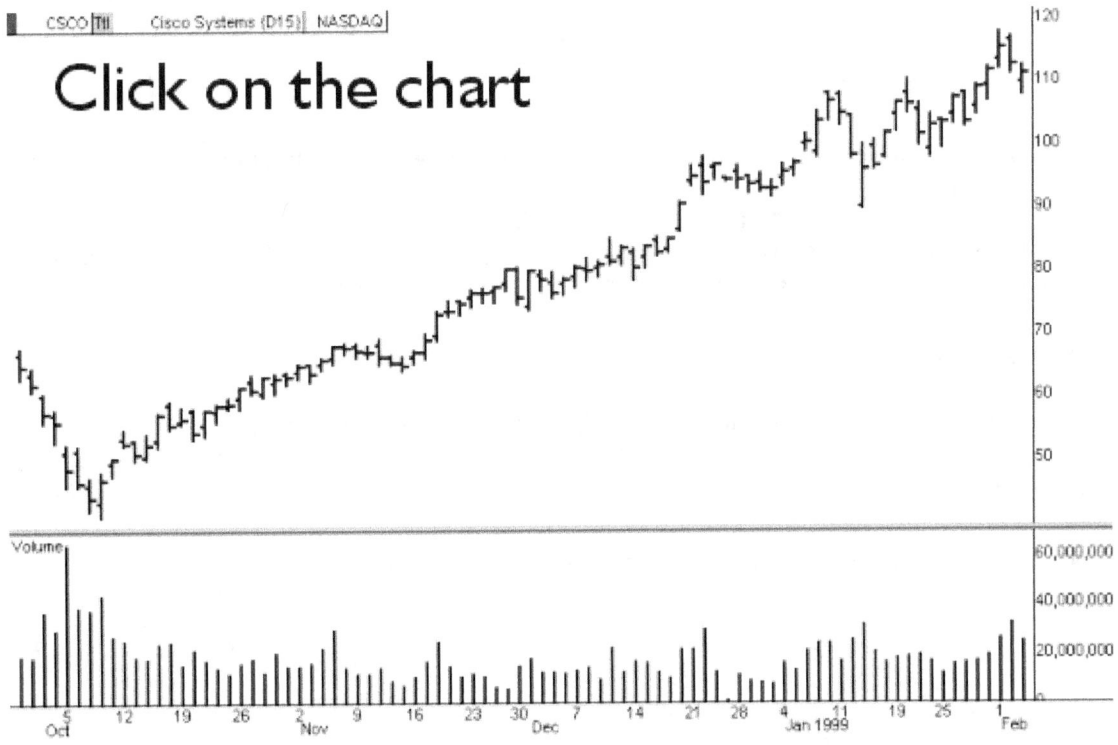

TBBLBG Patterns Revealed in CSCO

Notice how these patterns **follow one another in stair-step fashion**. This is one of the **primary characteristics** to which you must pay attention. I'll restate it now as a rule, just so you'll remember it better:

Generally, runaway markets contain many laps, gaps, and thrusts in the direction of the strong trend.

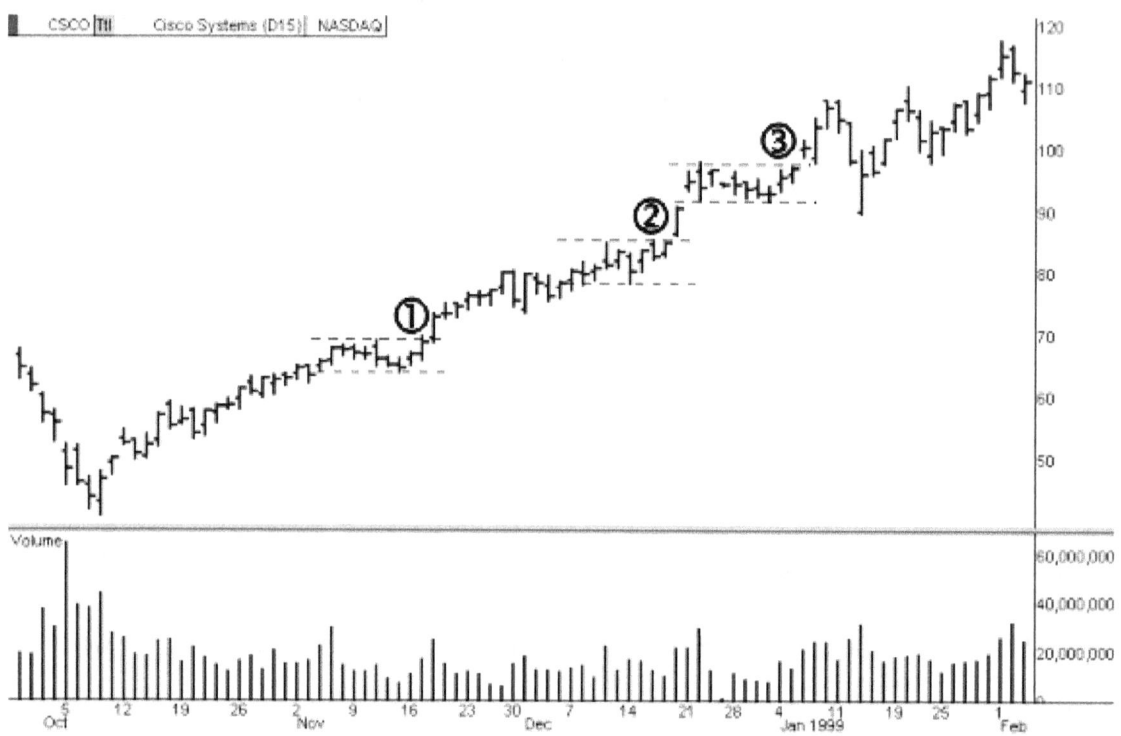

1) **Thrust Breakout**.

- The low of the breakout bar is a little under the close and below the high of the previous day's bar.
- Volume higher on the breakout bar than on the previous bar.
- The range on the breakout bar is greater than the average range of the previous 20 bars.
- The close of the breakout bar is in the upper third of the bar's range.

2) **Breakgap Up**.

- The low of the breakout bar is higher than the high of the preceding bar.

3) **Breakgap Up**.

- The low of the breakout bar is higher than the high of the preceding bar.

How to Jump On the Freight Train As It Leaves the Station

One of the key obsessions you ought to have is to identify runaway markets as early as possible. Like a freight train leaving the station, speed and acceleration develop fairly early on and it isn't long before it's barreling along at 80 mph. **I do everything I can to ride the first third of a runaway stock's rise to Wall Street prominence.** The risk of entering late in the game right before the stock fizzles out is vastly reduced.

So how do **you** do this?

The preceding TBBLBG patterns are the main runaway market patterns I search for when I'm looking for trading opportunities. **Now I'm going to show the patterns I search for when I want to verify the existence of a runaway market.**

Once again, I've analyzed and cataloged patterns quite meticulously using the past century's data and **found that there are certain patterns that occur far more frequently than others during the first third of a stock's rise to substantially higher prices.**

I cataloged and compiled the frequencies with which the most useful technical patterns occurred. What follows in the next pages are the results of this research.

Early Identification Pattern 1
Swing Breakouts on TLBLBG, 85%

Early Runaway Market Identification Pattern 1 -
Swing Breakouts on TBBLBG, 85%

85% of the 1,300 runaway markets I studied contained Swing Breakouts on TBBLBG's. These are basic swing patterns in which prices briefly pull back or consolidate and then resume the dominant trend by breaking out of the consolidation with a Thrust Breakout, Break Lap, or Break Gap.

In this and most of the examples to follow, I've drawn a schematic of how the pattern looks followed by an actual example of how the pattern looks when it occurs in the real world. The schematic will make the pattern easier to remember and the real pattern will help you to learn to recognize it better.

Schematic:

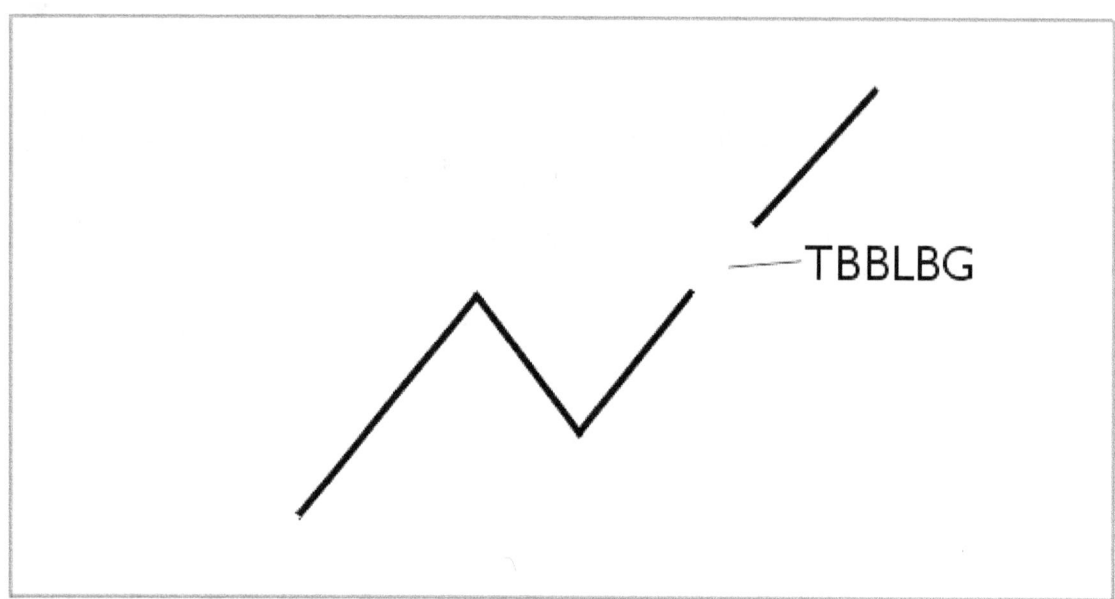

How it looks in the real world:

Early Runaway Market Identification Pattern 2

82% of the 1,300 Runaway markets I studied contained Breakaway Gaps. These are patterns in which a stock in a strong trend pauses and trades briefly in a consolidation pattern. A breakout occurs in which the breakout bar gaps higher. The low of the breakout bar is higher than the high of the preceding bar.

Schematic:

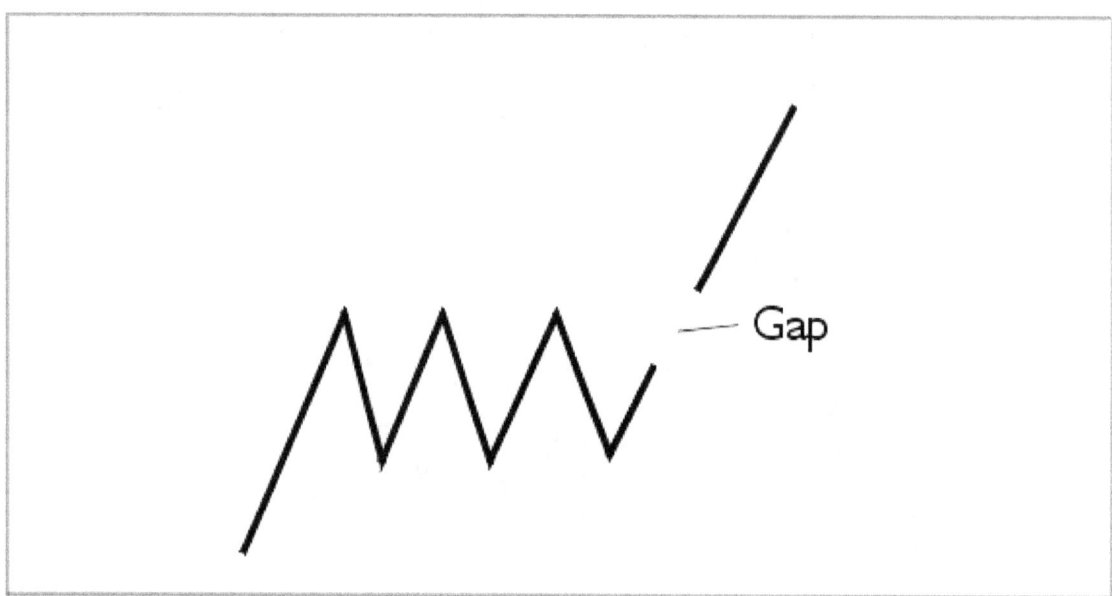

How it looks in the real world:

Early Runaway Market Identification Pattern 3 - Generic Flags and Triangles, 69%

Sixty nine percent of the 1,300 runaway markets I studied contained Generic Flags and Triangles. Other than fulfilling the classic shape these patterns are known for (shown below), there are no other requirements (such as a tight range or TBBLBG). It is important, however, to remember that I look for these in the context of a trend continuation. Therefore, you're looking for powerful trends in which you see flags or triangles occurring when the stock pauses or pulls back briefly.

Schematic:

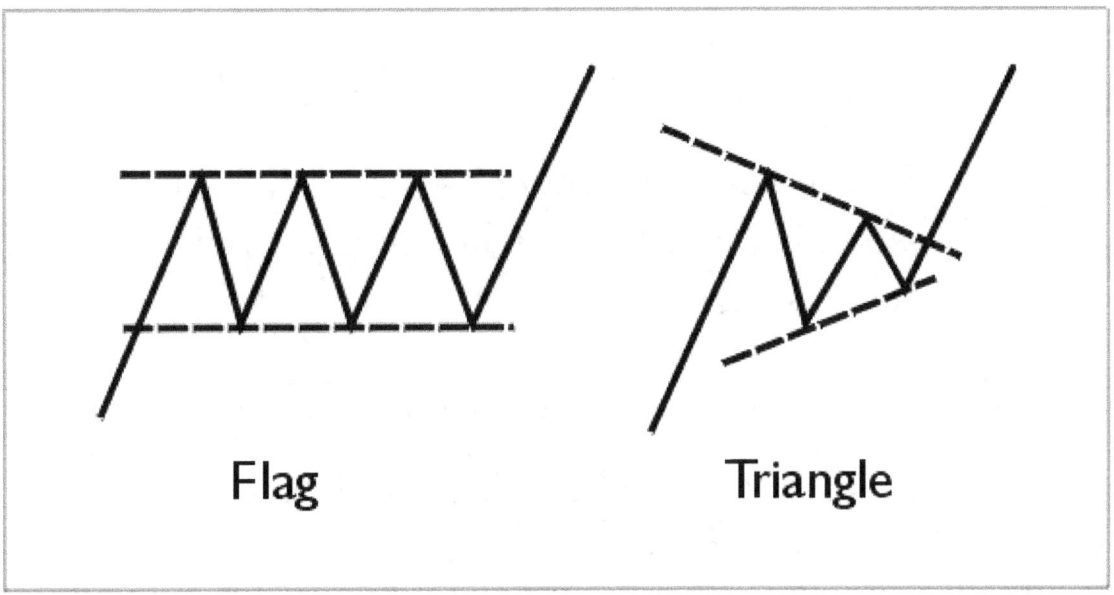

How it looks in the real world:

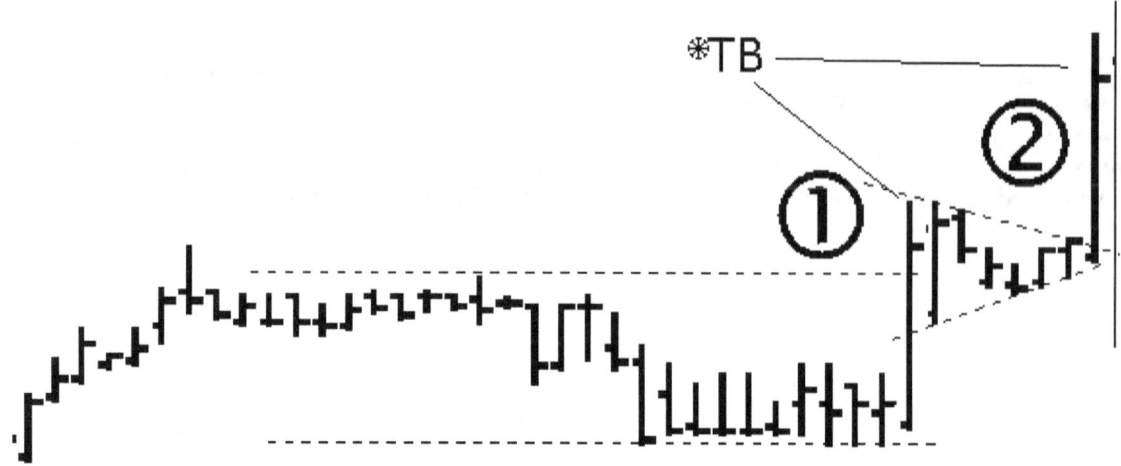

*Both these bars would be TB's only if their respective volumes are higher than their previous bars.

Please note that it was just a **mere coincidence** that this flag and triangle appeared in the same chart. When you look for them, they definitely do not have to be juxtaposed side-by-side.

Early Runaway Market Identification Pattern 4 - five-Day Runs, 46%

Fourty six percent of the time, runaway markets contain five-day Runs. These are strings of **five consecutive days in which each close is higher or lower than the previous one.** Frequently, these five-day Runs are followed by short reversals.

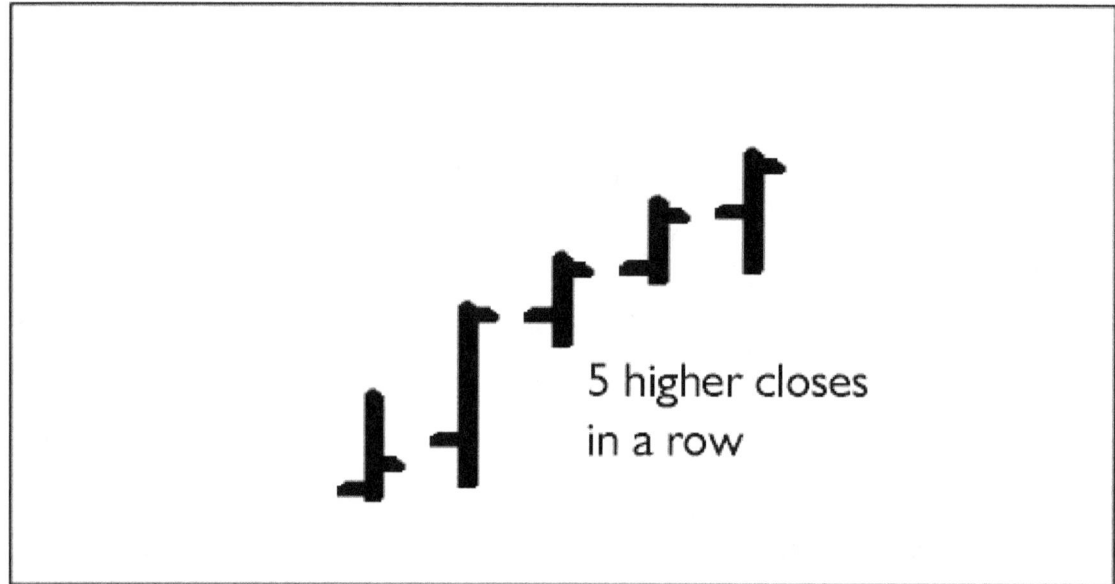

How it looks in the real world:

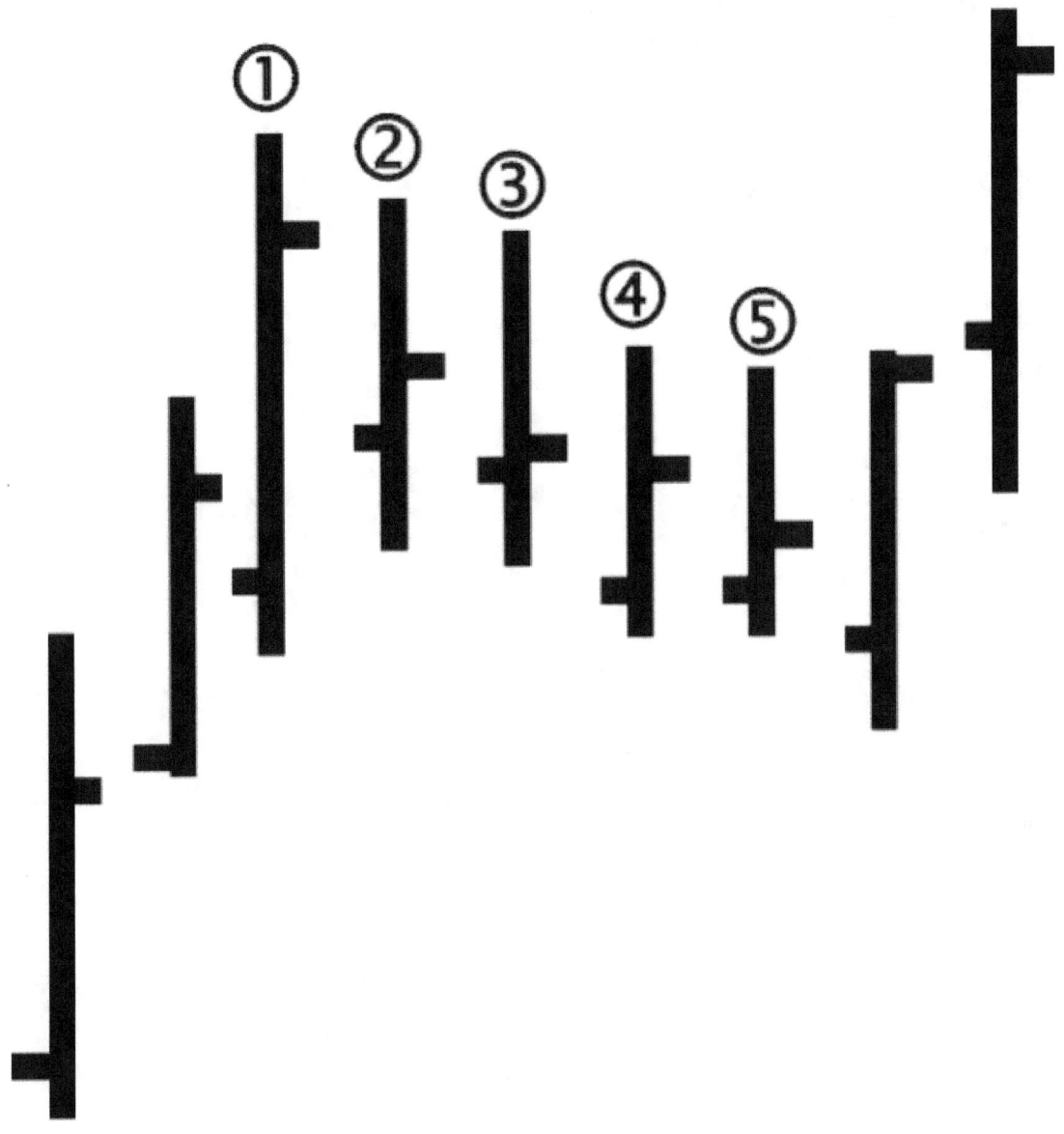

Early Runaway Market Identification Pattern 5
Runaway and Continuation Gaps, 32%

32% of the 1,300 runaway markets I studied contained Runaway and Continuation Gaps. This is a pattern which really conveys the clear message that you're in a <u>runaway market</u>. When an explosive price trend in which two or more gaps occur within short time frame, you're looking at a runaway market **that is moving at top speed.**

Schematic:

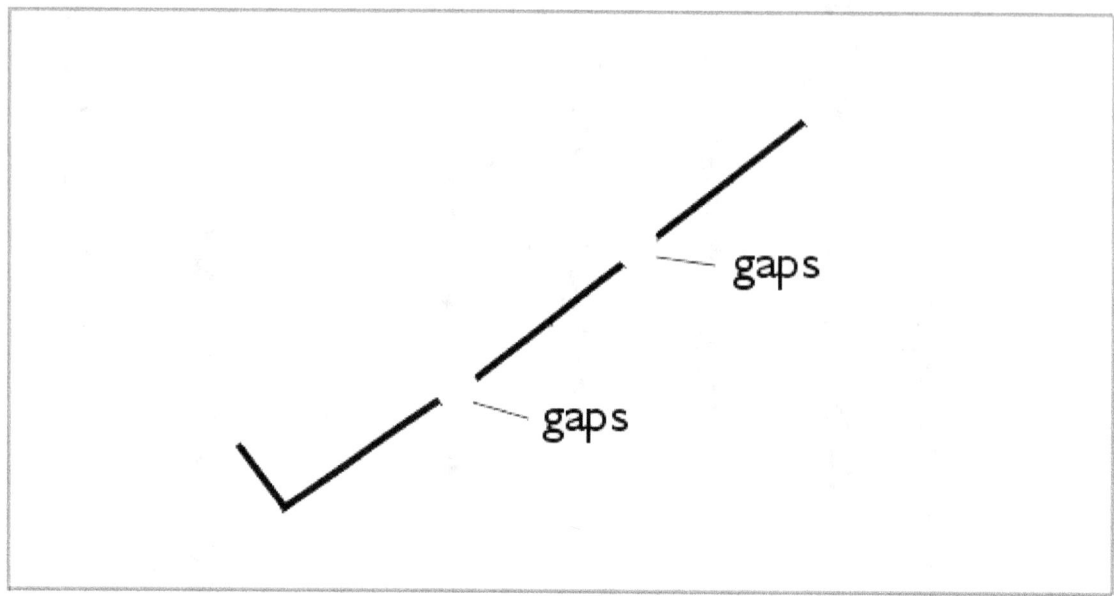

How it looks in the real world:

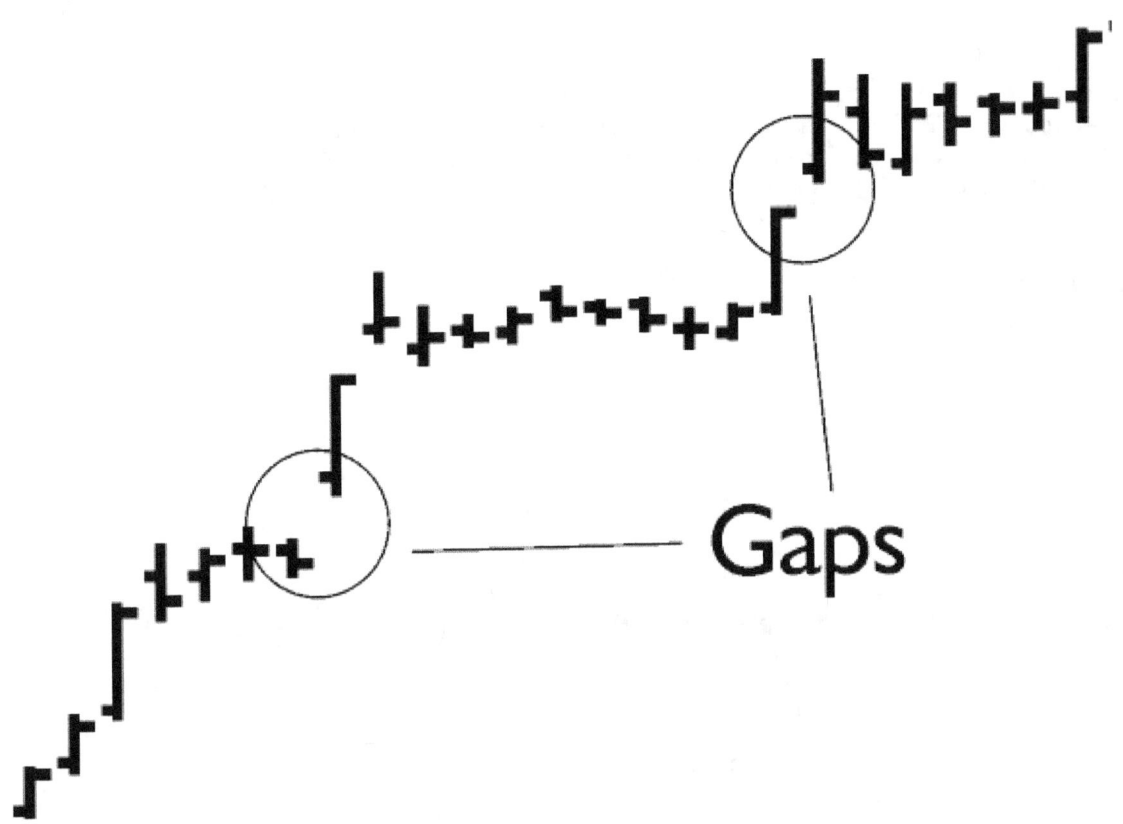

**Early Runaway Market Identification Pattern 6
Tight Range Breakouts on TBBLBG, 32%**

Thirty two percent of the 1,300 runaway markets I studied contained Tight Range Breakouts on TBBLBG. This is where a strong trend pauses in tight consolidations. These sometimes reflect indecision between buyers and sellers and their lack of resolve to bet in one direction or another. Once this indecision is resolved, resumption of the dominant trend ensues with the breakout occurring on a TBBLBG.

Schematic:

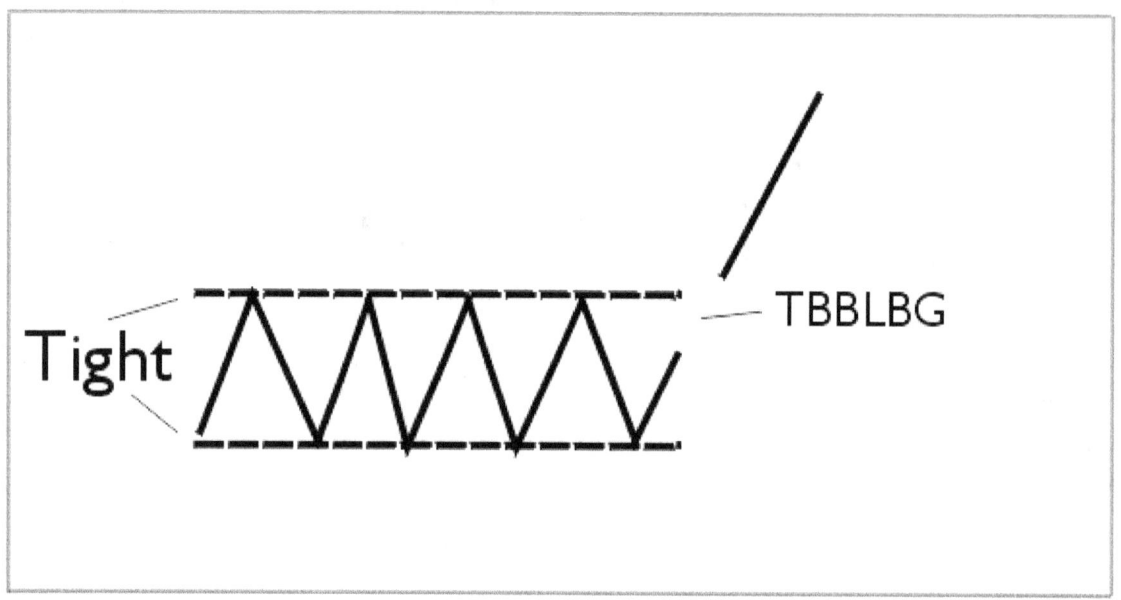

How it looks in the real world:

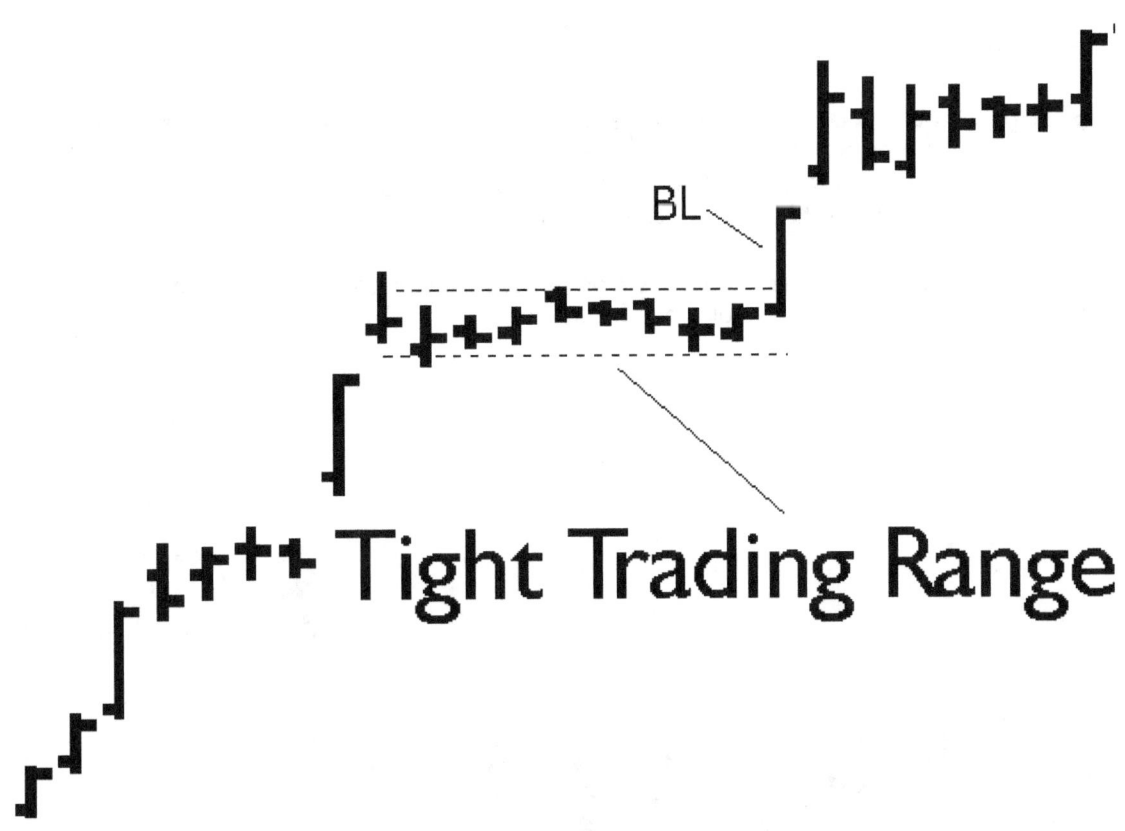

Early Runaway Market Identification Pattern 7 - Thrusts, 27%

27% of the runaway markets I studied contained Thrusts. Thrusts, by definition, are breakouts from consolidations in which:

- **Price breaks above resistance on a day whose range is two or more times the average range of the preceding 20 days.**
- **The volume is higher than the volume of the prior day.**
- **The close is in the top one-third of the day's range.**

This is one case for which I couldn't draw a schematic of the pattern that was any more illustrative than a real-life example. So I have only one picture for you to look at. It's the real thing.

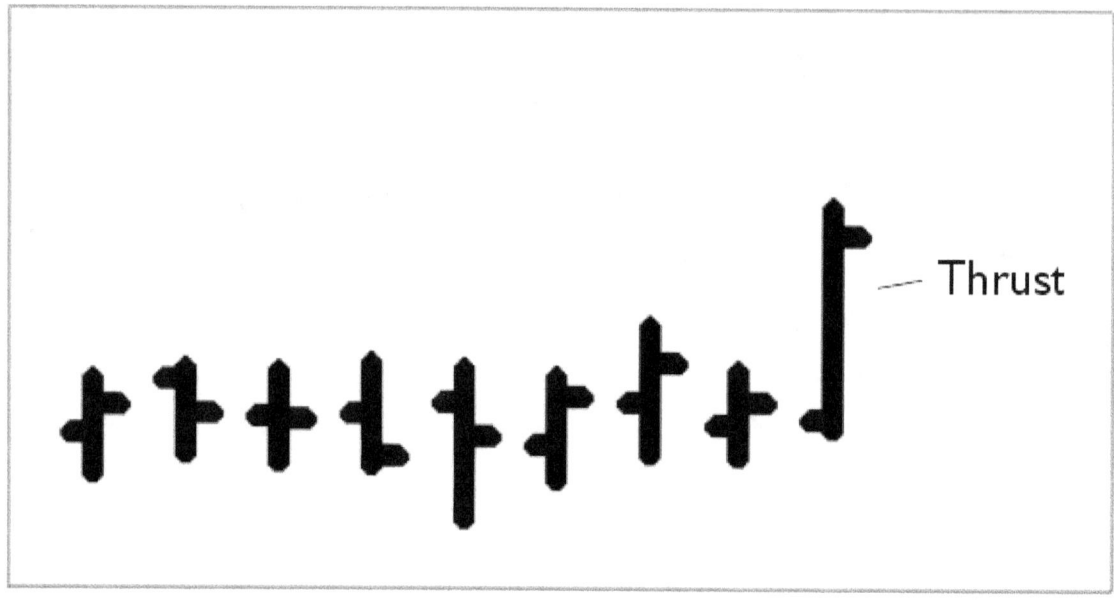

Early Runaway Market Identification Pattern 8
"N" Corrections

Finally, 19% of the 1,300 runaway markets I studied contained "N" Corrections. These are market consolidations within a down-sloping channel. Sometimes these "N" Corrections are easily mistaken as market reversals as opposed to minor pullbacks. That is, **they fool people into thinking that a strong trend has ended.**

Schematic:

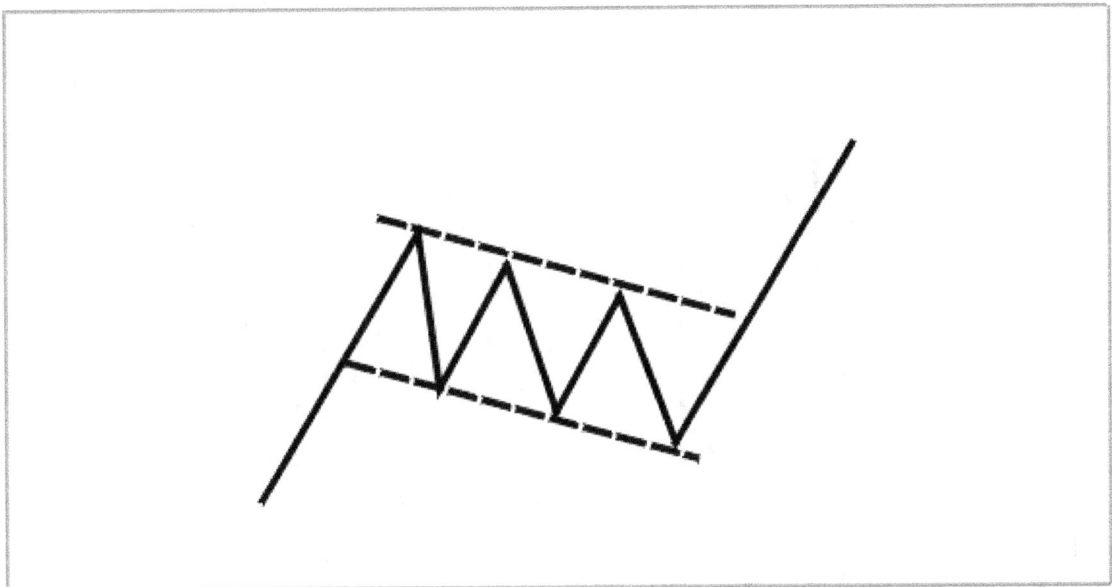

How it looks in the real world:

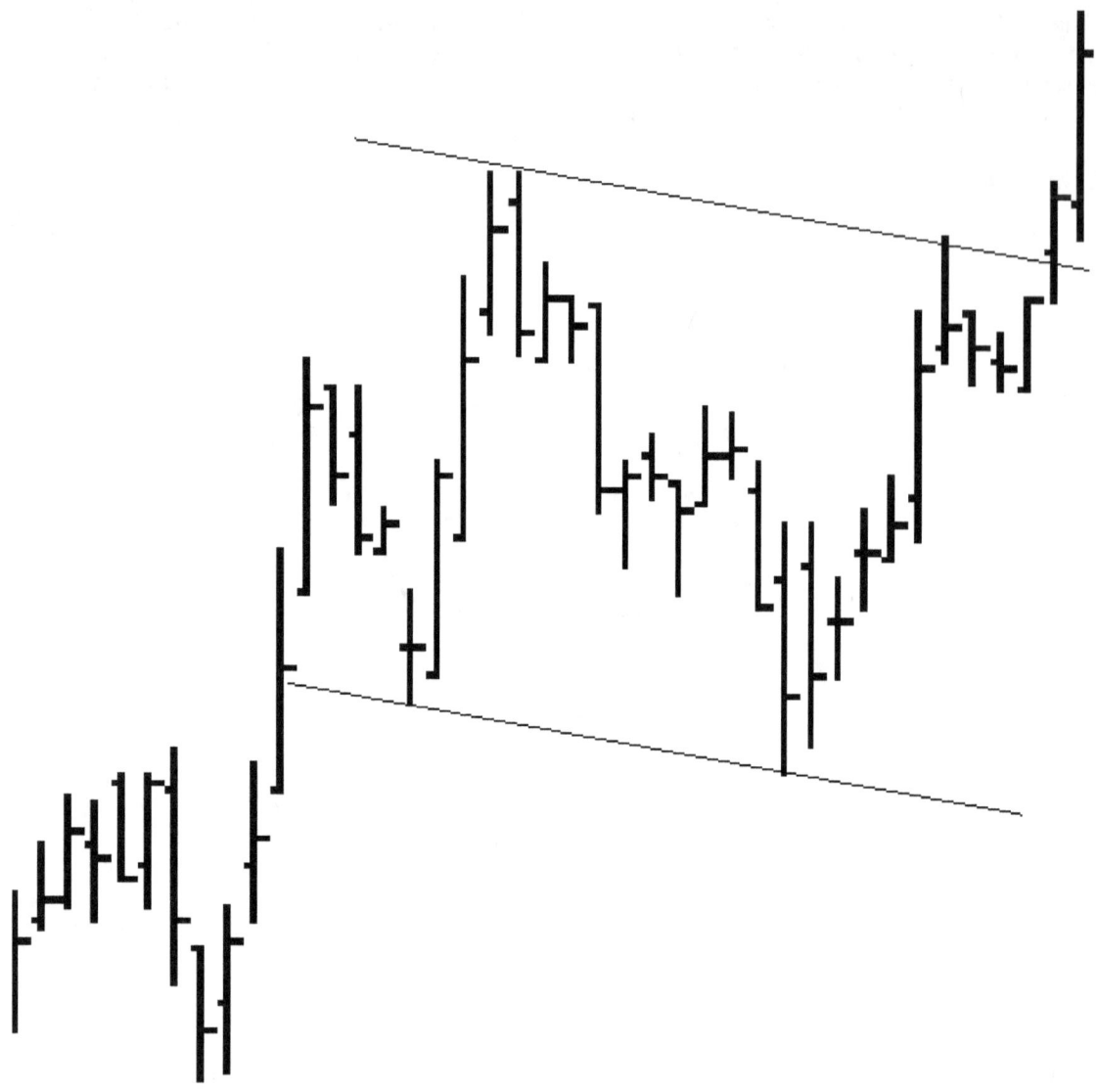

There you have it. You have now seen the eight patterns that occur most frequently during the first third of all the runaway markets I've studied. Now let's take a look at another factor you have to consider before you trade in runaway markets.

Fuel

Once we find stocks that have exhibited the types of technical patterns described in the previous section, we take a closer look at each stock and look for something called **Equity Fuel.**

The concept of Fuel is simple: We are looking for **valid reasons that the trend we have identified will continue well into the foreseeable future**. Remember, we are not in a stock just for a two-point move. Rather, we enter every trade with the hope that it will be a home run--that is, **return a high profit with minimal risk.**

Once we have seen the technical patterns and have verified that Fuel exists, we have a **good candidate for further appreciation.**

Criteria for Runaway Stocks with Fuel

The following is a simplified version of the criteria I use. A deeper into the the macro-economic issues underlying fuel is available in my book, the Hedge Fund Edge.

1) Must have **five or more Runaway patterns in a 21-day period.** These are the patterns I've described in the previous pages.

2) The stock **has not fallen below it's 200-day moving average** once the uptrend has begun.

3) The stock must have a **relative strength ranking of at least 65 during corrections and at least 80 if it is making new highs.** This ranking is available in the TradingMarkets.com site.

4) EPS ranking according to Investor's Business Daily is **80 or higher.**

5) **Relatively Undiscovered Stock.** Institutions own less than 16% of the total capitalization. Traders should begin taking profits once a stock reaches 40% or higher institutional sponsorship. This figures can be found in Investor's Business Daily.

6) Low Debt. The company should ideally use its own internal growth to finance its expansion. **Long-term debt should be less than 50%.**

8) Positive Fundamentals. There should be a simple, straightforward reason for earnings growth to continue. It could a **new product, technology gap, change in management, or other type of competitive edge** that makes sense for continued upward momentum in stock price.

Closing Remarks

If you've been a trader for a while, perhaps you're saying to yourself, **"This is way too simple to be that good."** Or you're recalling that you've seen these patterns before in "beginner's" books on technical analysis and that you've graduated to Gann, Elliott Wave or the Omnipotent Order of the Markets.

Well, it's important to note that much of what I've shown this week you IS fairly simple.

But keep in mind that a **disproportionate degree of focus on methodology** is what trips up most traders. There is a great deal of information that you must absorb and many direct market observations you must make yourself before you can reach the point of true understanding. I'll be discussing these things in Weeks 4 through 10 as well as deal with issues of practical application. For example, this week I've shown you the patterns I look for in runaway markets. In later weeks of the course **I'll lead you through some exercises that will help you to recognize these patterns.**

And remember, even though recognizing the patterns is relatively easy, it doesn't make trading easy. Trading and the discipline of money management a genuine challenge for most people. **But I know it's a challenge you will succeed at if you are willing to put your mind to it.**

By the way, I'm really excited about good discussion that I've seen via the message boards. I've spent a couple hours reading and answering questions so far and I've thoroughly enjoyed it. Many thanks. Your input will help to shape the content for the coming weeks.

What's in Store for Next Week?

Have you been wondering when the bull market in U.S. stocks we've been in is going to end?

Next week, I'll be showing you the telltale signs that will help you **detect the onset of bull and bear markets** through the use of Liquidity Cycles. For the past 17 years—and especially over the past 5 years—traders have been blessed with one of the **biggest bull markets ever**. There have been an abundance of stocks that fit my Runaway Market criteria. But as sure as I'm sitting here typing this, **it's going to be over someday**—maybe next week or maybe 5 years from now. Whatever the case, you have to be prepared to read the signs. This is what I'll be teaching you next week. Until then. . .

Profitable trading,

Mark Boucher

A Brief Note:

One word before we dig in. In college, you probably ditched Economics 101 when your professor started using terms such as yield curves, money supply, short-term interest rates, inflation rate, Consumer Price Index, etc. But let me reassure you that the information I am about convey is about as important as any technique or market pattern I describe during the course of these 10 weeks. Like each of my other weekly topics, I cannot imagine that I could have achieved any level of trading success without understanding the Liquidity Cycle.

Also, if you make it to the end of this week's topic, I will also share with you my opinion about where we are currently in the Liquidity Cycle and what may happen to the stock market if I'm right.

The Shocking Truth

The truth is that you and I as traders are living in a real-life version of the Truman Show. The only difference is that **we are all "Truman." I like to think some of us are less Truman than others, however.** This brings me to this week's exciting topic: **Liquidity Cycles.**

In Week 1 on Money Management, I said that it is only by understanding the financial markets that you can achieve a lifetime of success and contentment as a trader. I will now reframe this in the context of the "Truman Show Concept."

> **The more you truly understand the financial markets, the less of a Truman you will be and the more you will be like one of the viewing audience which derives "entertainment" from the show.**

The entertainment value I'm speaking of is, of course, **trading profits.**

My premise is this:

> You and I have to live in the Truman world. We work, produce, buy stuff, sell stuff, and consume stuff under the delusion that it's all within the framework of a wonderful free market system that is not subject to outside interference. We are under the delusion that many of the realities, struggles and triumphs we face--the amount of money we have in the bank, whether or not we have a job, or can afford a good education for our children--are based on natural fluctuations in the health of the economy. **We are under the delusion that bull and bear phases in the stock markets, business cycles, inflation, deflation, recession, and depression are all the result of the natural forces of the free market system.**
>
> **The real truth is that the government, in large part, through a kind of bizarre, twisted, altruistic meddling is writing the**

script. The major business cycles that influence how much money we have in the bank, whether or not we're gainfully employed and whether we can afford a decent education for our children are under the direct control of the government. Yes, we have freedom. But like Truman, we only have freedom within the confines of the cage the government holds us in.

This cage is called the Liquidity Cycle, which is what your marriage vows refer to when the minister says "through plenty and in want." **Most relevant to traders is that the Liquidity Cycle has a direct and exact correlation to whether the stock market is going up or going down.**

This week, I will teach you what I know about the Liquidity Cycle. **By learning about the Liquidity Cycle you will become less of a Truman and more of a spectator watching the show.**

You will be "entertained" by bigger and more consistent trading profits because you'll understand the underlying forces that drive the long-term cycles out of which bull markets and bear markets are made. This is important because many of you are new to the markets and your only experience as a trader may be through trading this wacky and wonderful bull market we've been in. After reading a trading book or attending a seminar, you got excited and discovered that by merely by buying a stock you can make money. I wish it could always be that easy. The truth is that it's all going to be over soon. **And what you have could all be taken away from you-- unless you understand Liquidity Cycles.**

Let me ask you a couple of questions:

- You do want to be able to anticipate **the next bear market** don't you?
- You do want to know **when to sell all those high flying Internet stock of yours** before the current bull market comes to a crashing end, DON'T YOU?

I thought so.

Stick with me for the next hour and I guarantee that your prowess at economic-speak will not only help you achieve instant popularity in social settings, but also will help you take a giant step toward understanding the markets far, far, better than the vast majority of traders. It is this understanding that I believe is essential to success in trading.

Who's Really Controlling the Stock Market?

For the stock market to go up, people have to want to buy stocks. That means money has to be flowing into the market. That money has to come from someplace. In our U.S. economy, there are three main sources:

1. **People are building up their savings and investing more.**
2. **People and institutions are shifting their money** out of other kinds of investments (such as real estate or precious metals) into the stock market.
3. **The government lowers interest rates** and increases money supply which stimulates business expansion; that in turn improves wages, job security, savings, and the ability to invest.

By far, the most powerful of the above three factors is 3). It is also the least understood of all three factors. There is tremendous leverage in understanding how the government artificially pumps money into the economy, because **by mastering this one topic you will understand a great deal about the root causes and the tell-tale signs of bull and bear markets.**

Interest Rates: There's More Than Meets the Eye

Just about everybody who trades or invests has some glimmer of awareness that the lowering or raising of interests has some relevance to the stock market. However, **peoples' understanding of this concept is usually too superficial to be of much use.** When news services **report a change in interest rates, one of two things usually happens:**

1. **Nothing,** because the event has already been anticipated and is discounted by the market.
2. **A big, jolting move in either direction that is quickly followed by a resumption of whatever trend was already in place.**

Even though there is tremendous attention paid to this form of government intervention, in the normal course of people's trading in the markets, it seems to have little relevance. Or does it?

It certainly does. In reality, **what the government does by lowering or raising interest rates is extremely important to traders**, and in fact, viewed from larger perspective, **it has a high degree of predictive power for bull markets and bear markets.**

Would you like to know **how to anticipate the onset the next bear or bull market?**

Then you must understand the **Liquidity Cycle**.

Understanding the Liquidity Cycle

The Federal Reserve System is the Central Bank of the United States. It was created by an act of Congress in 1913 and assigned the task of "fostering a sound banking system and a health economy." In the following sections I will explain to you the Central Bank's (**also known as the Fed**) role in the Liquidity Cycle and then let you decide whether it actually accomplishes this.

In the diagram below, you see what I call the **Liquidity Cycle**. Other people call it the **"boom-bust" cycle.** If you're at least 20 years old, this may strike a familiar chord because you have lived through different portions of the Liquidity Cycle and have been negatively affected by it, either directly or indirectly. You or someone in your family may have gotten laid off, the business you owned went through hard times, or you lost a bundle in the stock market.

The Liquidity Cycle

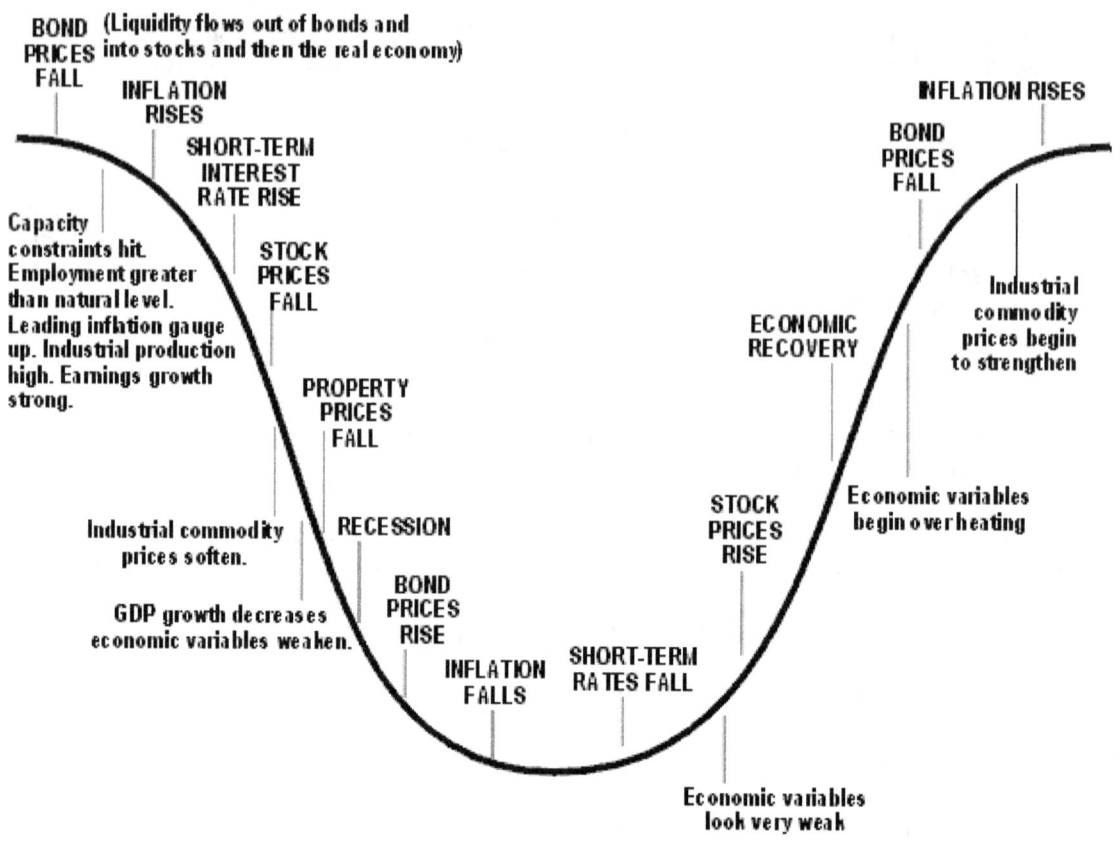

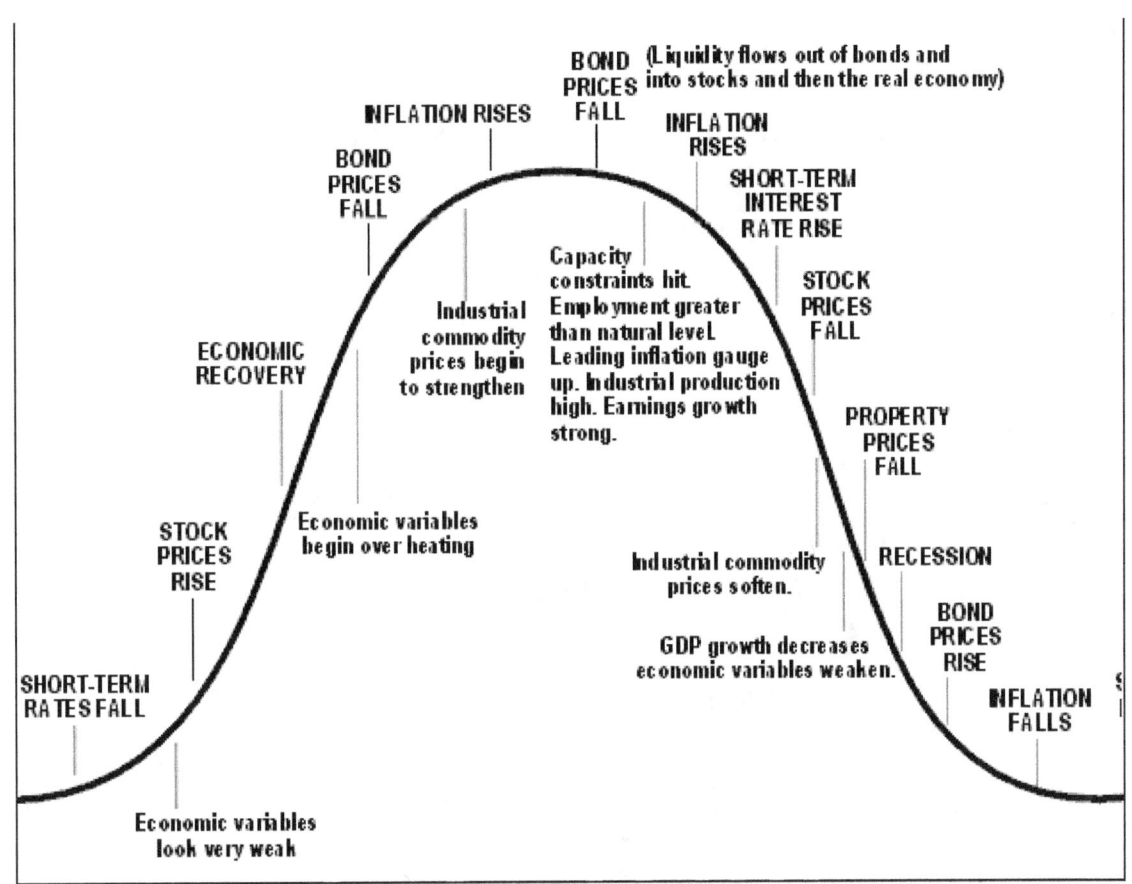

What's kind of funny about this is how the news media commonly refer to this as a "**business cycle**," the implication being that business or the economy goes through a natural ebb and flow between good times and bad times. **But it really doesn't have anything to do with business because the whole phenomenon is created by our government's Central Bank.** I call it the Liquidity Cycle because it has to do with the amount of available money (liquidity) that is floating through our economy.

If you look at the behavior of the Central Bank, historically, you'll see that

- the Central Bank usually takes action in order to allow the government to **spend beyond its means during a recession or depression** and to **kick-start an economy that is probably already distorted by virtue of earlier intervention by the Government.**

The Liquidity Cycle from the Bottom Up

Right now, we're going to examine the Liquidity Close close-up. In the following pages, I'll take you through its different phases and describe what the Central Bank does and the mischief it causes in the economy, the stock market, and the lives of individuals. As we go from stage to stage, you'll understand how, **by watching Central Bank over the course of time, you can be one step ahead of other traders.**

You will also understand the degree of control that a relatively small handful of people have over the state of the economy as well as the direction of the stock market. This hopefully will awaken you from being a Truman. **Sure, it can be scary, but it can also be profitable.**

The best place in the Liquidity Cycle for us to start is the "**kick-start**" activity the Central Bank does at the bottom of the Liquidity Cycle. From here everything will come into focus.

To move forward, **CLICK ON THE WORD "RECESSION"** in the Liquidity Cycle diagram below:

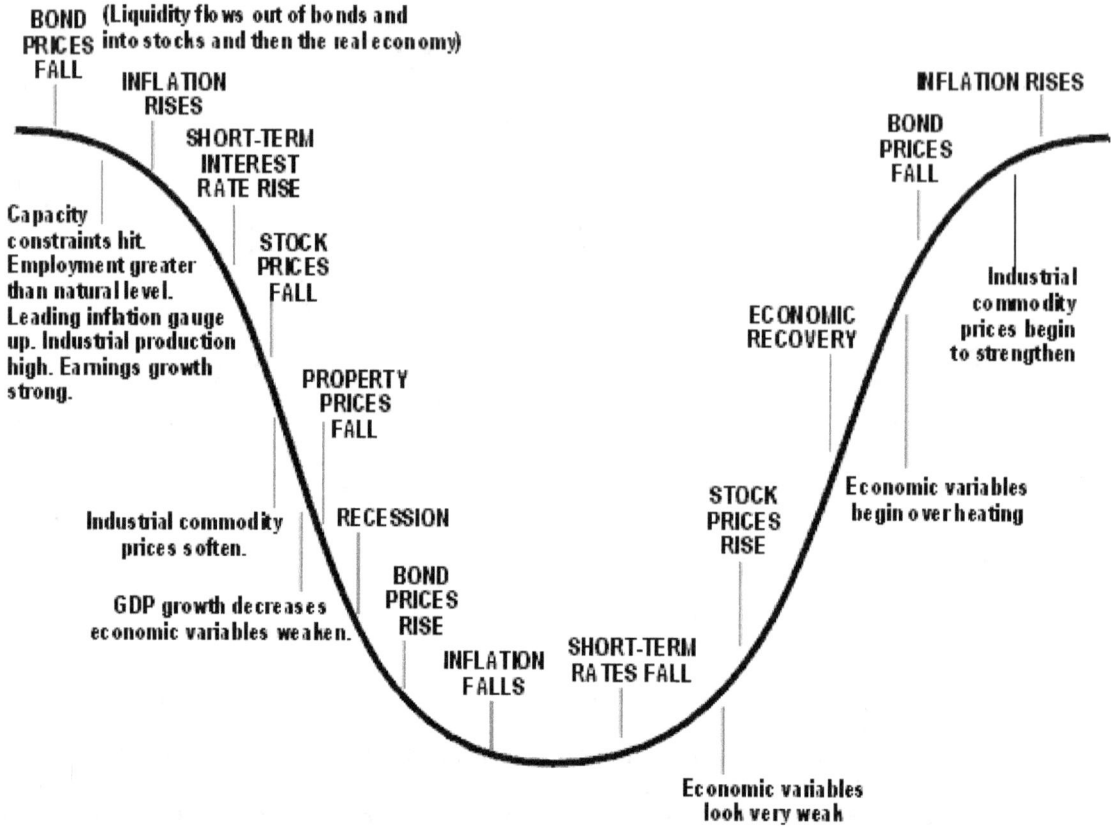

Recession

In a recession, the following happens:

- The **GDP (Gross Domestic Product) slows and then reverses to negative.** GDP is the total business production of the country.
- Real estate, bond prices, **stock market prices, and inflation are falling.**
- **Company earnings are falling** and balance sheets are deteriorating.
- **Banks cut lending** because they're worried about getting back their principal.
- **People are generally pessimistic** about the future.

As the recession deepens, the Central Bank realizes that the downward slide has such momentum that **it can pump up money supply without boosting inflation**, at least in the short-term. The following illustration not only shows the **faulty reasoning** behind this, but also how the **Central Bank underestimates the real severity of inflation** when it merely watches the **Consumer Price Index (CPI)**. In addition, you will understand a bit better what the **CPI numbers represent and what they don't represent.**

The Island Economy

10 people are stranded on a deserted island. Totally isolated from civilization, the 10 people develop their own economy. Everybody counts all the money they brought with them, and between them, **they find that there's a total of $1000 for everyone on the island** (or $100 for each person).

Each person is assigned a job. Some fish. Some pick coconuts. Others built huts. Prices are established for each good and service by island supply and demand forces. The total value of all these goods and services is $1000.

At times, there is a shortage of one thing or another like coconuts. The price of coconuts would increase. But when that happens the price of something else like fish has to drop because if people spend more on coconuts, they have less money with which to purchase other fish. Demand drops on fish and the price of fish has to be lowered. Also, there is only the same total $1000 in circulation. **The sum total value of absolutely everything could never be worth more or less than $1000.**

But then, **one member of the group (a fellow by the name of Central Bank or CB) finds an extra $500 in cash somewhere.** CB doesnít tell anybody else about, but slowly begins to add it to the money supply by spending an extra dollar here and an extra dollar there until he has spent $120 out of the $500. **Because there are more dollars competing for all goods and services, demand increases and becomes slightly out of balance with supply which causes prices to rise.** The "real" inflation rate has risen 12 percent because the sum of the price of everything had gone up 120/1000 or 12 percent.

Soon the other members of the group notice the rising prices and try to find out whoís got the extra money. Failing to do so, they appoint someone in the group to be an economist whose job is to study the inflation. Since it would take too much time and effort to track the price of absolutely everything in the economy (real inflation), one person suggests that he **monitors the price of coconuts in order to watch inflation.** This works because in the growing island economy, coconuts are an ingredient in virtually every meal as well being a critical component of clothing, housing, fishing, and almost every sector of the island of the economy. Soon, this economist is

CPI for short) as a way of determining when any islander is spending money that wasn't in the official pool of $1000.

With all this taking place, CB decides he's better off not spending any more new money for awhile. One day, however, he finds a box with more money in it--$100,000 to be exact! **CB then begins to realize that he can spend the money however he wishes, at least until the Coconut Price Index begins to head higher.**

With his new found wealth, CB tries to use his new buying power as surreptitiously as possible. Knowing that the CPI Index is based on coconuts, he keeps his spending channeled towards other products and services. **The first thing CB does is to have the hut-builder build him a bigger hut.** The hut-builder **gets paid $40** for this extra service and spends **only $2 on extra coconuts. The rest he spends on fish, savings, and other goods.**

The economist, **notices a small increase in the price of coconuts and declares a minimum increase in inflation with his CPI number.**

The important thing to notice is that this:

> With coconuts representing only 10 percent of the original $1000 economy, the $2 increase in demand had only raised coconut prices about 2 percent. **Thus, the economist reported CPI inflation of 2%.**
>
> But is that a true reflection of the amount of inflation? No. Remember that CB actually spent $40 to build the hut. **The real rate of inflation is actually $40/$1120 = 3.57%.**
>
> **There is a significant difference between the real inflation number of 3.57% and what is reflected in CPI inflation of 2%.** It was only after CPI inflation began to pick up steam that CB had to curb his spending again.

In our real economy the net result of the Central Bank's pumping money into the economy generally results in the same things as in our Island Economy example. Inflation creeps back into the picture, **but is not noticed soon enough because the Consumer Price Index (CPI) lags behind the real rate of inflation.** The reason for this is that the CPI is calculated from what is considered to be a representative portion of the goods and services of the entire economy.

How Interest Rate Cuts Affect the Stock Market

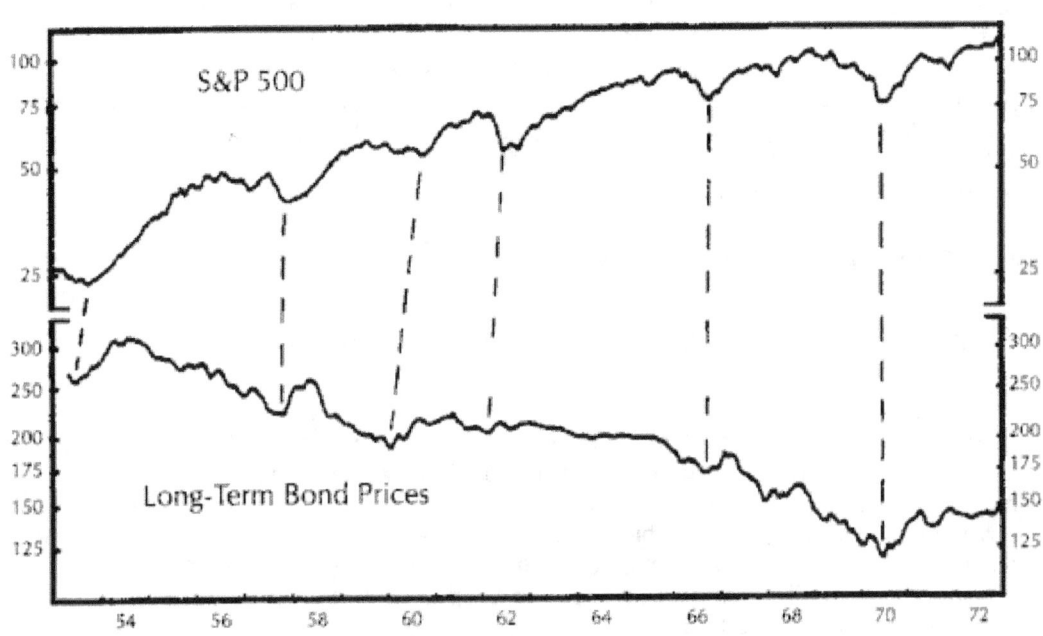

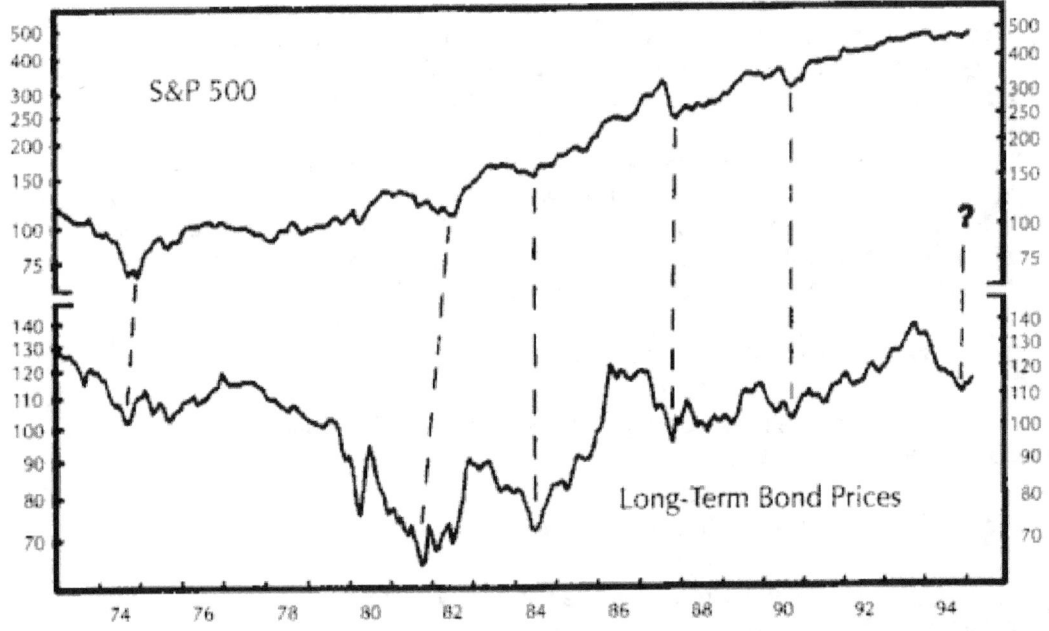

How This Works in the Real Economy

In our real economy the Fed increases money supply a couple different ways:

- **It can simply print money** and use that new cash to buy government bonds from the Treasury Department.
- **It can cut interest rates.** Let me explain how this works: Banks operate under a fractional reserve system. That means that when you deposit $1 in the bank, the bank can loan out more than $8 based on that dollar. The government requires that banks keep only a certain fraction of their total loan activity on their books as assets. In recessions, banks tend to loan out less money because they're worried about losing principle on loans from companies with bad earnings or declining asset values. So—the Fed **increases money supply by creating an incentive for banks to loan out the maximum possible amount of money** on their reserves. To do this, the **Central Bank simply cuts the discount rate.**

Now watch where the money flows to. . .

From Fed to Banks to the Government Bond Market

The discount rate is the short-term interest rate the Central Bank charges member banks to borrow from it. Once the discount rate has dropped far enough below long-term government bond interest rates, **banks have a new way to make money.** They borrow as much money as they can legally and loan to the government bond market at the higher long-term interest rate, profiting from the difference. Doing so, banks are increasing the money supply going into the economy. **Eventually, long-term rates also drop in response to more money heading toward long-term bonds.**

From Bonds Into Stocks

As the newly created money flows from the Fed to Banks and then to the government bond market, **interest rates begin to drop for all forms of borrowing in response to lower short- and long-term rates.**

Bond investors are more apt to take profits and investment in the lower-yield bonds slows. In addition to bonds yielding less, as borrowing costs are reduced, investors begin to anticipate a recovery in corporate profits because **one of the biggest costs that businesses have (borrowing) has been reduced.** The theoretical value of companies goes up when rates fall.

This drives money out of the bond market and into stocks.

So—to sum it up, the new money shifts from the Fed to the Banks to government bonds and then to stocks.

From Stocks to the Real Economy

As stock prices rise and corporations can suddenly borrow at lower rates, existing public companies can also more easily **float secondary stock offerings**, and companies without publicly traded stock existing can sell **Initial Public Offerings** (popularly known as IPOs) to raise capital. **The money**

sloshing around in the bond and stock markets thus begins to make its way into the real economy as corporations access both stock and bond markets to raise capital for expansion, and as individuals borrow more in response to lower interest rates. This is why, as we'll see, **bond prices usually lead stock prices, and stock prices usually lead the economy**. It's not that investors are good at predicting the future, it's just that bond and stock markets are the first recipients of money that ultimately hits the real economy later.

Business expansion ultimately causes economic activity to pick up and this leads to a recovery from the recession. This entire process takes a while; **anywhere between 6 to 18 months may pass** after the Central Bank's action before measurable results begin to occur in the economy. **This time lag makes the Fed's job very difficult.** Picture yourself steering a huge ship in which your steering does not affect the ship's movement until 6 to 18 minutes after you made the adjustment.

In the chart below, you can see how interest rate cuts ultimately affect stock prices. This is a chart of the relationship between bond prices and stock prices since 1954. (2 Graph above)

If you carefully examine the slight slanting of the dotted lines, you'll see that **virtually every major stock market advance since 1954 was preceded by a bond market rally**, which reflects declines in interest rates. This is a case of simple cause and effect, and is one of the **most valuable and accurate tools we have for determining the right time for shifting in and out of the stock market.** As you can see, the relationship between interest rates and the stock market, while extremely useful, is not a short-term one. That is why **you don't need to have stroke every time Alan Greenspan twitches.**

This cause and effect relationship also illustrates very clearly the degree of power that Central Bank and government policy has over the stock market and the state of the economy. **Most everyday people are heavily affected by it as well, just as Truman is affected by his carefully contrived make-believe world.**

Now, as the economy begins to pick up, we move further up the Liquidity Cycle, shown once again below:

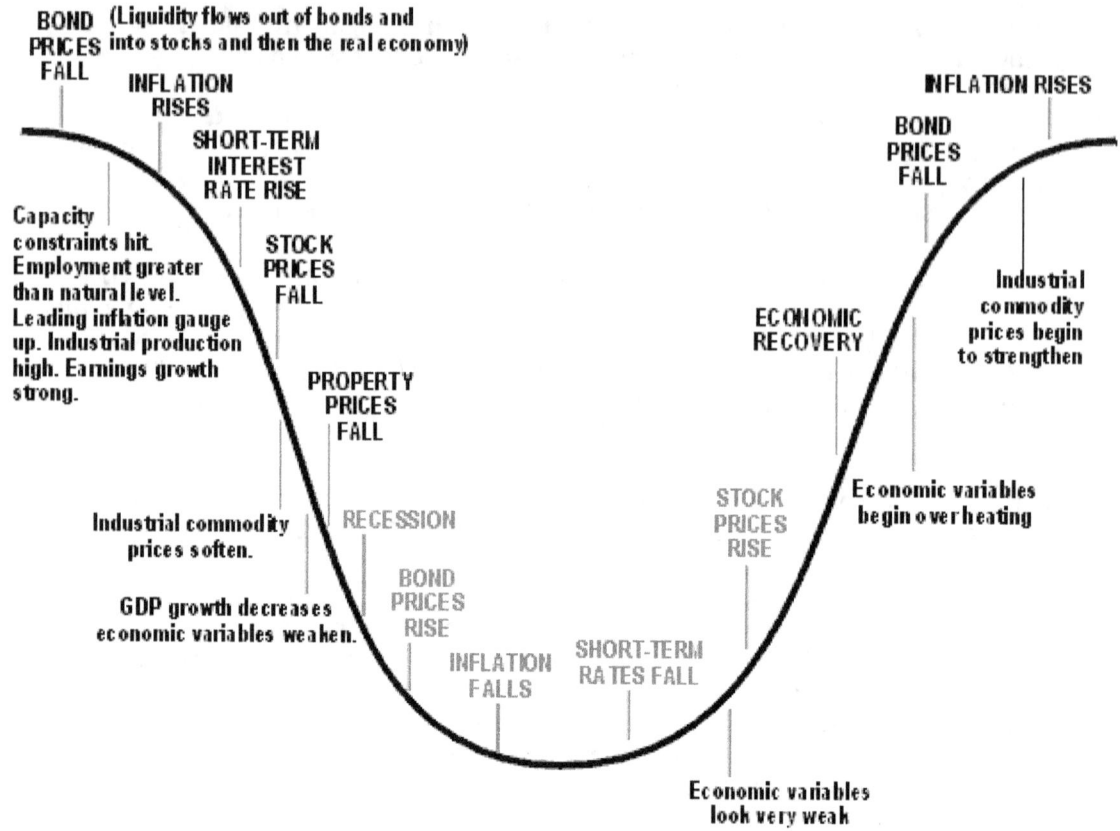

Economic Recovery: What's Wrong With This Picture?

What could possibly be wrong with:

- **record lows in unemployment?**
- **a booming stock market?**
- **low interest rates?**
- **low inflation?**
- **general optimism about the future?**
- **increasing corporate earnings?**
- **good GDP growth?**

Indeed, with the economy picking up steam, printing money seems like a **magic elixir** for whatever ails the economy. Politicians slap each others' backs and **whoever is lucky enough to be president at the time gets high approval ratings** no matter what he does in the Oval Office.

I don't need to tell you that the time we are now living in bears a lot of resemblance to these good economic times.

The problem is that **you can't get something for nothing** in economics. The recession was already a result of distorted free-market forces. Now the **Fed has simply added to the problem** through its Band-Aid solution of increasing Money Supply.

Let's go back to our Island Economy Story and examine some sticky situations that can develop.

The Island Economy (continued)

Watch what happens if we **stir things up** in the Island Economy. In the real world, we could have a war, or some natural disaster. For our friends on the island, let's give them a **surprise monsoon.**

Day after day, rain is pouring. The demand for roof building services rises very quickly.

Let's examine two possible scenarios. First, what would happen if CB **could not** spend any of the extra money he had found. In this case, the price of roof building services would be bid up only with the existing money supply. **When the price for roof-building soars, the price of other goods, like berries and fish fall commensurately**, and the price of absolutely everything else remains the same. The only way that many islanders can afford more roof-building services is by limiting their diet to fish and coconut juice and forgoing eating berries. The price of berries drops to almost zero. **Because people can't afford to eat as much due to their higher spending on roofs, prices of other foods drop as well due to the decreased demand.**

Meanwhile, the only way for the berry-picker to make any money is to become a roof-builder. Soon, however, after a week of intensive roof-building, everybody has adequate roofs. Demand on roof building drops and the berry picker returns to berry-picking.

This analogy shows how a free-market economy would adapt to crisis. There is no distortion of money supply. **The island allocates its time-labor-capital-resources in way that allows an easy return to the norm after the crisis is over.**

Now suppose however, that **CB DOES HAVE ACCESS TO HIS NEW MONEY.**

With the new money getting introduced into the economy, **CB bids the price of roofing-services to double** what it would be without the new money. The berry-picker and the fisherman see dollar signs and the decide to quit their normal occupations and borrow money from CB in order to build their own roof-building factories. The ventures look promising due to the high profits, but unfortunately, they're unaware that much of the incredibly high demand for roofing services resulted from the **artificial temporary increase in money**

spending at such a high rate once his own roof is built.

The new roof-building factory comes on-line, but with disastrous results. Once everybody is happy with their new roofs, demand drops, and the price of roofing services plummets. The two new factories built by the berry-picker and the fishermen **start going down hill.** They borrow more money to stay in business. But eventually, **they go bankrupt and lay off all their employees.** The island is now poorer for the time and capital misallocated to building the factories and for the loans on the factories which defaulted.

Here's what you should take notice of:

> A boom-bust economy developed here out of the **artificial stimulus** of money creation. The islanders were **unable to differentiate** between real relative demand increase and artificial and temporary new money created demand. Once the pace of new money creation (or spending in this case) slowed, prices shifted, and the allocation of resources became unstable and had to be corrected.
>
> New money creation creates a temporary and artificial source of demand in an economy. As the economy re-allocates and adjusts its resources of capital, labor, and time to the prices created by temporary increases in money supply, it is misallocating resources, and once the temporary pace of money supply creation slows down the misallocation becomes clear and must be adjusted. **This creates a boom-bust cycle.**

What implications does this have for the real world? In the Liquidity Cycle chart below, **click on the big "?"** over on the far right.

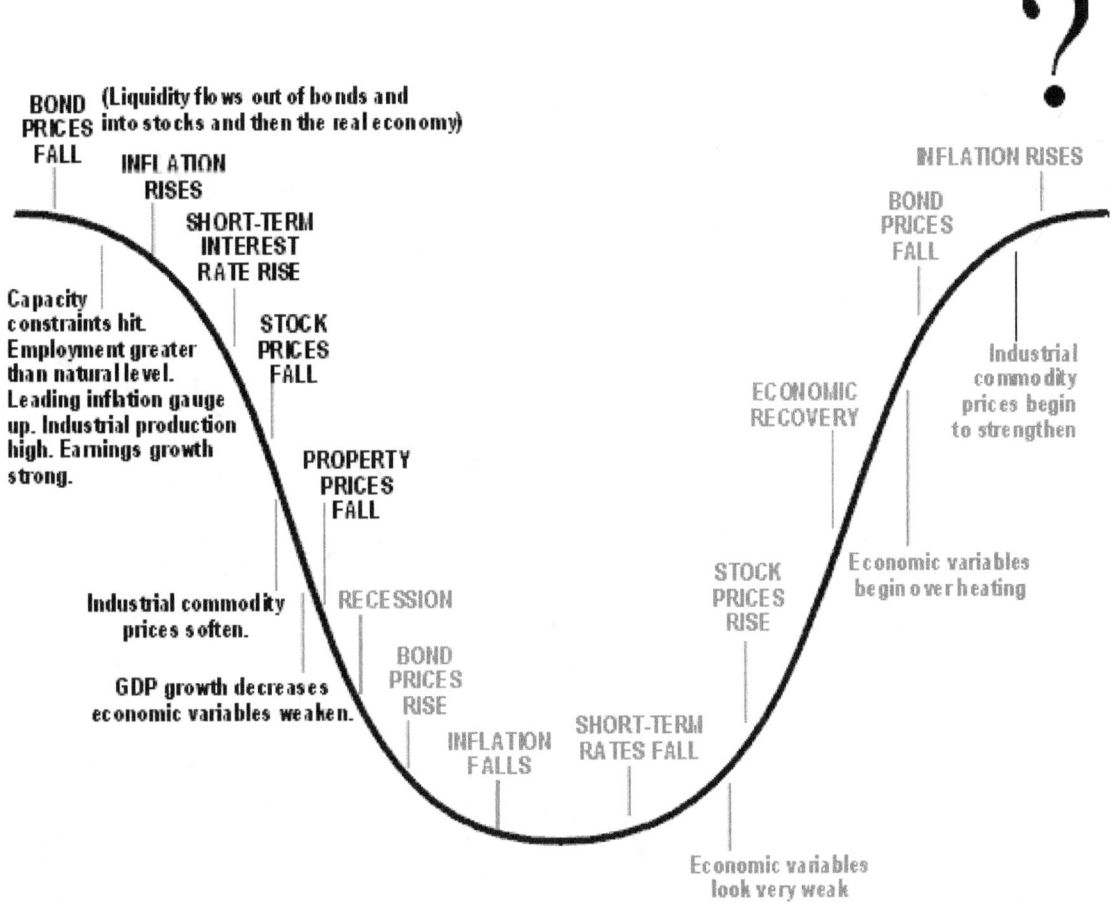

Welcome Back, Recession!

For us, in the real world, there are many problems that lurk on the horizon during an artificially induced economic boom:

1) **Inflation comes back eventually.** As in our island example, new money added to the system causes demand beyond that which would be generated by the free market. This causes prices to increase. There is a great lag time, however, between the point at which new money is introduced and inflation becomes noticeable. What makes inflation particularly insidious is that it can be far easier to cause than it is to get rid of. Inflation can last over several Liquidity Cycle booms and busts.

2) **Over-capacity.** Businesses operate under the assumption that the artificial demand is real and that customers really want more of their products and services. So they increase their production capacity to a level that greatly exceeds the real demand. Once the rate of money creation slows, this artificial demand will dry up overnight and business are left with over-capacities. The plant closures and layoffs begin.

3) **Excessive Speculation.** The funny money flows into hot areas of the marketplace, pushing prices beyond well beyond free-market levels. One result of this was the real estate boom that occurred during the 1980s and its ultimate unraveling in the early 90s.

4) **Excessive Debt.** With the low cost of borrowing, the debt that companies and people take on becomes excessive.

5) **Overvaluation in stocks.** The bond market reacts to high inflation by choking off the inflation through higher interest rates. Interest shifts away from real assets like real estate to the stock market, which benefits from an environment with low inflation and low interest rates. Eventually, the stock market becomes highly overvalued. Real estate values, and that of other hard assets such as gold, crash.

In the Liquidity Cycle chart below, click on the word "**Recession**."

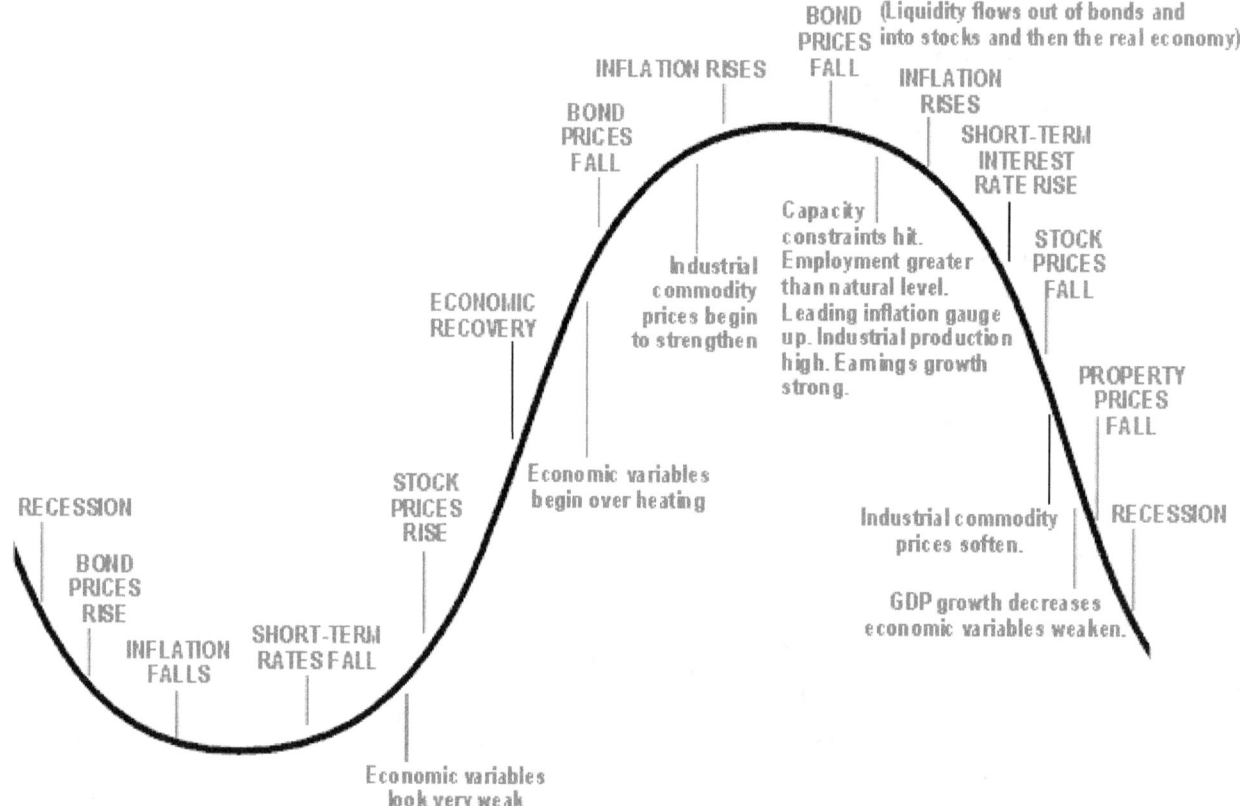

And the World Keeps Turning

Eventually, as people begin to notice inflation creeping back into the picture, the Fed is forced to throw in the towel and **raise interest rates again.**

The house of cards collapses. The **artificial demand dries up**. Companies that invested a lot of money for new production capacity and hiring are caught **holding the bag**. Bond prices, stock prices, and eventually real-estate prices fall as demand drops off.

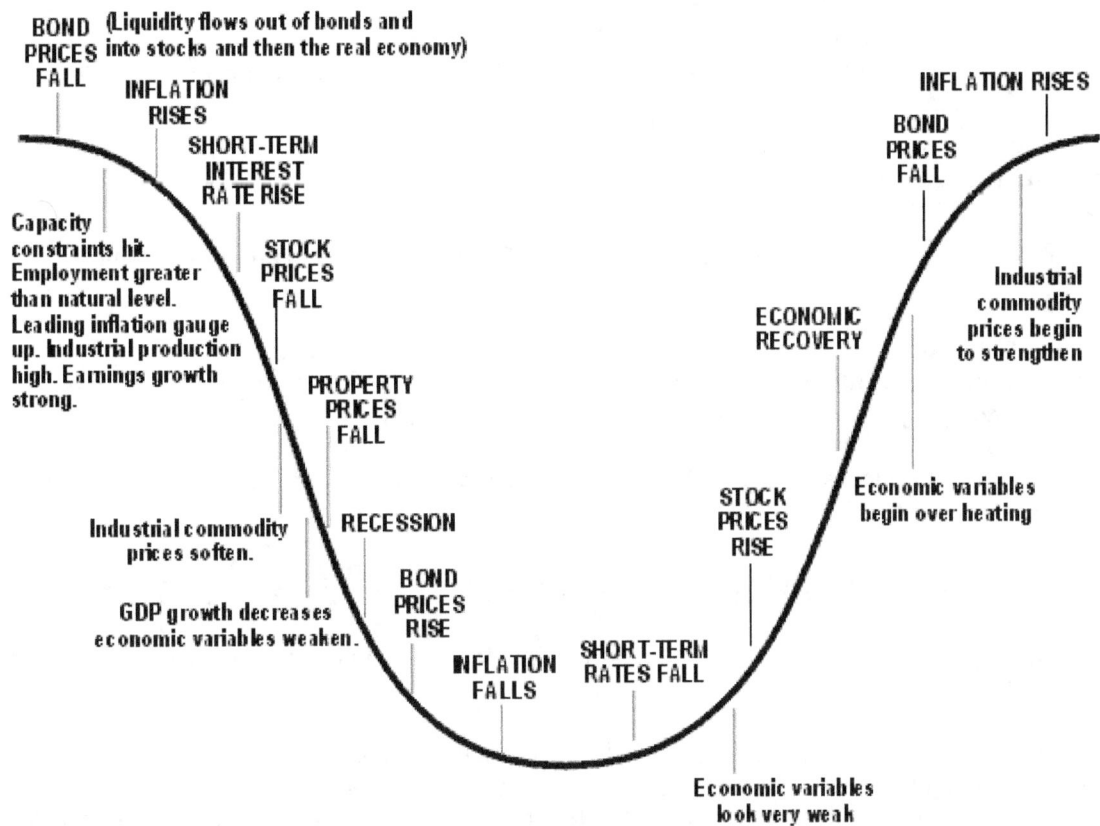

As you can see, the Fed **wields tremendous power** by controlling interest rates artificially rather than allowing free-market forces to be in the driver's seat. The Central Bank's actions have a direct impact on average people. In many cases, **the effects can be devastating**. The Truman analogy used at the beginning of the course is really not all that farfetched because peoples' lives are getting impacted, but they don't know that the **Fed is the one pulling the strings.**

Fortunately, if you are aware of the Liquidity Cycle and how the pendulum is occasionally given a shove by the Fed, you are one step ahead of the game. This can be especially advantageous if you are a trader or investor.

General Rules for Using the Liquidity Cycle in Trading

In this section, I'll give you a taste of what I look for in various monetary and economic gauges in order to figure out where we are in the Liquidity Cycle at any given time. I have developed and tested systems which help me to know whether it is safe to be stocks. If you want to know about these systems, you might want to refer to my book, "Hedge Fund Edge" (1999, John Wiley & Sons, NY).

I also use the services of the Bank Credit Analyst Research Group. I highly recommend that you explore their website at: http://www.bankcreditanalyst.com/.

Monetary Gauges

Let's say we're looking for an environment in which stocks perform well. This is what I need to see:

- T-Bill rates rise at a **slow rate**.
- Corporate bonds are **moving up or flat**.
- When the **yield curve steepens** (the ratio of 30-Year Treasure Bonds to Three-Month Treasure Bills increases)

Economic Gauges

In addition to the above monetary gauges, I look at confirmation in the following economic gauges:

- **The economy slows down** as shown in lower Capacity Utilization Rates
- **Industrial production growth is not high** as reflected in Industrial Production Index.
- **Unemployment is increasing** (this seems to go against common sense, but historically that's the way it's been).
- **When Inflation and Gross Domestic Product growth are not moving up at too fast a pace.**

Putting the Pieces of the Liquidity Cycle Puzzle Together

The Liquidity Curve is a basic model that tells us what to expect and watch for **as we move from one phase of the cycle to another.**

One of the trickiest aspects of the Liquidity Curve is that it **leads economic statistics**. Economic statistics are **lagging indicators** that help economists to gauge the relative health of the economy. Since the stock and bond markets are the first to feel the effects of new money printing, they will be strangely out of sync with what you hear economists and journalists talking about in the news media.

Normally, people think that the worst time to buy stocks is during a recession when economic statistics look horrible. However, what we've learned about the Liquidity Cycle makes this view incorrect and even dangerous.

In actuality, when economic variables are weak and the Fed begins lowering rates, **that is the best time to get into stocks and bonds**. As we said earlier, the effects of lowered interest rates are typically not seen in the economy for 6 to 18 months. **In the face of continued bad news about the economy, stock market prices can start moving up much sooner.** If you were watching the markets between 1994 and 1995, this will have a familiar ring.

Conversely, the riskiest time to invest in equities or to be heavily biased toward long positions if you're a trader, is **when the economy looks good but the bond market is beginning to head lower** (which is a reflection a rise in interest rates).

My Opinion About the Current Markets and Closing Remarks

Right now the economy is **starting to show signs of overheating** and the **bond market has already witnessed its first phase down**, with long-bond futures prices having dropped from 135 to 114 since last October. The Fed is reluctant to hike rates, however, because the rest of the global economy is still just recovering from a global deflation scare last year. Since mid-1997 there have been an unprecedented 220 global interest rate cuts by central bankers around the world trying to fight off deflationary forces.

In April we started a **more typical change in leadership in the stock market** - with cyclicals, commodity plays, and small-cap value taking over leadership from the overdone high techs and "internuts." However the bond market reaction has been so severe that it has cut short this takeover in leadership.

The bond market has had a huge correction. My suspicion is that the **first phase of the bond market decline is over or nearly over.** If bonds can consolldate or rally from here for a month or two, selected stocks should have a blow-off rally. However investors need to watch our bond market like a hawk. Further declines below 114 will hit the stock market immediately. It is possible that bonds will keep declining and **stocks will take a much bigger hit in the months ahead.**

However the more normal cycle is that bonds undergo a bear market rally, and during this rally **stocks make their final highs**. Then when bonds turn down again, **stocks turn lower as well.** This is probably the best base model for now. But investors must realize that the game is getting old, the risks are getting high, and bonds must be watched closely.

If bonds do rally and move lower, the **decline in stocks will likely be bigger than we have experienced since 1982.**

In addition, investors may want to watch foreign markets for relative strength if they are trying to play this final potential rally. Asia is still cutting rates, as is Europe. Stocks in these countries may therefore outperform our own if a final blow-off rally materializes. Realize however, that when the U.S. market sells off in earnest, no foreign stock market will offer a place to hide. Commodity market systems and funds offer the best diversification.

Here's What's in Store for Next Week

Whether the market goes up or down, I bet you're still determined to **make money trading.**

Next week we'll return to the trenches with an overview of my favorite technical indicators and how I use them in both up and down markets. For many TradingMarkets.com members who've been following this course, this is the week they will have been waiting for because they want to put all those 300 indicators in their charting software to work.

Well, for me there are **only a small handful** that are worth looking at and I will be happy to share them with you next week.

Best regards,

Mark Boucher

P.S. I want to encourage you to reread this week's content on Liquidity Cycles until it sinks in. When you grasp the big picture, you will be able to think one step ahead of the crowd. The Trumans of the world are just now becoming convinced that we're in a bull market and that it's easy to make money in the stock market. Very few people are thinking about the possibility of a bear market in stocks. Still fewer are thinking about where they'd shift their money when this happens.

A Dose of Reality

In trading, most of what are touted as hot new ideas are actually old ideas that through time get updated, modified, re-invented, or synthesized with other ideas. Over the years, my main emphasis has been to find **principles that work** - no matter what the source. An idea that I come up with is not necessarily better than an idea someone else comes up with - it is the profitability of the application of an idea that determines its merit, not its originator. Many traders spend so much time reinventing the wheel, that they ignore some great previously formed methodologies. **I sought instead to find everything that worked, period.**

I also feel that a caveat is appropriate here. I was very fortunate to have spent many years with a Stanford Ph.D. Tom Johnson and some of his students doing research on indicators and models and what worked in various markets. One of the hot topics at the time that we did a lot of research on was called "pattern recognition" which used many of the indicators we will learn. In fact pattern recognition was such a popular topic that when we began raising money for hedge fund management we got lots of sponsorship due to our pattern recognition work.

In the first hedge fund that I co-founded with one of the students I had done research with, Tom Johnson and I applied pattern recognition almost exclusively. We found a large number of patterns (using the indicators you will learn) which had phenomenal reliability of 65% or higher on stock, futures, and foreign markets going back to the 1870's. **We thought we had found a nearly flawless trading strategy.**

However one of our partners was not satisfied with the long-term reliability of our approach. He wanted to know, year by year and month by month, what the profit, loss, and drawdowns were. In computing this we learned something shocking: most indicators and patterns based on them tend to all fail at the same time, usually during changes in a major trend. This meant that while an indicator might be reliable 70% of the time over the long run, it would go through long periods of one to two years at a time where it might be only 20% or 30% reliable, creating **totally unsatisfactory** drawdowns.

We were panicked! We had already launched a hedge fund trading much of our own and our partners` money on a strategy that made money certainly, but had some nasty drawdowns along the way despite incredibly high long-term profitability. What we learned in researching how to correct this problem was that vehicle selection **is much more important than what indicators you use or what pattern-recognition methods you use to enter and exit a trade.** We found that systems which chose trades by technical action regardless of selection based on Relative Strength and Fuel, almost all had very high drawdowns during some market phase.

The point I want people to understand clearly is this. Most traders spend way too much time trying to learn indicators and tweak a particular system based on several indicators into the perfect "holy grail" system. I cannot name one top money manager or even great trader who attributes his success to an indicator, or even to a purely mechanical system. Can you? **Traders, in my opinion, are far better off to focus most of their attention on vehicle selection**, where over 70% of gains come from for most investors. However, once you've spent most of your time finding the strongest potential longs with room on the upside, and the weakest potential shorts with room on the downside, then it pays to know several reliable ways to use indicators for entry/exit techniques. **Indicators are important, but only after vehicle selection is completed.**

With the preceding caveat in mind, I want to thank Ralph Dystant, George Lane, Welles Wilder, Gerald Appel, H.M. Gartley, and Joseph Granville for their hard work and ingenuity in developing the tools that I will be talking about in the following pages.

Enter Week 5

Introduction

Many traders have a mystical attraction to computer-generated indicators that causes tunnel vision to set in to the point that they embrace an oversimplified version of the financial markets.

I suppose it has a lot to do with the fact that indicators like the ones I'll discuss this week give the market a comforting sense of order that you just cannot see by looking at a conventional bar chart alone. After all, what could be more reassuring to the trading novice than to see a nice oscillating pattern like this:

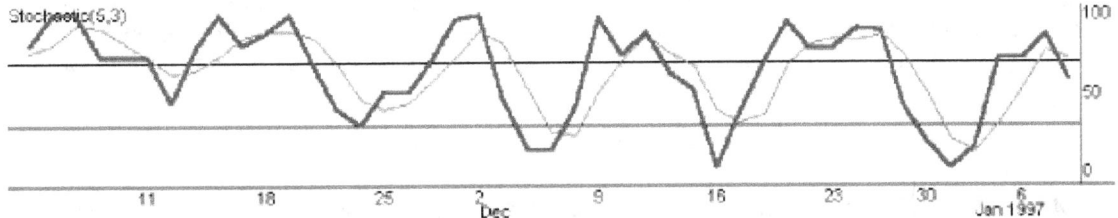

Like a bouncing ball, it goes up and down in a predictable trajectory. You'd get the idea that the markets and trading are not so difficult to understand after all. But looks are deceiving and indeed, these types of indicators are but a **mere sliver** of the big picture that you must grasp to trade profitably over a long time period. So as we delve into this week's topic, try to have some perspective relative to the topics covered in other weeks of the course.

I continue to be glad that we covered Money Management and some aspects of Market Selection in the earlier weeks because now we can look in-depth at some technical tools knowing we're standing on a firm foundation. For teachers there is always the temptation to start with the stuff that students will find most interesting. Usually, that means talking about some super-duper trading system. However, through my own experience, I know (and have said repeatedly) that trading does not revolve around a trading system. I'm trying to illustrate that when you put first things first, you will be a better trader and will succeed no matter what kind of trading methodology you wind up using. When you complete this course, I want to you see that you've not only increased your knowledge, but improved your ability to apply that knowledge.

What is an Indicator?

The term "indicator" refers to a formula that crunches raw market data such as open, high, low, close, and volume in a specific way, and plots the result as a series of dots. The resulting line typically fluctuates in a manner which sometimes produces patterns that coincide fairly consistently with certain kinds of market behavior.

Some of the indicators we'll be discussing this week often display cyclical behavior. That is, plotted over time, they cycle through peaks and troughs which reflect the up and down movement of market prices--for this reason, these types of indicators are also called oscillators. Indicators, as described here, are considered by market technicians to be useful for identifying ideal points at which to be buying or selling a security. There are a couple inherent limitations that need to be considered, the most important of which are:

1) **Oscillators assume cyclicity**. That is, they try to find cycles where none may exist. The trick to using them involves the interpretation of a past pattern and making a supposition about what it says about the future.

2) **Oscillators don't work most of the time.** Oscillators should only be used to trade with a strong trend--never against it. Trying to using an oscillator to pick a top in a runaway up-move is usually financial suicide. However, using an oscillator to catch a reaction against a strong up trend can help pinpoint low-risk levels to buy into the trend.

Some Indicators I Like

In the following pages, I will show you some indicators I find useful under specific market conditions. **You probably have heard of stochastics, RSI, MACD, and OBV** because they are stuffed into most of the off-the-shelf market analysis programs these days. In fact, it wouldn't surprise me if many traders pay little, if any, attention to these because of all the more exotic "better mousetraps" out there. But the fact is, because these indicators have been around for awhile, many smart traders have researched them and discovered **nice techniques for using them that are not widely used**. Combined with other tools that I discuss in other weeks of the course, these indicators, when used properly, are some additional arrows to add to your quiver.

The Stochastic Oscillator

The Stochastic Oscillator compares where a stock closed today relative to its trading range over a past period of time. It consists of two lines, %K and %D. In the following pages, %K is a blue line and %D is red line.

%K is calculated is as follows:

$$\frac{(\text{today's close}) - (\text{lowest low of the last x periods})}{(\text{highest high of the last x periods}) - (\text{lowest low of the last x periods})}$$

where x is the number of time periods you're looking back. In the following examples, **our look back period is 5 days.**

A moving average of %K is then calculated by using the number of time periods you specify. This is called Slow %D or SD. In the following examples, **we calculate SD using a value of 3 days.**

Popular Uses

The Stochastic Oscillator is typically used to indicate either overbought or oversold conditions. That is, price movement in the markets is thought to exhibit the behavior of a **rubber band**. Stretched too far in one direction, it'll tend to **snap back** in the opposite direction. So, when a market has moved up too far or to fast, it will tend to take a breather and move down a bit before going up again.

The stochastic oscillator that is at 70% would indicate an overbought condition in which today's close is near the top of the range over the past x number days.

In this case, the conventional interpretation, which is the way in which most people tend to use Stochastics, **is also the least effective approach to using it unless you're in a** Runaway Market.

Now, let's explore some of the ways I use the **Stochastics Oscillator**.

My Parameters

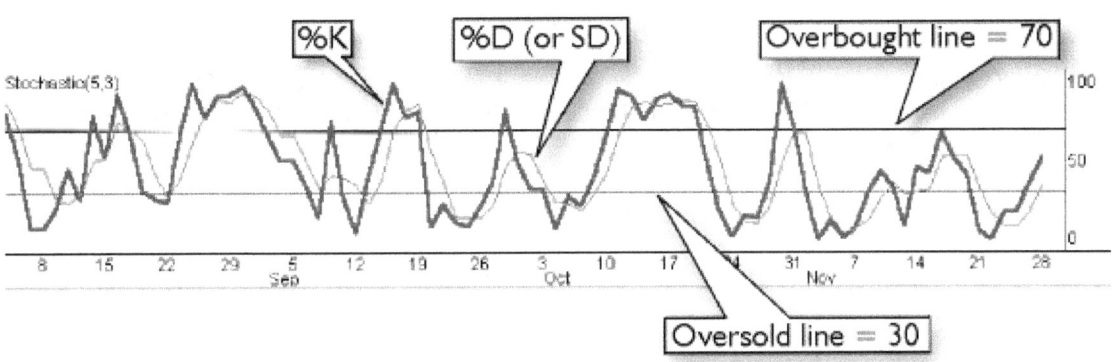

All of the following examples use 5 %K and 3 %D. Unless otherwise noted, the line that defines the pattern or signal is the %D, which I call SD (for slow %D). This is the red line.

In addition, I use 30 for the oversold line and 70 for the overbought line.

Please note that my settings are probably different from the default settings on your market analysis program.

Definitions

In the examples I'll be showing in the following pages, I'll be using some terms that you probably have not heard before in the context of the Stochastic Oscillator. Please note that it's only necessary that you become familiar with these terms so that you don't get confused. **You don't have to memorize them.**

Here are the definitions:

Stochastic Rally: This occurs when the Slow %D (SD) moves from below the 30 line to and passes above the 70 line. When SD moves back to 30 line, the rally is over. In the example below, the red line crossing from A to B and from E to F are stochastic rallies.

Stochastic Decline: This occurs when the SD moves from above 70 to and passes below the 30 line. When SD moves back above the 70 line, the decline is over. In the example below, the red line crossing from C to D and from G to H are stochastic declines

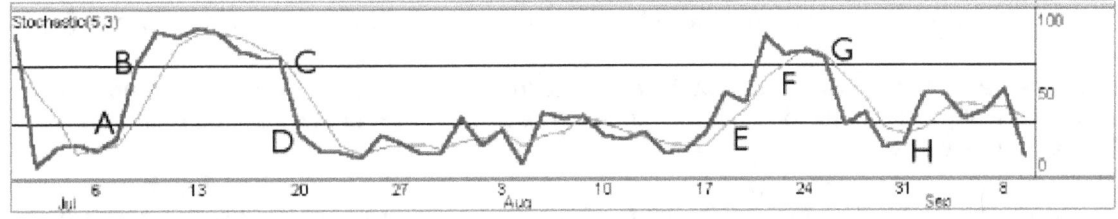

The following definitions for Stochastic Cycle High and Stochastic Cycle Low are a little tricky, but if you refer to the picture and read both definitions a couple times, you'll be fine.

Stochastic Cycle High: This is the highest high in the price of a market that occurs between the previous Stochastic Cycle Low and the end of the Stochastic Decline that immediately follows it.

This definition is tricky because we haven't defined what a Stochastic Cycle Low is yet and because our definition requires that we refer to a point on the bar chart and a point in the stochastic oscillator.

In the chart below, you'll see a Stochastic Cycle Low at 1). The next Stochastic Decline (as defined above) is at D. The highest high in the price of the stock that occurs between 1) and D is at 2).

If you don't know what the previous Stochastic Cycle Low was, then you find the Stochastic Cycle High by finding the highest high between the beginning of a Stochastic Rally and the end of that Stochastic Rally. The beginning of the stochastic rally is B and the end of the stochastic rally is D when the stochastic decline begins. The highest high in the price of the stock between these two points is at 2.

Stochastic Cycle Low: This is the lowest low in the price of a market that occurs between the previous Stochastic Cycle High and the end of the Stochastic Rally that immediately follows it.

In the chart above, we pointed out that 2) was a Stochastic Cycle High. The end of the next Stochastic Rally is at F. The lowest low in price between those two points is at 3). This is the Stochastic Cycle Low.

If you don't know what the previous Stochastic Cycle High was, then you find the Stochastic Cycle Low by finding the lowest low between the beginning of a Stochastic Decline and the end of that Stochastic Decline. Again looking at the stochastic oscillator above, we see that at a Stochastic Decline begins at D and the end of that decline is at F, when the stochastic rally begins. The lowest low in the price of the stock between these two points is at 3.

Uses for Stochastics

We can use stochastic cycle highs and lows to find support and resistence, as well as to define a trend. Referring to the chart above, once a new low below 3) was made, 2 days after the high at 4) stochastic cycles have made lower highs and lower lows, which confirms that the trend is down.

We can also use past stochastic cycle highs and lows to determine where we place trailing stops, and to determine levels from which we can calculate retracements (we'll cover these techniques in later weeks).

How to Identify Weak Markets Using the Flutter Pattern

In a market in which price is bouncing up and down within a certain price range, the Stochastic Oscillator tends to fluctuate up and down. In fact, a market can be moving in a "gentle" up or down trend and still produce an oscillating stochastic pattern.

However, in a market that is moving very powerfully in a given direction, the stochastic oscillator will behave differently. In a strong downtrend, it will move from a high reading to a low reading and then as the trend continues, **"flutter"** in the low range.

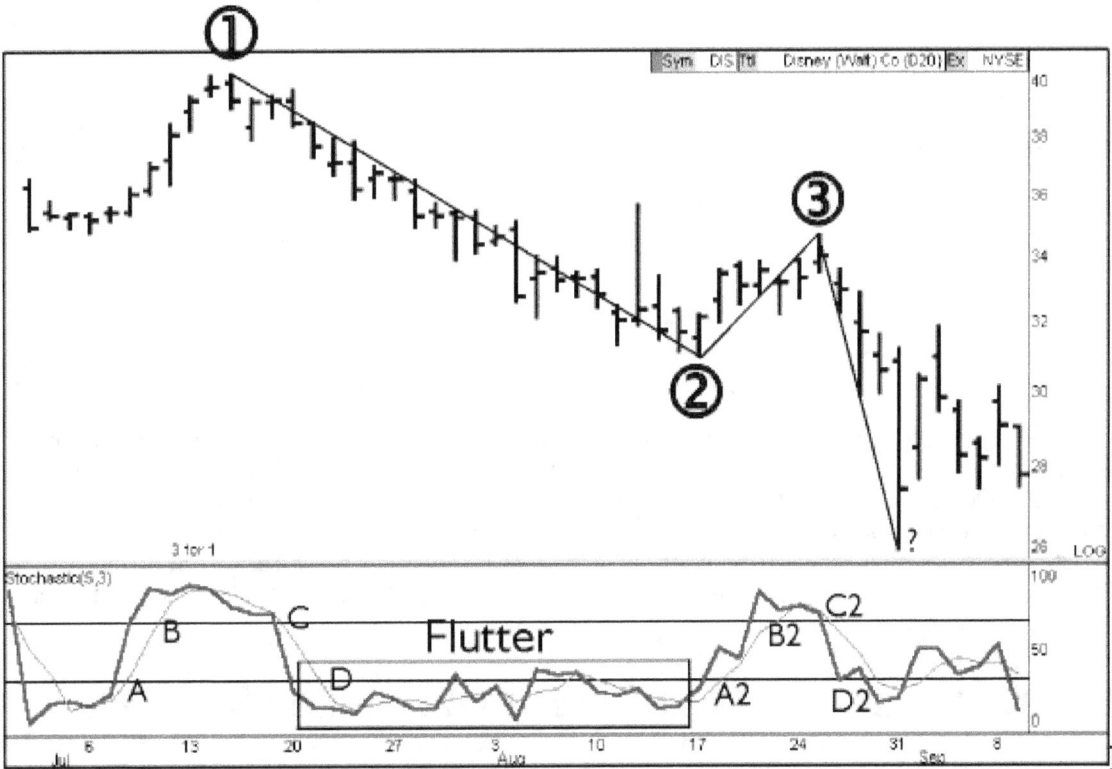

) is the highest high between A & D so it becomes the first stochastic cycle high on the chart. However, after D, SD (the red line) fluctuates around the 30 line without going back above 70 for quite some time. This is the flutter pattern. Finally at B2, SD moves above 70 again and we look for the lowest low between 1 and B2 for the stochastic cycle low; that turns out to be the low at 2). Remember, **as long as SD does not rally above 70, a decline may still be intact.** The next stochastic cycle high is shown at 3).

When you are in a short position, this type of flutter is useful for confirming that the downtrend is continuing. Besides using a trailing OPS, you can also use the crossing back above the 70 line as a signal to start watching for additional short sales once the downward trend resumes.

How to Identify Strong Markets Using the Flutter Pattern

In the following example, we see what happens when a market makes a **very strong and sustained move to the upside.** As you can see, the Stochastic Oscillator moves above the 30 line and then bounces around for a while as price continues soaring higher.

1) is the highest high between A and D so it becomes the first Stochastic Cycle High on the chart.
2) is the lowest low between 1) and B2 so it becomes the first Stochastic Cycle Low on the chart. However, after B2, SD fluctuates around the **70 line without falling back below 30 for an unusually long period of time.** This is the flutter pattern that occurs in a very strong market. When you are a long position, this pattern is helpful for **confirming the strength of a rally.** Besides using a Trailing OPS, you might also consider looking to add to your long positions when SD crosses back below the 30 line.

How to Identify Possible Market Bottoms Using Stochastic Divergence
Variation 1: Retest Non-Confirmation Bottom

One of the first things that is taught in most basic technical analysis books is how to use stochastic divergence to find market tops and bottoms. I looked at the instructions that came with one of the most popular charting software packages on the market. I found that description of how to use Stochastic Divergence **left out many important details.** So while you may already be familiar with this particular tool, you have to ask yourself if you're using it profitably.

Let's look at the following example for identifying possible market bottoms.

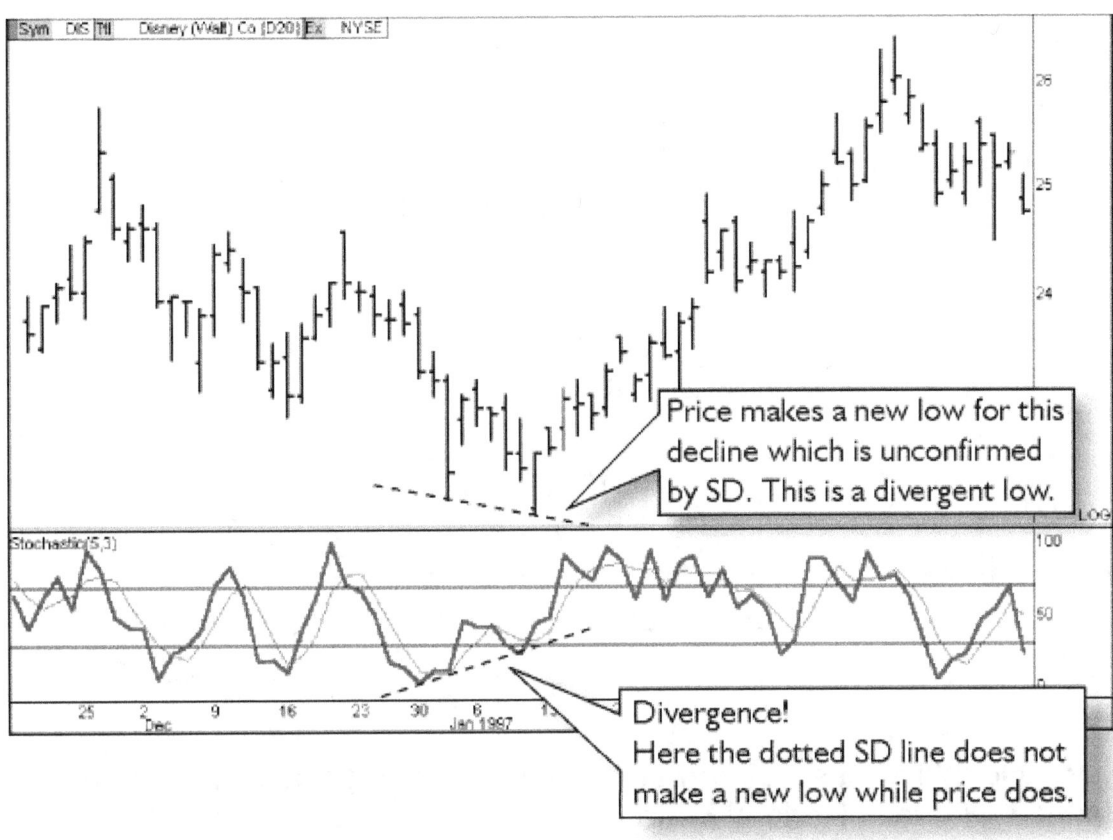

1. Typically, price will make a low, a rally attempt which fails, and then a lower low (Double Bottom).

2. SD declines below 30 and then rallies.

3. On price's failed rally attempt, SD makes a top, but that top must be below the 70 line.

4. SD then goes down to retest the previous low.

5. While the stock makes a new low, SD's low is higher than the previous low.

How to Identify Possible Market Bottoms Using Stochastic Divergence
Variation 2: Sliding Non-confirmation bottom

In this instance of divergence, price makes one steep plunge into new low territory and turns up. Sometime prior to the final price bottom, however, SD begins to slide up, diverging with price

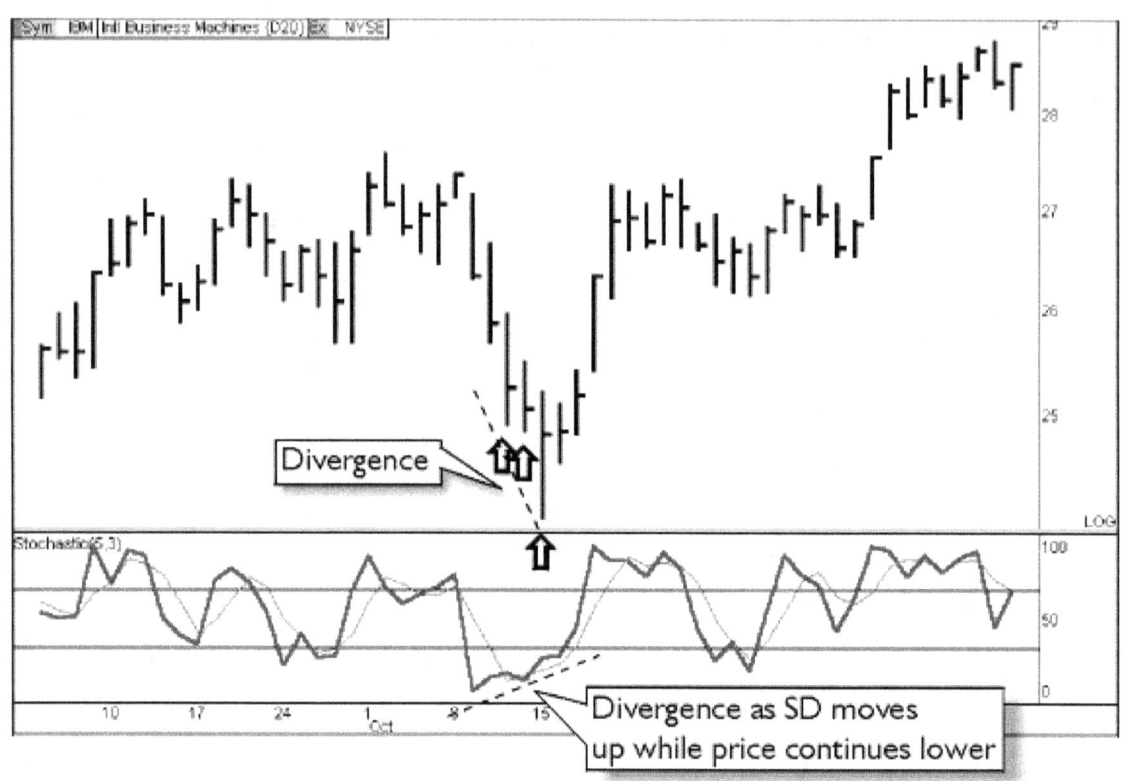

How to Identify Possible Market Bottoms Using Stochastic Divergence
Variation 3: Floor Traders' Bottom

This pattern is a Stochastic Divergence with an added twist that occurs in the price pattern

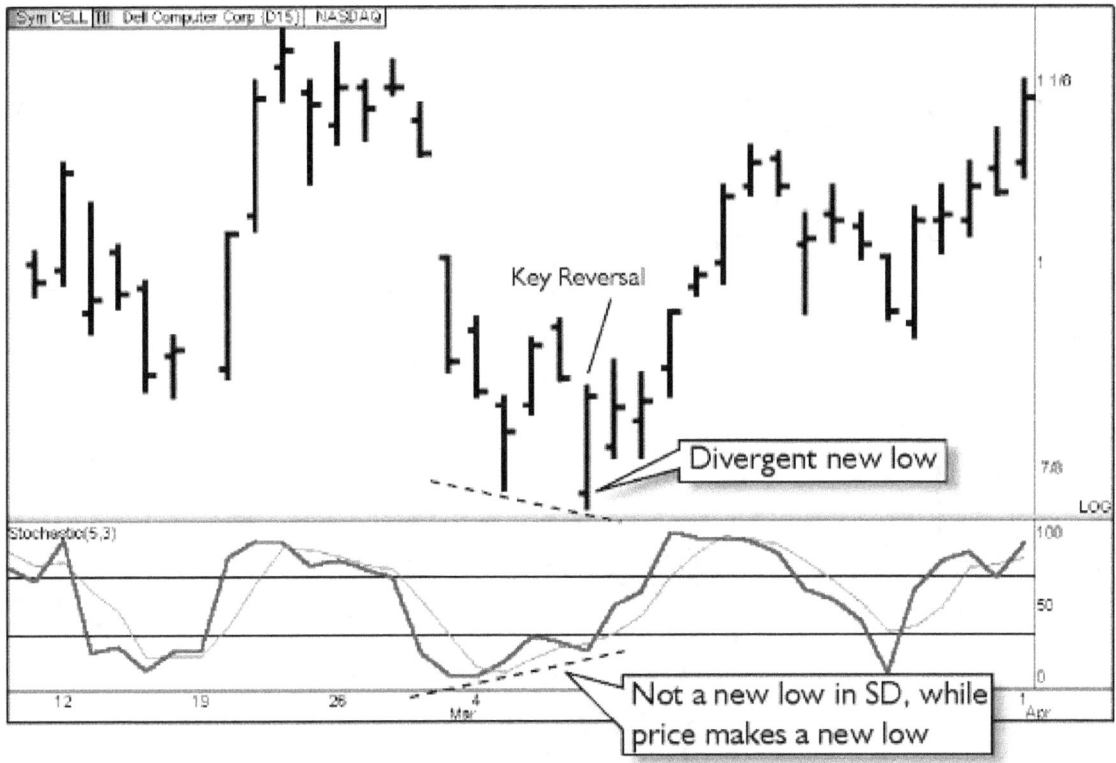

As with Stochastic Divergence, price typically makes a short-term double bottom.

1. The new low in price is a single day in which the floor traders have gunned the stops--pushing prices below the previous low in order to activate sell stops of position traders.

2. The ensuing flurry of protective sell stop orders will then allow floor traders to cover their shorts, initiate new longs, and **force prices up for the remainder of the day.**

3. The low day always closes in the top half of the range for that day. This one bar pattern is known as a **Key Reversal.**

4. While the above price action is occurring, SD has declined below 30 at least on the first half of the double bottom and has not penetrated the 70 line prior making its final low.

5. **The final low in SD is higher than the previous low.**

How to Identify Possible Market Tops Using Stochastic Divergence Variation 1: Retest Non-Confirmation Top

In this case, price typically makes a new high, pulls back a bit, and then makes a higher high which becomes the final top. While this is occurring SD makes a new high, pulls back and makes a bottom that is above the 30 line, and then re-tests its previous high. SD's second high does not reach the level of its previous high, diverging with price.

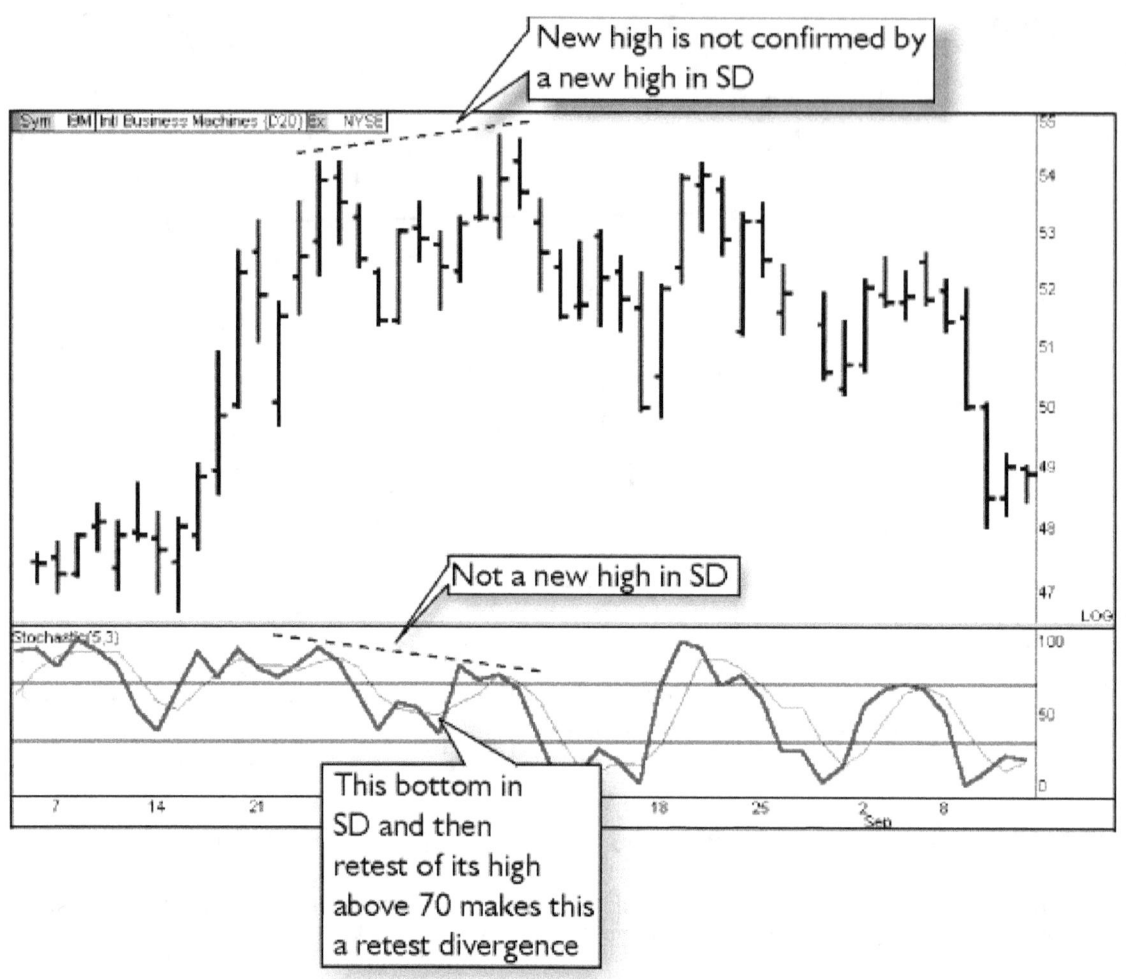

How to Identify Possible Market Tops Using Stochastic Divergence
Variation 2: Sliding Non-Confirmation Top

Price makes one steep stab to new highs, makes a final tops and then declines. Sometime prior to the final price bottom, however, SD beings to slide down, diverging with price.

How to Identify Possible Market Tops Using Stochastic Divergence
Variation 3: Floor Traders' Top

This is the reverse of the Floor Traders' Bottom in which price makes new high after one or more previous attempts. Typically, the **trading range of that day is large** since floor traders initially take prices higher in order to trigger limit buy orders among position traders. Once those orders get executed, floor traders sell their stock and establish short positions and the **high day closes in the bottom half of the range.**

While the below price action is occurring, SD has risen above 70 for its first top and has not penetrated the 30 line prior making its final top. The final top in SD is lower than the previous high.

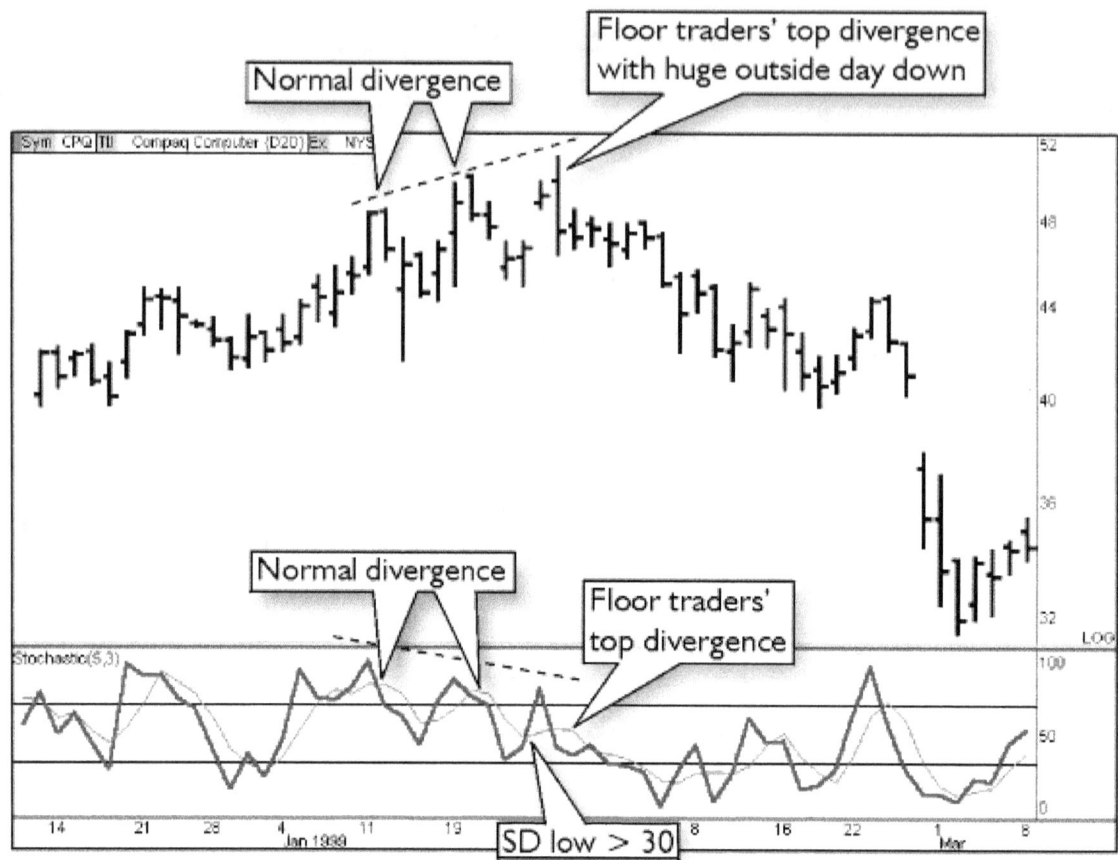

How to Find Major Market Bottoms Using Stochastic Divergence Across Monthly, Weekly, and Daily Time Frames

If you've been following these weekly lessons since day one, you'll already be aware that nothing I've talked about so far constitutes tradable buy or sell signals. Rather, they are nice confirmations that add to your confidence level when many other pieces of the puzzle fall into place. In the following example, you have a stochastic divergence setup which is more potent because it occurs in several different time frames. All other factors, such as market selection and relative strength, should be in place, but certainly a setup such as this carries more weight.

The following setup occurred in Disney during the last quarter of 1998.

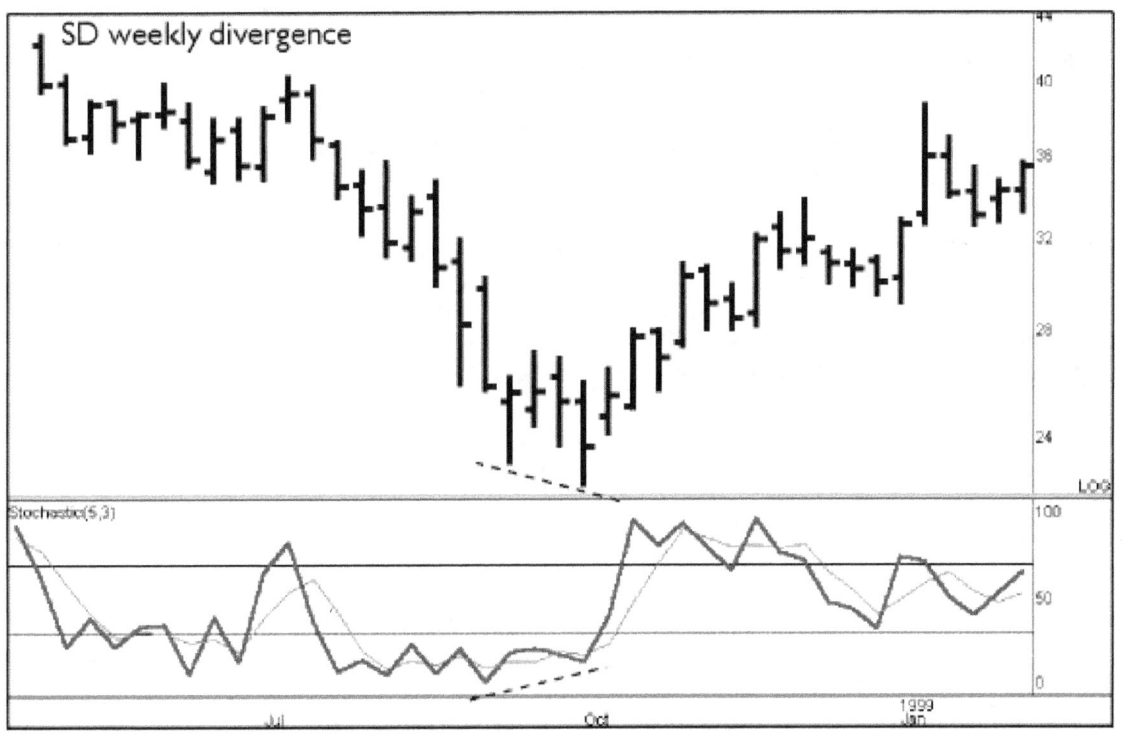

Monthly, weekly, and daily SD divergence exists all on the same day.

How to Find Major Market Tops Using Stochastic Divergence Across Monthly, Weekly, and Daily Time Frames

Here is another powerful example of divergence which occurs across monthly, weekly, and daily charts. Particularly interesting in this case of Compaq Computer is how the divergence took shape during a time when the company was announcing record corporate earnings. All of that unraveled during the first quarter of 1999 when the company being posting disappointing earnings. **Somehow, the stochastic oscillator was able to anticipate this.**

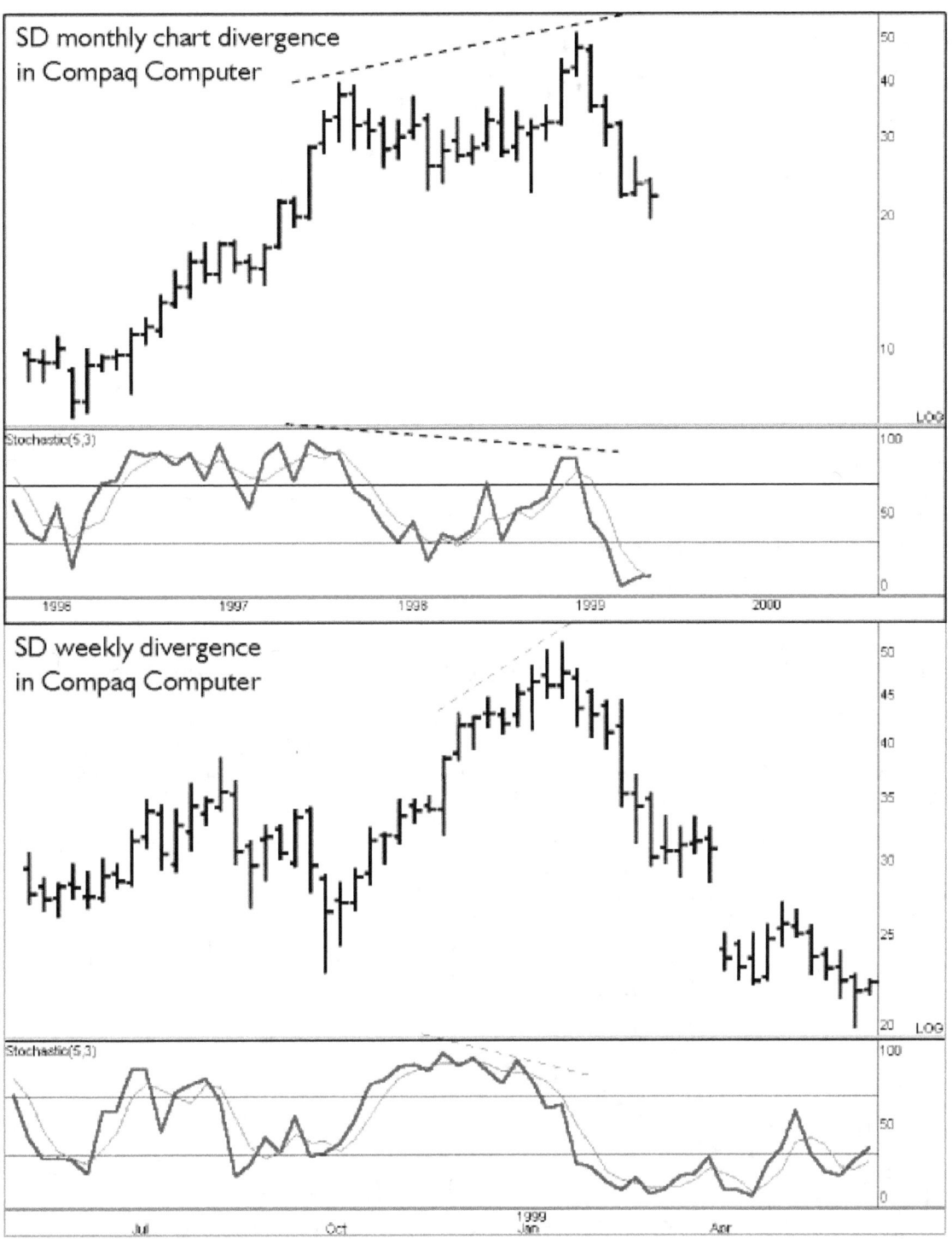

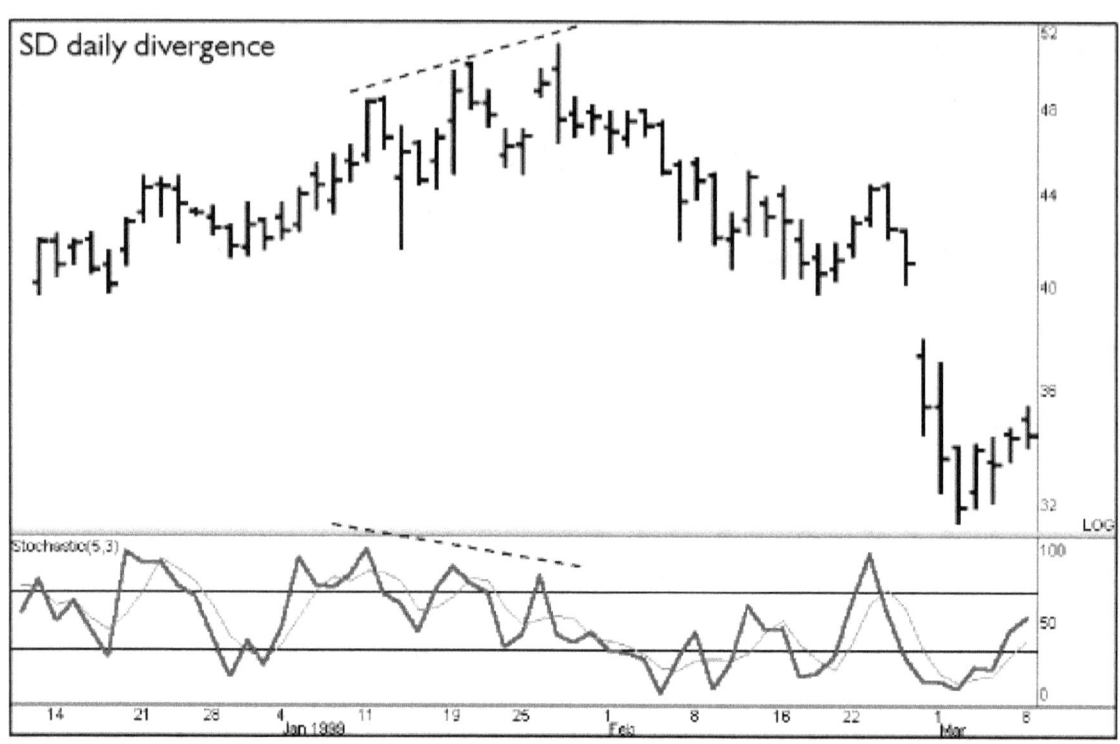

How to Find Pyramiding Opportunities by Catching a Reaction in a Strong Trend

In Week 3's lesson on Runaway Markets, I showed you how I use patterns to catch trading opportunities when markets consolidate or react during strong trends

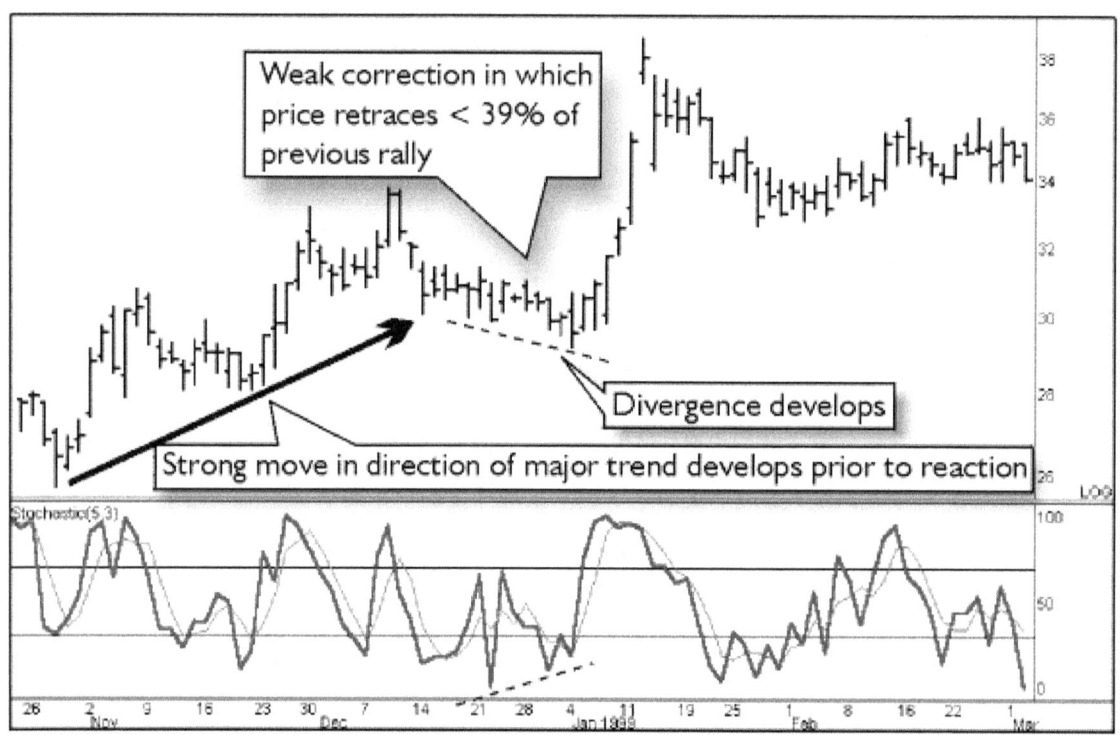

Using stochastics, you can identify this same kind of trading setup. First, you must identify a market in which a strong trend is in force. Review our discussions on Relative Strength and Runaway Markets to find ways of doing this. Let's say that you bought into a stock at a lower level. The stock moves enough that you can move your correction that coincides with a divergence pattern. The correction must be less than 39% of the preceding rally. Once SD turns up, an excellent buying opportunity has developed.

How to Find Pyramiding Opportunities by Catching a Reaction in a Declining Market

Here, we find the opposite case, wherein we have the opportunity to add to a short position when a strongly declining stock makes an upward correction of less than 39% of the preceding decline.

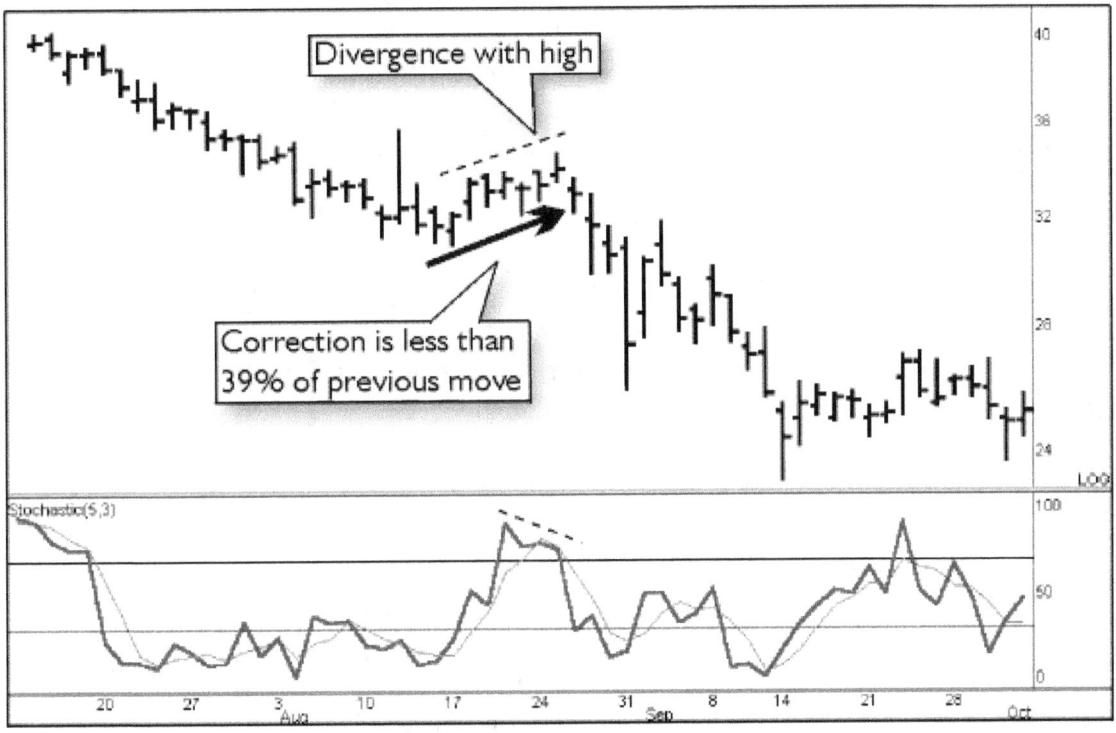

As you can see, when price makes a new high, SD fails to do so and diverges. An excellent short selling situation has developed.

How to Identify Possible Buying Opportunities in a Runaway Bull Market

If you have identified a runaway stock that is shooting up like a rocket, a possible buy signal exists when SD drops below 30 as long as the stock corrects less than 39%.

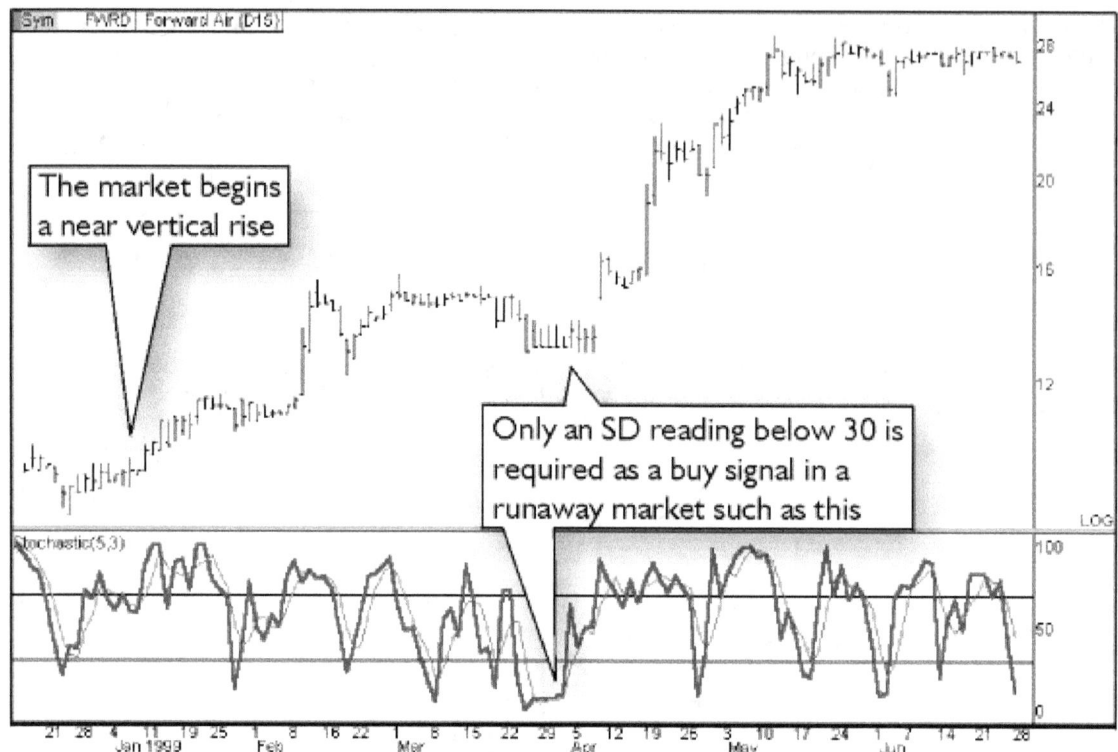

How to Identify Possible Shorting Opportunities in a Runaway Bear Market

The same kind of setup discussed previously applies to markets that are on a rapid, out of control decline.

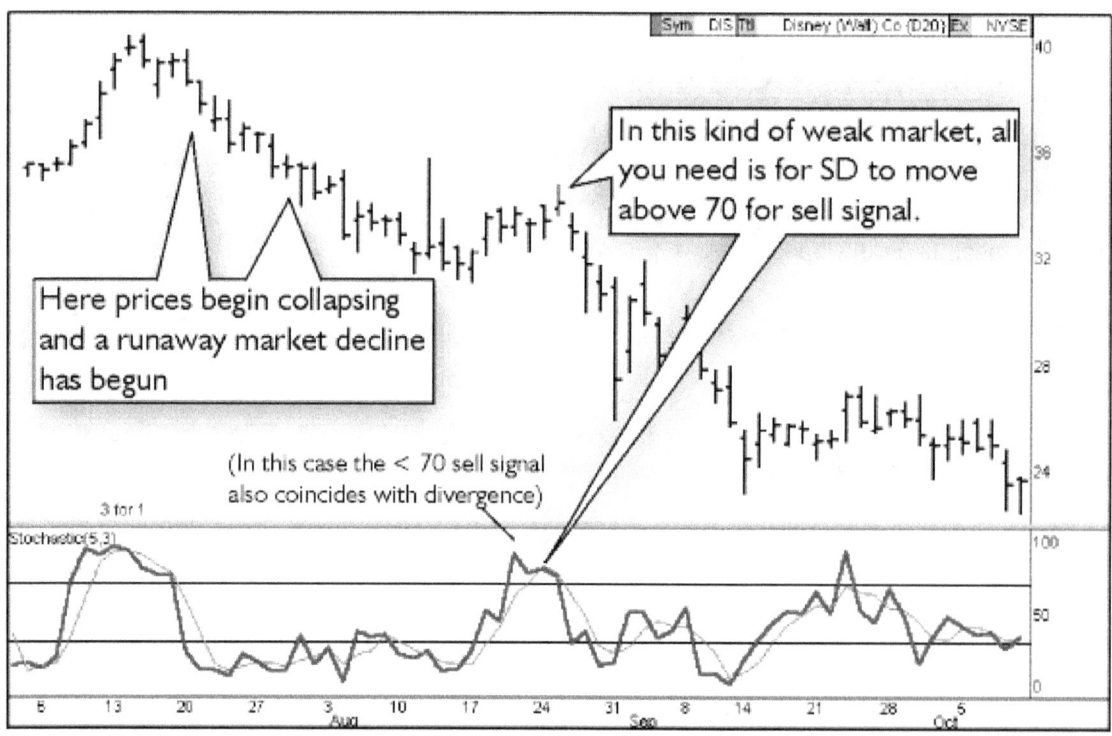

If you find a stock that meets the criteria of a runaway market and it corrects less than 39% of the preceding downtrend, look for a possible shorting opportunity when SD moves above 70.

Relative Strength Index (RSI)

The Relative Strength Index (RSI) is one of the first oscillators that became widely used back when charting software first appeared in the early eighties.

It was first introduced by Welles Wilder in an article in Commodities (now known as Futures) Magazine in June, 1978. The RSI formula is:

RSI = 100 - [100 / 1 + (U/D)]

U = An average of upward price change.

D = An average of downward price change.

Note that the name "Relative Strength Index" is **not the same thing** as "relative strength" as used in Week 2 of our course. In fact, its rather misleading to call it the "Relative Strength Index" because the RSI does not compare the relative strength of multiple securities, but rather the **internal strength of an a single security.**

Popular Uses

Most traders start out using the RSI as an overbought and oversold indicator. The conventional wisdom is to sell when RSI is overbought condition and buy when RSI is oversold

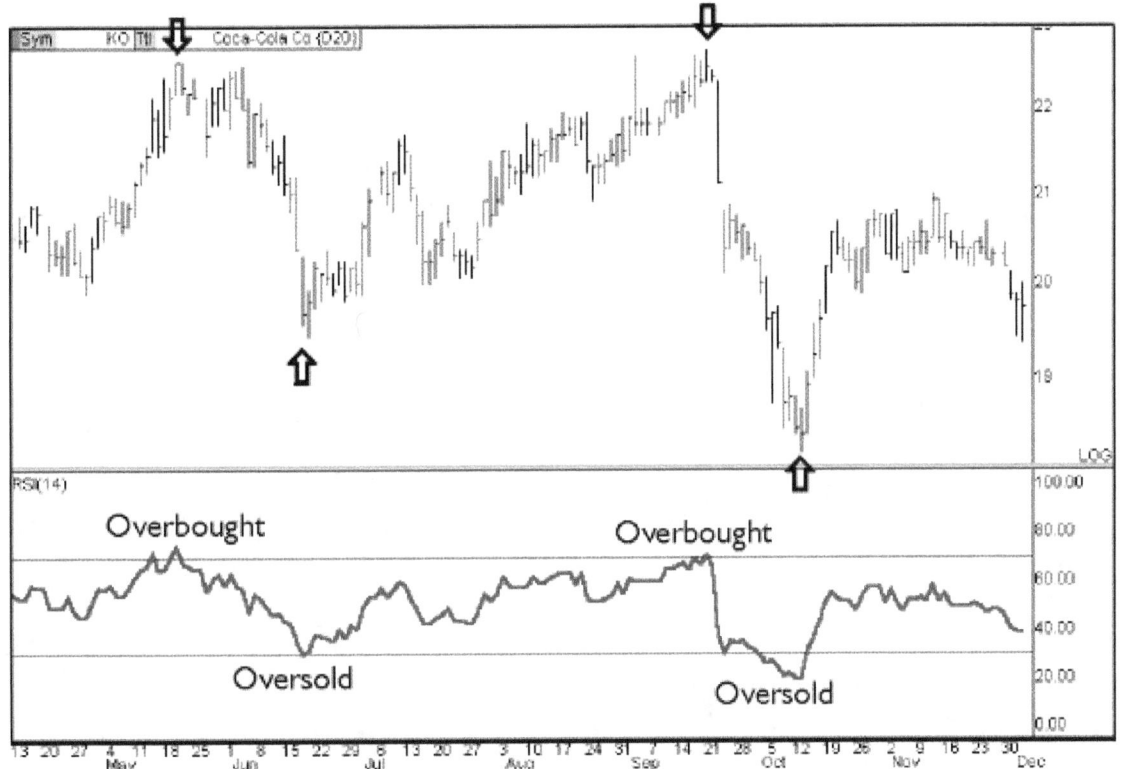

Applied haphazardly, this doesn't work very well--and certainly nowhere near as well as the example above depicts.

Now, let me show you how I prefer to use the RSI.

My Parameters

All of the following examples use a look-back value of 14, which is the default setting on most charting programs.

As with the stochastic oscillator, I use 30 for the oversold line and 70 for the overbought line

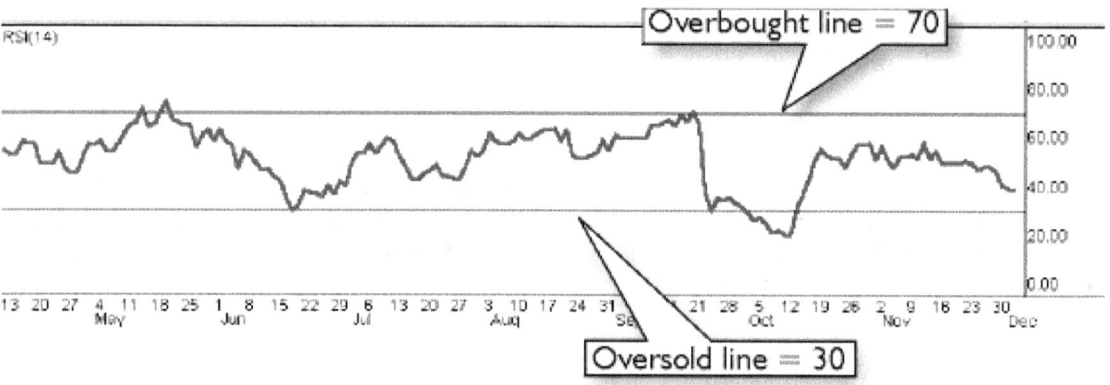

How to Find Potential Market Bottoms Using RSI Downside Divergence

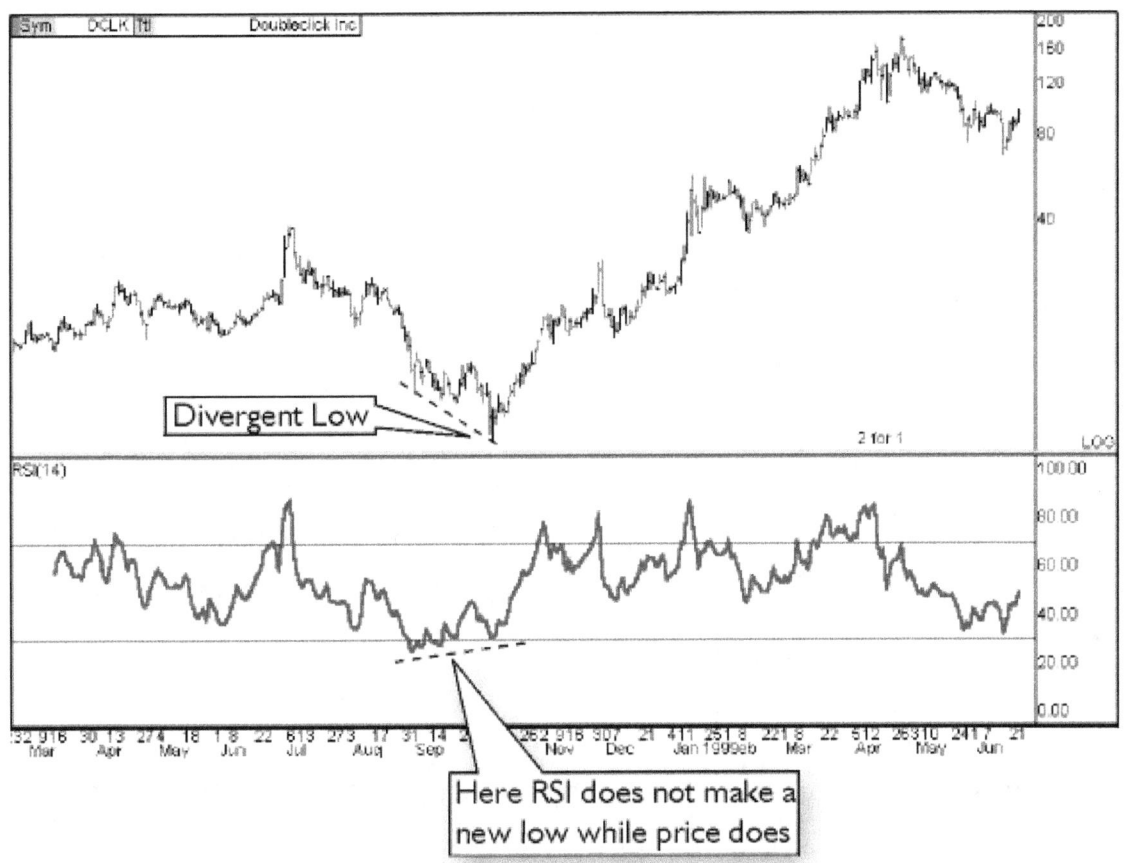

This setup is quite similar the one for Stochastic Divergence.

1) RSI dips below 30 on a price decline.

2) Price makes a new low

3) RSI does not confirm the new low in price.

Once this occurs, a divergence exists.

How to Find Potential Market Tops Using RSI Upside Divergence

Once again, we're looking for price to make a new high that is not confirmed by RSI.

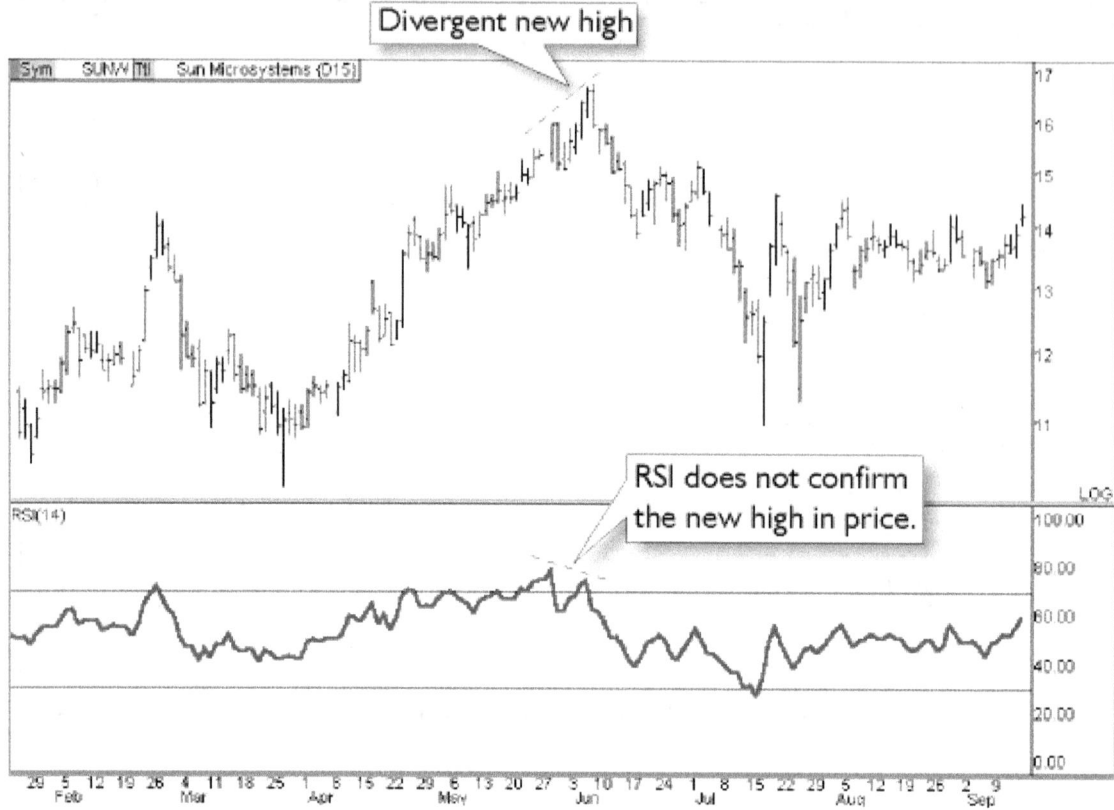

1. RSI moves above 70 on a rally in price.

2. Price makes a new high.

3. RSI does not confirm the new high in price.

Once the divergence exists you have a potential selling opportunity.

How to Find Possible Major Market Bottoms with RSI Weekly and Daily Divergence

Occasionally, you'll find RSI divergences that coincide on both weekly and daily Charts. This is a potent indication that in combination with other agreeing factors described elsewhere in my 10-Week Course, can constitute a powerful buy signal. Here's one of these instances that occurred in AOL.

Here's the weekly chart:

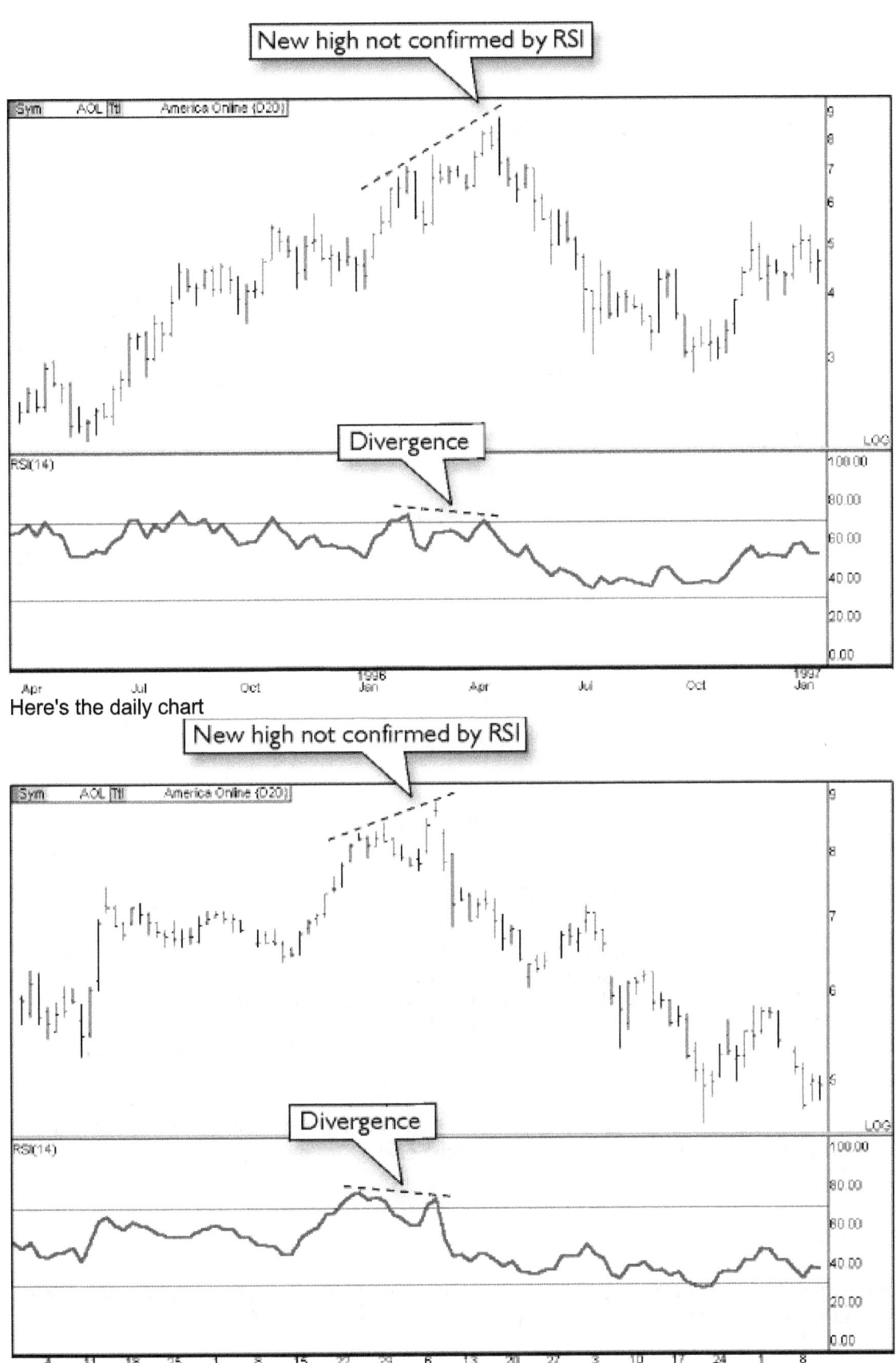
Here's the daily chart

How to Find Possible Major Market Bottoms with RSI Monthly Divergence

An event that rarely occurs is a RSI divergence on a monthly time frame. When it happens, pay attention.

Moving Average Convergence-Divergence (MACD)

Many books about technical analysis will say that the moving average convergence-divergence (MACD) indicator is "the difference between the 12-day and 26-day exponential moving averages." However, its creator, Gerald Appel, defines the indicator as the difference between the 0.15 and 0.075 exponential moving averages. When expressed in decimal form, the 12- and 26-day exponential moving averages are actually 0.153846 and 0.076923 exponential moving averages.

The above calculation results in the MACD line. A 9-day exponential moving average called the "signal line" is overlaid on the MACD. In the following examples, the blue line is the MACD and the red line is the signal line.

Popular Uses

The most popular approach to using MACD is to buy when MACD crosses above the signal line and sell when MACD crosses below the signal line as shown below.

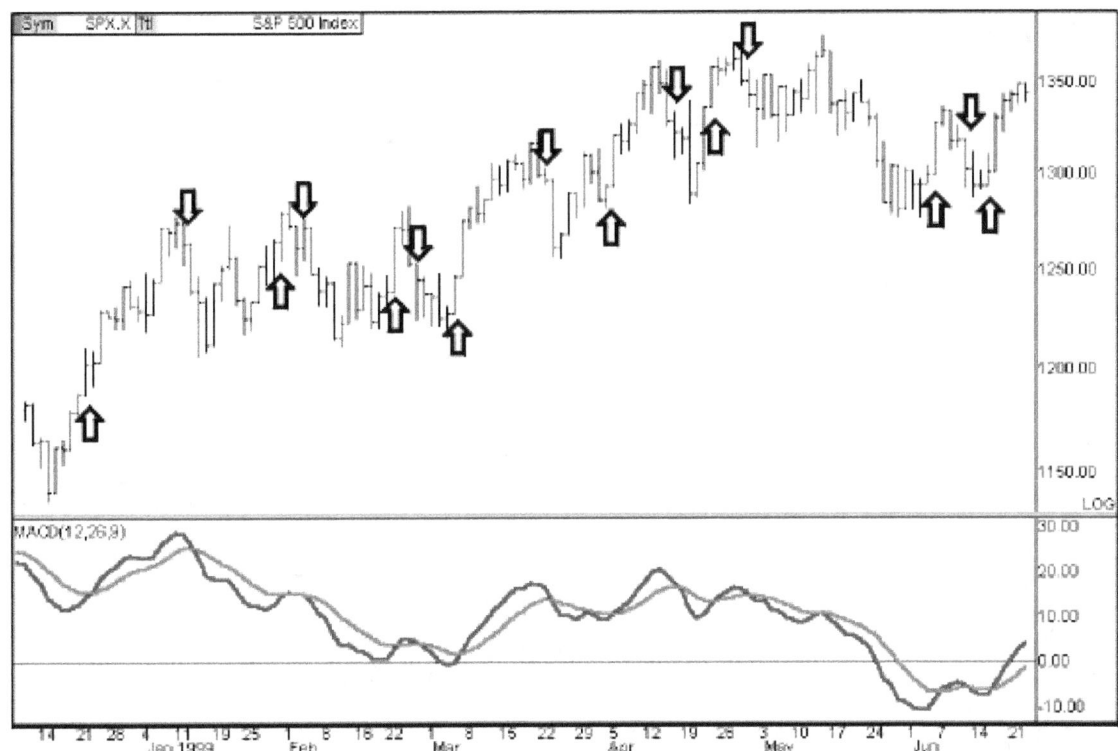

Like most mechanical oscillator-based systems, this approach produces **too many signals** with a **very low percentage of profitable ones**. It is especially bad in whipsaw markets.

Now let me show you how I prefer to use MACD.

How to Identify Potential Market Bottoms Using MACD Divergence

Here, a new low in price is not confirmed by a new low in the MACD line. A buy signal would be issued when MACD crosses above the signal line while the divergence remains intact.

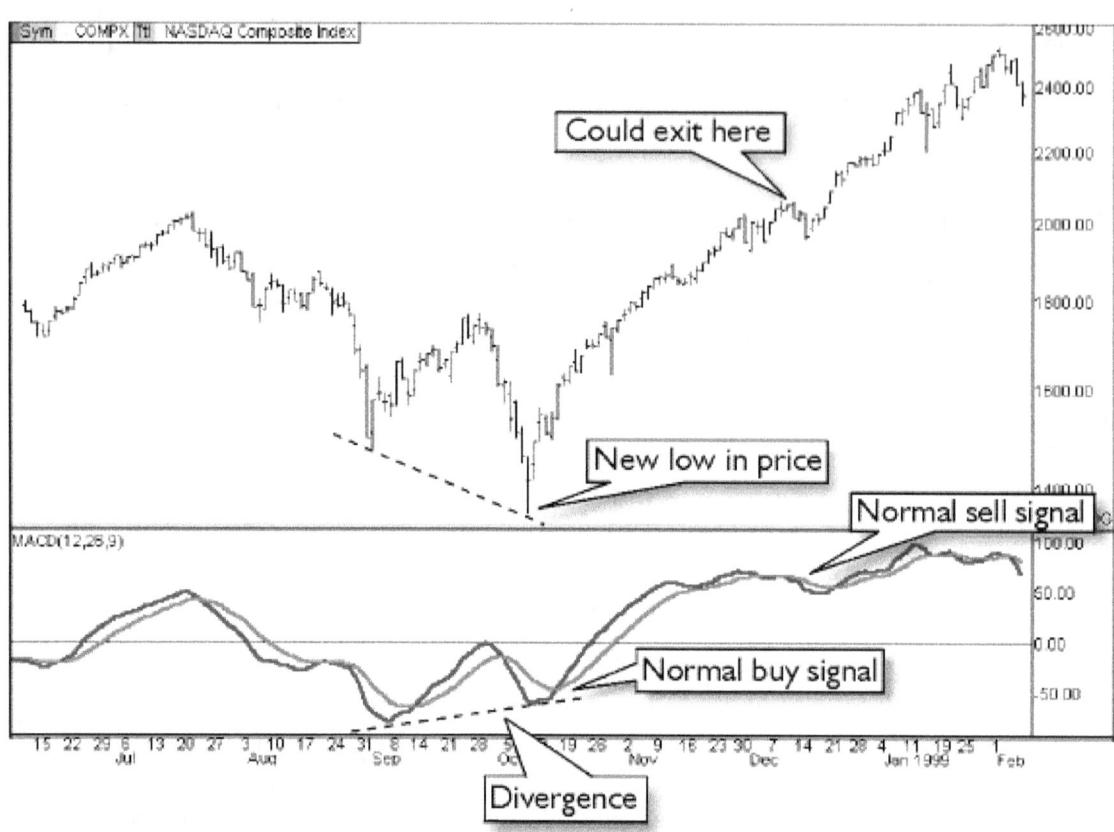

Note, however, that when a market is in a nice trend, MACD can provide with good signals at which to partially or fully exit your position.

How to Identify Potential Market Tops Using MACD Divergence

Once you see the divergence occur between price and MACD, wait until the "normal" sell signal occurs before entering a position. The normal sell signal occurs when the MACD line cross under the signal line.

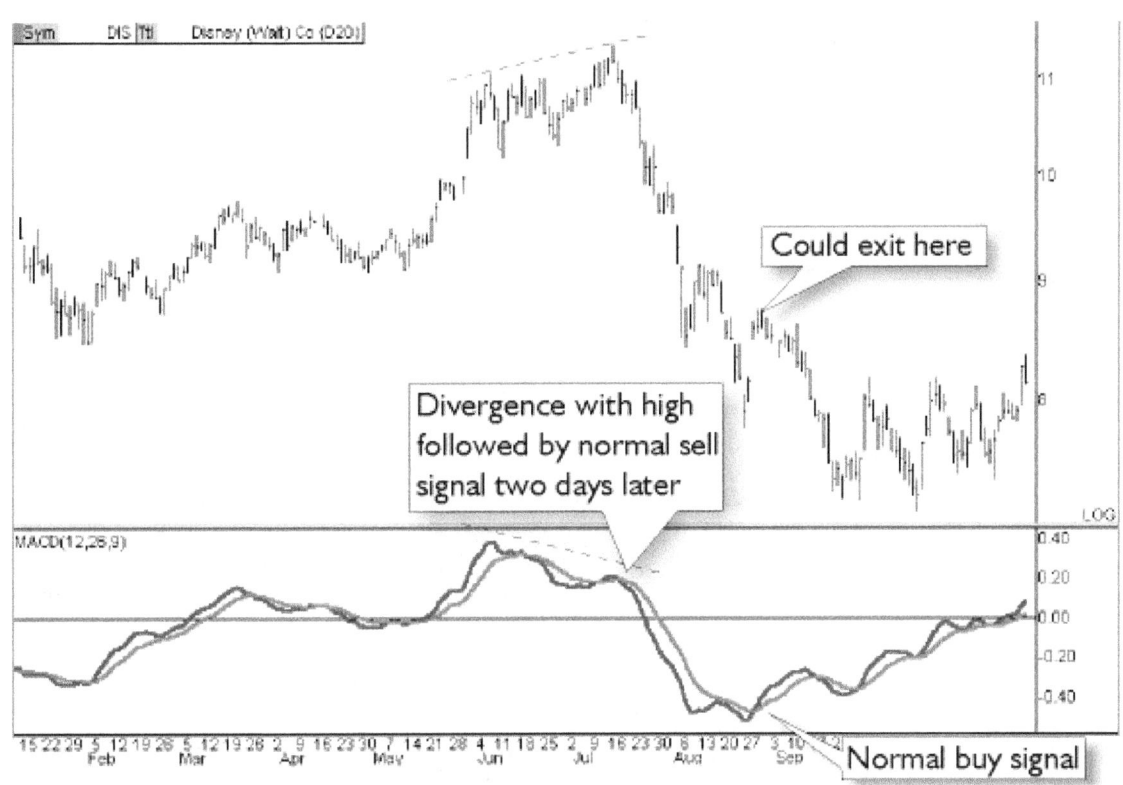

As with buy signals, MACD can be used to help you find good points at which to lighten or exit your position.

On-Balance Volume

Created by Joe Granville, On-Balance Volume (OBV) keeps a running total of volume and relates price changes to changes in volume. The idea is to show accumulation and distribution taking place that might not be visible by the standard volume bars you normally see in most charting software.

The classic OBV is calculated by adding today's total volume to a cumulative total when price closes higher than yesterday's close and subtracting today's total volume from the cumulative total when the price closes lower than yesterday's close. If price remains the same, then the OBV is not changed. The actual amount of the price change is irrelevant and only the direction of change is significant for these calculations.

Popular Uses

The premise behind OBV is that volume trends lead price trends and that changes in OBV generally lead changes in price. The way I use OBV is pretty close to the way most people use it, except that numerous other independent variables have to be in place for me to see a trading opportunity. Generally, I look for divergences and breakout patterns. These are shown on the following pages.

How to Find Potential Market Bottoms Using Downside Divergence

Look for price to make a new low that is not confirmed by OBV

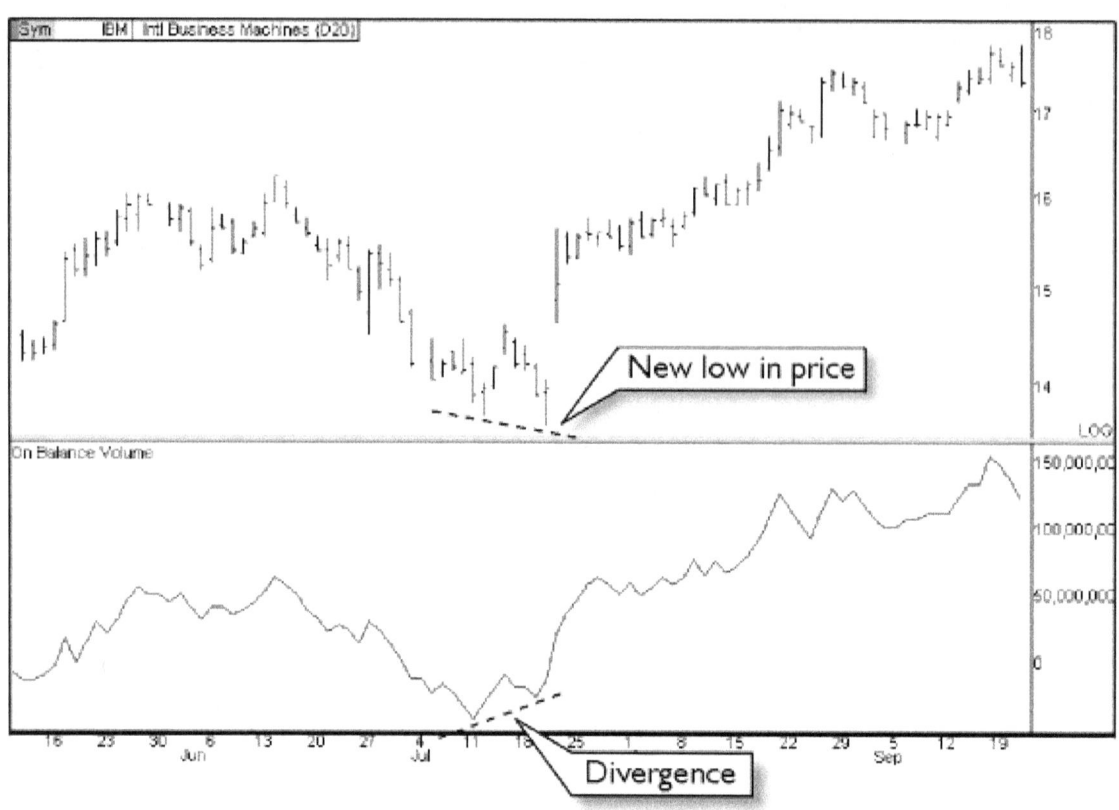

How to Find Potential Market Tops Using Upside Divergence

Here is the classic divergence pattern once again. A new high in price coincides with a lower high in OBV.

How to Find Trading Opportunities in Breakouts Using OBV

In my discussion of Runaway Markets in Week 3, I showed you a number of useful patterns in which price consolidates in the midst of strongly trending markets. I look for trading opportunities to occur when price breaks out from these patterns. Another thing I sometimes look for is for a similar pattern in OBV to breakout simultaneously or prior to the price breakout as shown below

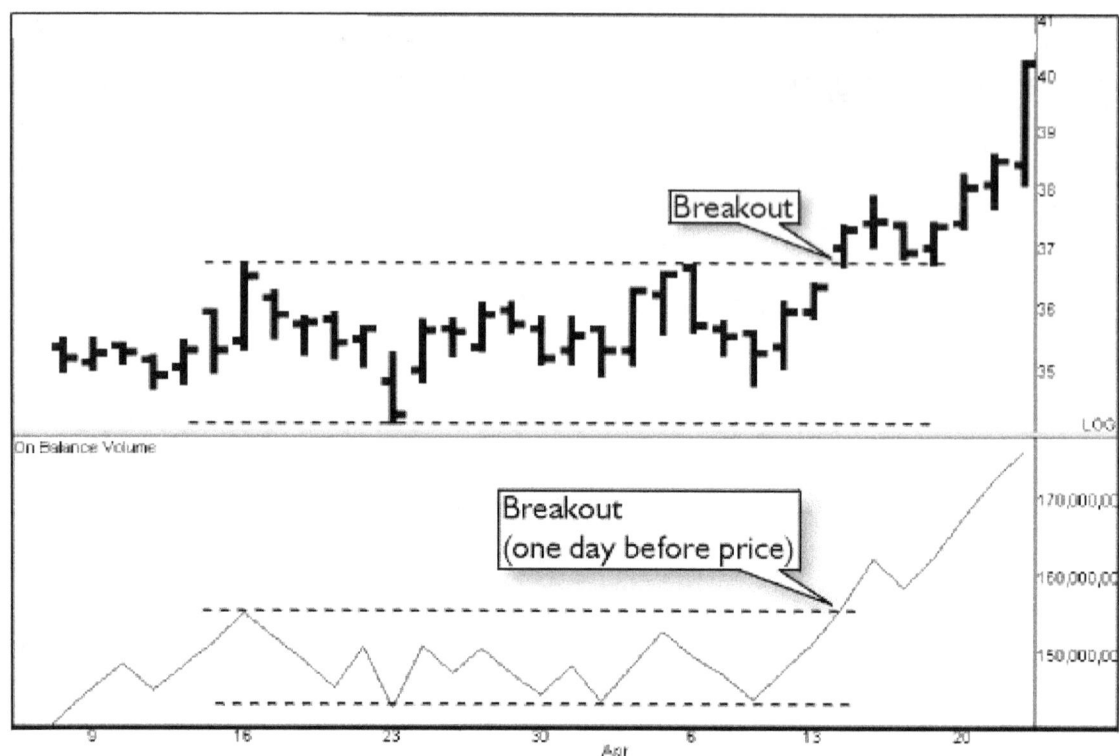

This is acts as a confirmation which increases my confidence that a viable trade is at hand.

Breakout Tips

Since I trade breakouts much more often then reactions, let's review how we can increase the reliability of a consolidation (trading range) breakout:

1. Make sure that the consolidation corrects less than 39% of the prior move.
2. Make sure OBV or any other good volume accumulation/distribution indicator breaks out before price does.
3. Make sure that the breakout occurs on a TBBLBG pattern.
4. Make sure the breakout occurs on higher volume than the previous day and, ideally, on higher volume across several bars.
5. Make sure that market has been in a runaway trend prior to the beginning of the consolidation.

With these five tests you can increase the reliability of your breakout setups by 15%!

the Quiz

Question 1: What stochastics pattern do you see in this Amazon chart?

Answer: It's a Sliding Top divergence.

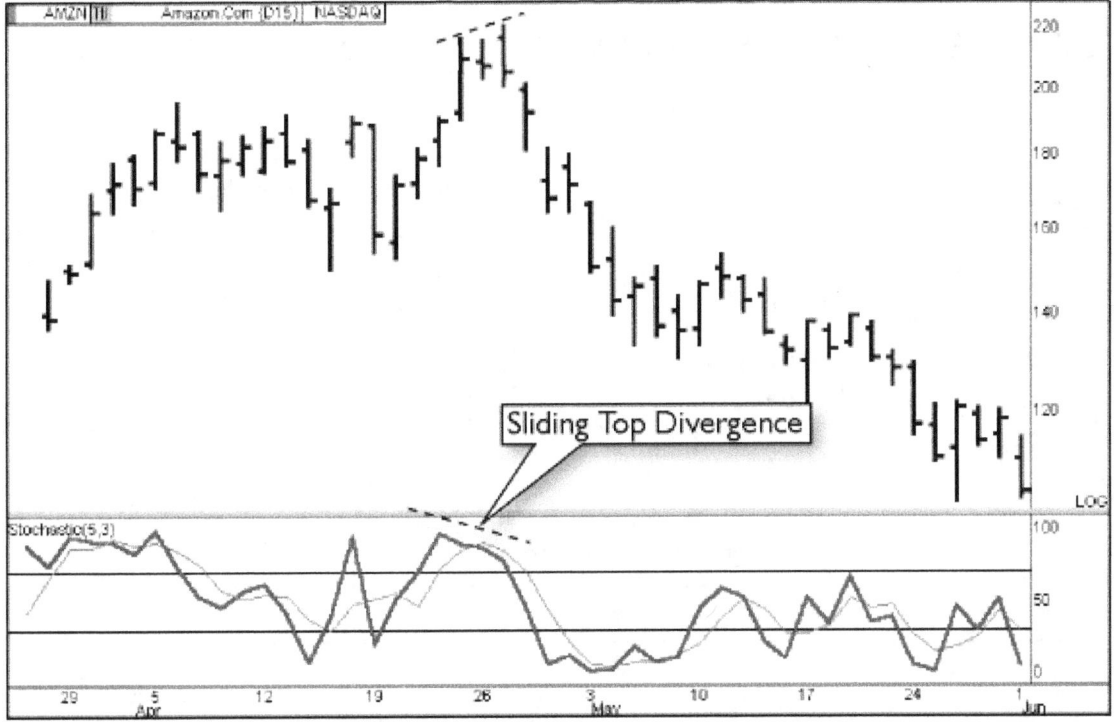

Question: What trading opportunity do you see here?

Answer: Once you have identified all the factors that need to be in place for a runaway bear market, you can enter short positions when SD moves above 70.

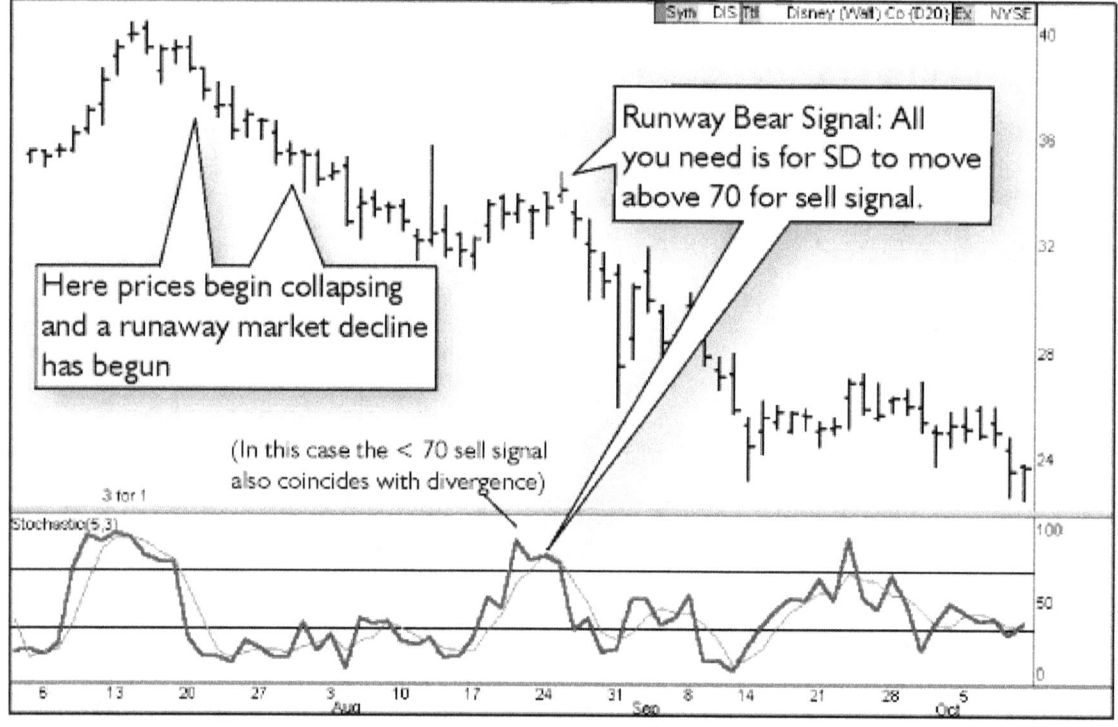

Here prices begin collapsing and a runaway market decline has begun

Runway Bear Signal: All you need is for SD to move above 70 for sell signal.

(In this case the < 70 sell signal also coincides with divergence)

Question: This is a monthly chart of AT&T. What RSI pattern do you see here?

Answer: It's divergence in the monthly time frame.

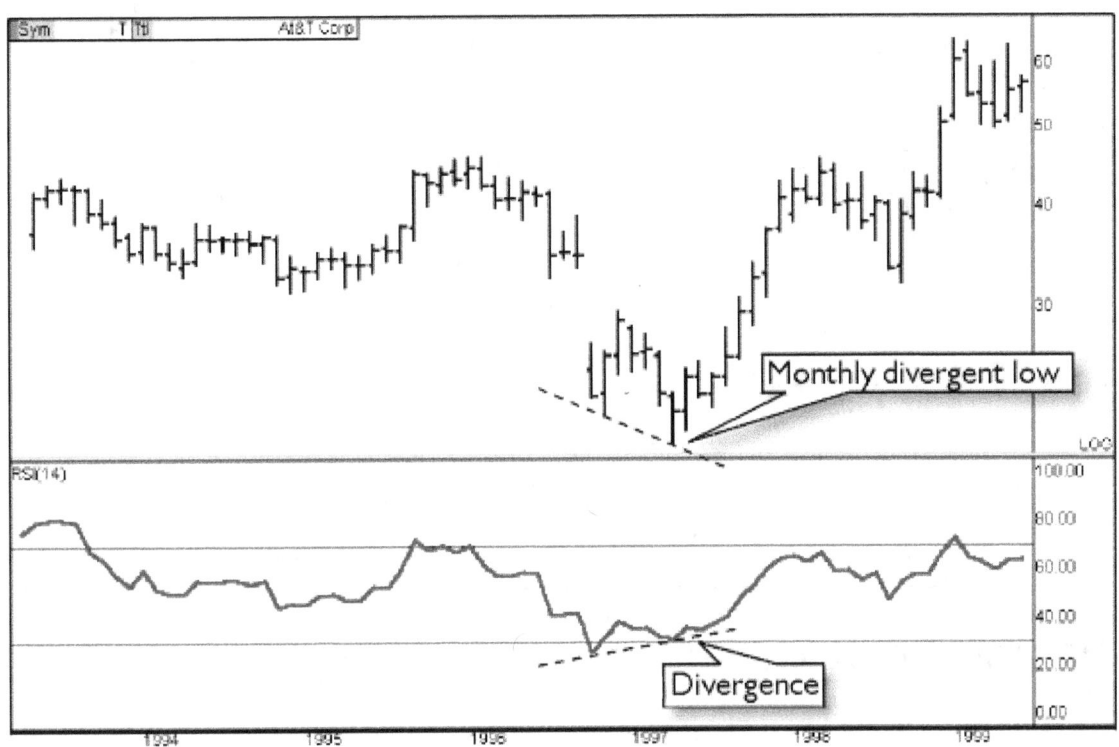

What stochastics pattern setup do you see here?

Answer: It's a Floor Trader's Bottom

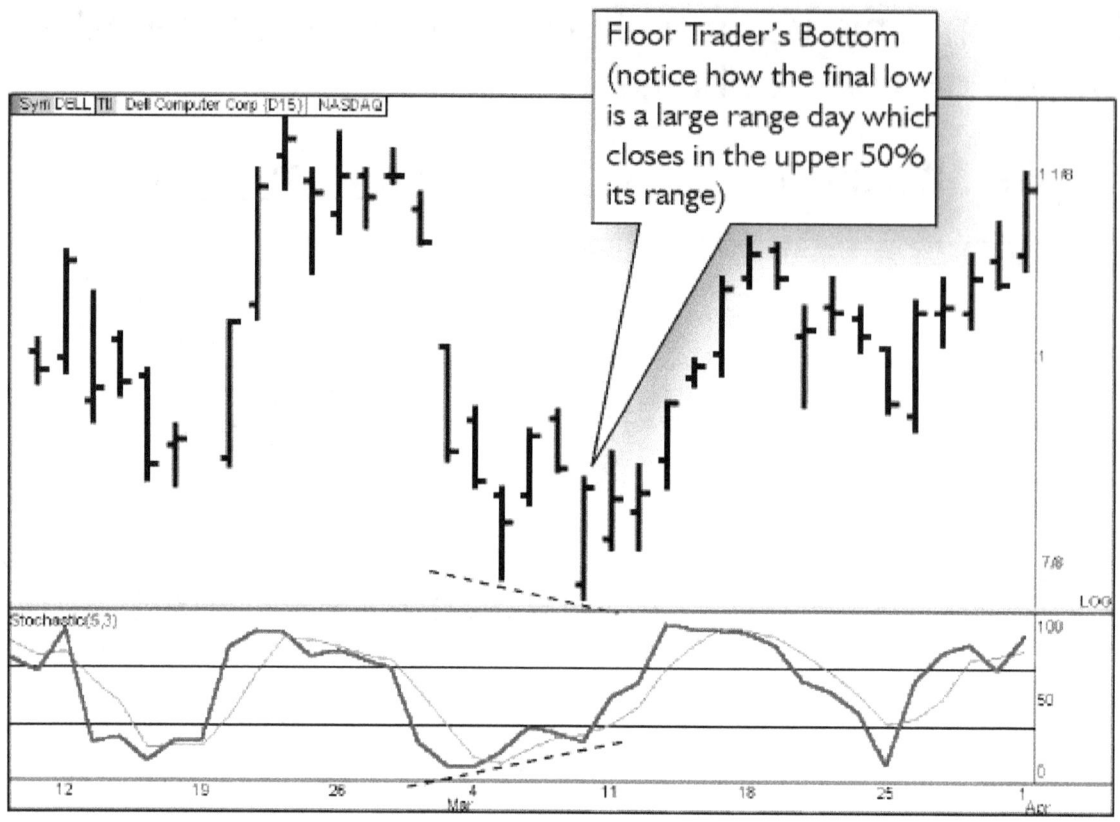

Closing Remarks

Most traders either **overuse or misuse indicators**. Before looking at:

- momentum oscillators such as stochastics and RSI
- accumulation/distribution indicators such as OBV, Volume Accumulation, William's A/D, Power Index, Money Flow (or any other other type of tool that is similar to OBV)
- short-term trend detection tools like MACD

--remember J. Paul Getty's most important rule of success:

"GO WHERE THE OIL IS."

In trading, going where the oil is means **finding the strongest trends via relative strength and runaway market criteria** in stocks and/or futures that have room to continue in the direction of those strong trends. To try and use indicators without first finding strong trends with fuel is to shoot your rifle before aiming at your target--you're just wasting ammo at best, and you may hit something you don't want to.

Only after you've found your target vehicles should you even consider looking at indicators.

Secondly, only use indicators to go with the strong trend--never to fade it. I showed you this week how to use weekly, monthly, and daily divergences in stochastics and RSI to spot potential market tops and bottoms of significance. If you find a monthly-weekly-daily divergence setup top don't sell it short, rather use it to exit longs in that vehicle. If you find a monthly-weekly-daily divergence setup bottom you would only use that to exit a short if you had one in that position.

GO WITH THE TREND. Trying to use an oscillator to fade the trend is like picking a number in roulette--it might feel great when you win and it will return a lot on your bet that one time, but you're going to lose the vast majority of the time. In other words:

Don't spit against the wind.

If the trend is up, look for oversold reactions and divergences on reactions down as potential areas to buy or add to positions in the best vehicles you can find. If the trend is down, look for overbought reactions and divergences on corrections up as potential areas to sell short or add to short positions in the best short vehicles you can find.

Remember that

- a momentum oscillator that is overbought and/or divergent in a runaway trend up is virtually meaningless.
- a momentum oscillator that is oversold and/or divergent in a runaway trend down is virtually meaningless.

Most traders should not have more than 1/3 of their positions entered on reaction patterns, in my opinion. **The majority of your trades should be entered on breakouts of consolidation patterns to new highs in uptrending runaway stocks with top relative strength rankings and plenty of fuel (room to keep climbing). Most short sales should likewise be breakdowns of consolidations or topping patterns in weak relative strength downtrending runaway stocks.**

The best pattern we looked at this week was in OBV. A breakout by OBV or another accumulation/distribution indicator prior to price, along with our other five criteria in a runaway uptrend stock with high relative strength rankings is the most reliable use of indicators we have yet discussed. Also valuable is the use of pyramiding via stochastics on reactions against a super-strong trend in a stock you are already long in.

When you are long a vehicle (stock or future) make sure you it doesn't conflict with a monthly-weekly-daily setup topping pattern. If it does, take at least partial (if not full) profits as soon as you see this pattern. The same is true in reverse for shorts and a monthly-weekly-daily stochastic or RSI potential bottom setup. Definitely--do not buy a monthly-weekly-daily bottom setup or sell short a monthly-weekly-daily top setup unless you're doing so as part of a market timing play where you're trying to trade the market in a particular direction for other reasons.

To sum it up, indicators can be very helpful tools, but they are **not holy grails**, and they are not the most important components of profitable trading. However, if you remember to focus on **vehicle selection first**, and to use indicators only to help you trade **with the trend**, indicators can become a helpful part of your trading arsenal.

We're Taking the Week Off Next Week

Next week, I'm going to take a mid-term breather from the course. With summer vacations kicking in around the 4th of July weekend, I figure that many of you won't even be around to read anything I have to say--so I might as well take a week off as well.

So, please be advised that **all future topics will be shifted forward by one week.**

Don't get get too relaxed though; when we get together again, I will be talking about one of the most powerful trading strategies you could ever utilize: Market Selection.

Best regards,

Mark Boucher

TradingMarkets.com Members, Welcome Back to the Course:

It was great for us to take last week off, wasn't it? Perhaps you've had time to reflect upon the material we've covered so far in the Course and the relevance that it could have to your own trading approach.

I certainly hope that my ideas have had some positive impact on you so far because whatever success I have achieved as a trader and hedge fund manager these past 21 years can be attributed to the very techniques I've been sharing with you. I want to pass these ideas to you out of the gratitude I have towards the great teachers who delivered me from my own ignorance during my initial years of struggle.

The bottom line here is that part of **your success as a trader depends on to the extent to which you're willing rely on objective analysis and use principles that go against the grain of the establishment**. What does the establishment teach? Review the content of magazines such as Technical Analysis of Stock and Commodities and Futures. Look at the financial web sites out there. You'll see these common themes:

1) **Strategies and Techniques.** There's always a hot new methodology that will somehow improve your trading results. Success is from some external source, not something from within yourself.

2) **Predict the future.** Figure the exact future dates when the market is likely to turn up or down. Make a fortune buying bottoms and selling tops.

3) **It's all in your head.** No matter what your trading strategy is, you can succeed as long as you have the right mental attitude.

While many of the ideas coming out of these themes may be valid and useful, they should not be your main focus. If you were to start with a blank slate and allow your trading approach to be completely reprogrammed, I'd upload the following into your brain:

- First start with money management. Understand the mathematics of how you optimize incremental gains and keep losses to a minimum and have the discipline to apply in your trading.

Secondly, focus on market selection. There's such a wide array of tantalizing, enticing, and irresistible trading products that opening the financial section of the paper is like walking into a Las Vegas casino. You've got Leaps, Diamonds, Spiders, sector funds for everything, options on everything, not to mention a pump and dumpers pushing a wide array of penny stocks. Instead of thinking that you're going to find the Holy Grail that will trade any of these vehicles successfully, you've got instead focus on identifying the small number of markets whose characteristics make their behavior most predictable.

Finally, once you've got a handle on money management and market selection, then **apply the best trading techniques** that you have available.

This week I'm going explain in detail my approach to market selection and share some trading ideas you can apply, once you know what markets to apply them to. In Week 3's topic of Runaway Markets, we covered some of this material already, but this time we'll focus more on the **"how to"** as opposed to the **"what is."**

You'll learn:

- How to put the odds in your favor with Market Selection
- How to identify Runaway Markets
- How I Trade Runaway Markets

Enter Week 6: Market Selection

Drilling For Oil (or Bananas)

In past weeks you've heard me say repeat J. Paul Getty's #1 rule for success, **"GO WHERE THE OIL IS."** In this section, I'll show you **how I find the oil and drill for it** in the stock market using **Market Selection techniques.**

With Market Selection, I am simply identifying markets that are easiest for me to make money off of. They exhibit uniquely predictable behaviors which increase the odds that the application of my trading techniques will payoff. The types of stocks which fit this profile are those exhibiting Runaway Market characteristics. Runaway Markets are stocks that are moving either up or down with great momentum and velocity, to the point that they seem out of control. By using various breakout trading techniques, I am essentially able to position myself in these stocks in sync with the dominant trend at the most explosive times of their movement.

This is somewhat counterintuitive to the average trader because typically, the time a stock exhibits Runaway Characteristics, it has already "bottomed out" and is within a strong established trend. When a large move in a stock has already taken place, particularly if new highs or lows are being made, there is tendency for people to think it's already moved too high or too low and that a correction is right around the corner. But one of the central characteristics of Runaway Markets is that to the casual observer they exhibit extremes in their behavior and **move farther, longer, and faster than seems reasonable.** That is the very thing that makes them such viable trading vehicles. Once you have identified such a market and trade in sync with it, you will find **your odds of making money dramatically improved.**

In the 60's, there was this documentary called the Endless Summer in which two surfers travel follow the summer season as it moves from continent to continent in search of the perfect wave. They finally find this wave in Australia. It's one which they can surf farther, longer, and faster than wave in the entire world. That is the type of wave I want to surf in the markets.

How to Identify Runaway Markets

Now that we know what we're looking for, I want to show you how to find them. In Week 3, I showed you the type of patterns that occur most frequently in Runaway Markets. This week, I will show you **a technique that uses these patterns in quantitative fashion to accurately identify Runaway Markets**. Before I do this, I want to remind you that you must look for Runaway Characteristics in the context of Fuel. That is, there has to be a **rational reason** for a stock to move either up or down to an **irrational extreme**.

Once we find stocks that have exhibited the types of technical patterns described in the previous section, we take a closer look at each stock and look for something called **Equity Fuel**.

The concept of Fuel is simple: We are looking for **valid reasons that the trend we have identified will continue well into the foreseeable future**. Remember, we are not in a stock just for a 2% move. Rather, we enter every trade with the hope that it will be a home run--that is, **return a high profit with minimal risk**.

Once we have seen the technical patterns and have verified that Fuel exists, we have a **good candidate for further appreciation**.

Criteria for Runaway Stocks with Fuel

The following is a simplified version of the criteria I use.

1) Must have **five or more Runaway patterns in a 21-day period**. These are the patterns I've described in the previous pages.

2) The stock **has not fallen below it's 200-day moving average** once the uptrend has begun.

3) The stock must have a **relative strength ranking of at least 65 during corrections and at least 80 if it is making new highs**. This ranking is available in the TradingMarkets.com site.

4) EPS ranking according to Investor's Business Daily is **80 or higher.**

5) **Relatively Undiscovered Stock**. Institutions own less than 16% of the total capitalization. Traders should begin taking profits once a stock reaches 40% or higher institutional sponsorship. This figures can be found in Investor's Business Daily.

6) Low Debt. The company should ideally use its own internal growth to finance its expansion. **Long-term debt should be less than 50%.**

8) Positive Fundamentals. There should be a simple, straightforward reason for earnings growth to continue. It could a **new product, technology gap, change in management, or other type of competitive edge** that makes sense for continued upward momentum in stock price.

How to Identify Runaway Markets

These next section is divided into two parts. The first part will show you the patterns that are characteristic of Runaway Markets. The second part will explain a technique for using those patterns to find Runaway Markets.

Part I: Runaway Market Patterns

In Week 3, we explained that most runaway moves contain many laps, gaps, and thrusts. We also described the technical patterns that are most often found in the initial phase (first third) of Runaway Market moves.

In the following pages I will describe **all the technical patterns**, most of which contain laps, gaps, or thrusts, that I look for in order to determine when a market is making a runaway move. Before proceeding any further, I suggest that you look back at Week 3 in order to familiarize yourself with laps, gaps, and thrusts.

These technical patterns are divided into three groups, Gap Patterns, Continuation Patterns, and Corrective Patterns. Let's start with Gap Patterns.

Gap Patterns
1. Exhaustion Gap Reversal

Here, the gap makes the final move up and runaway down move develops after the gap top

1. Exhaustion Gap Reversal

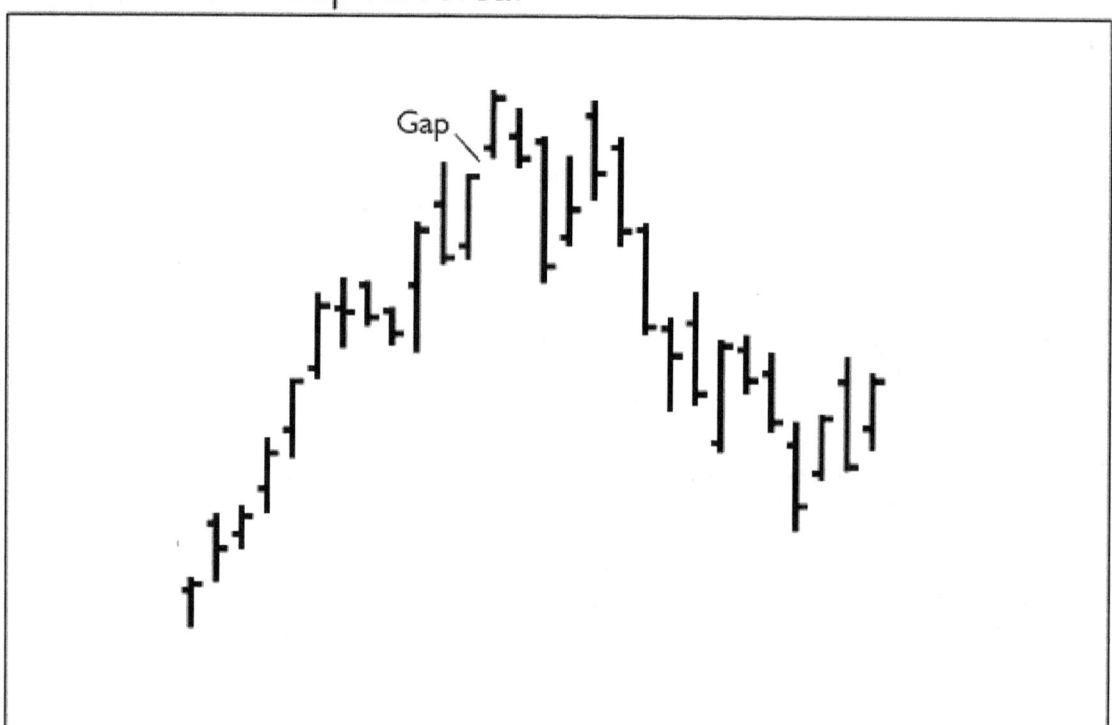

Gap Patterns

A gap on both sides of one or more bars is an island reversal because the bars separated by those gaps create an "island" of price action. Look for a reaction to a strong trend to end and return to the direction of the main trend on an island gap reversal.

Let's say that the dominant runaway move is in the down direction. As shown in the example on the left, a sharp reaction occurs to the upside terminating in an Island Reversal. The main trend down would then resume.

2. Island Gap Reversal

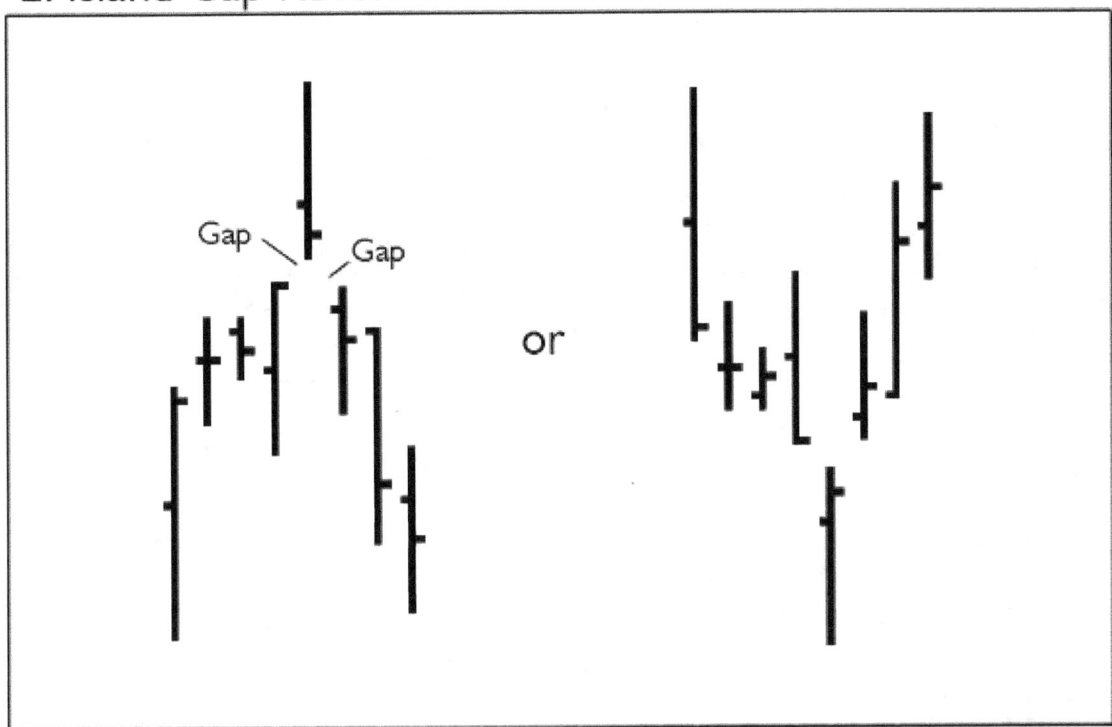

Gap Patterns

Here, prices run up and then form a consolidation that corrects no more than 38% of the prior up move. Prices then break out to new highs on a gap.

3. Breakaway Gaps

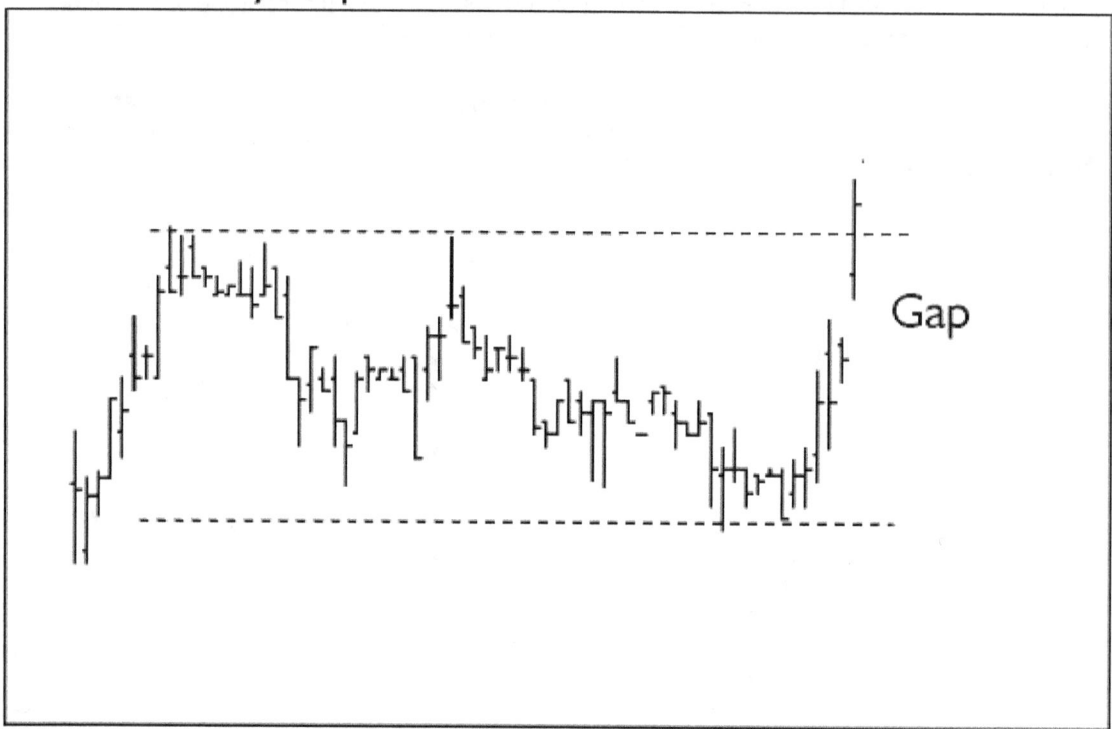

Gap Patterns

Instead of breaking out of a consolidation on a gap, prices here breakout on a lap.

4. Breakaway Laps

5. Runaway and Continuation Gaps

— Gaps

6. Gap Filling Corrections

Gap

Gap gets filled by correction

Now let's move on to **Continuation Patterns!**

Continuation Patterns
1. Flag with TBBLBG Breakout

1. Flag with TBBLBG Breakout

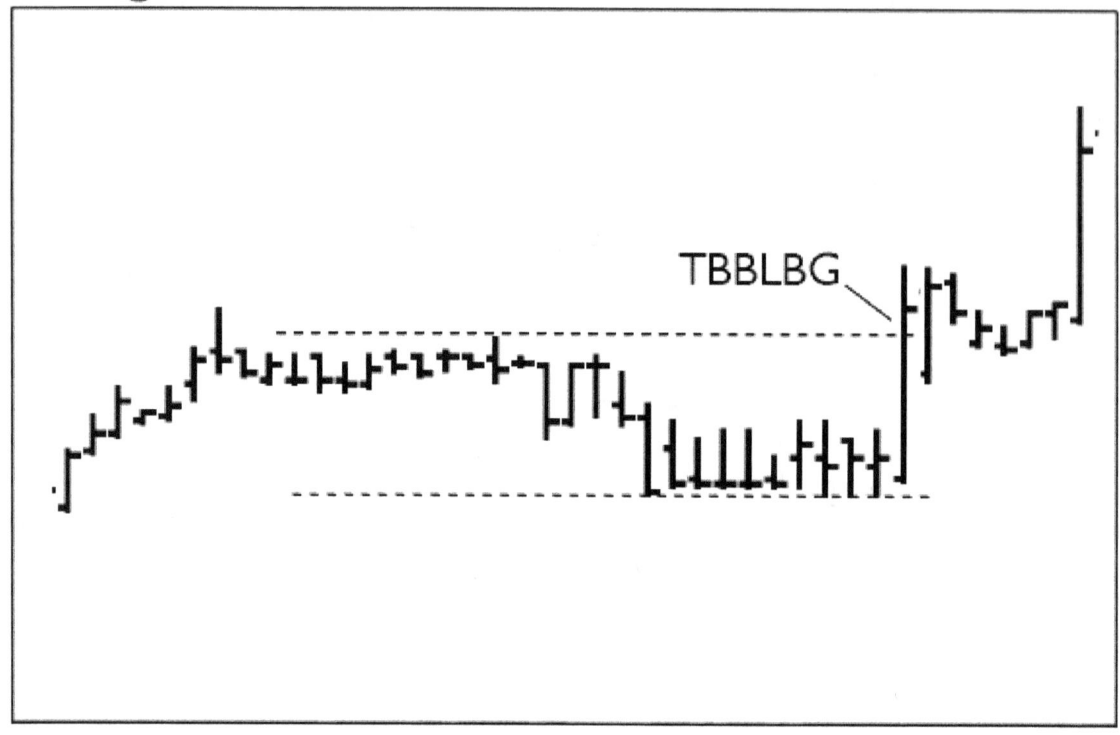

Again, prices rally strongly and then consolidate no more than 38% of the previous runup. The consolidation is broken by a thrust, gap, or lap.

2. Inside Day Flag with TBBLBG

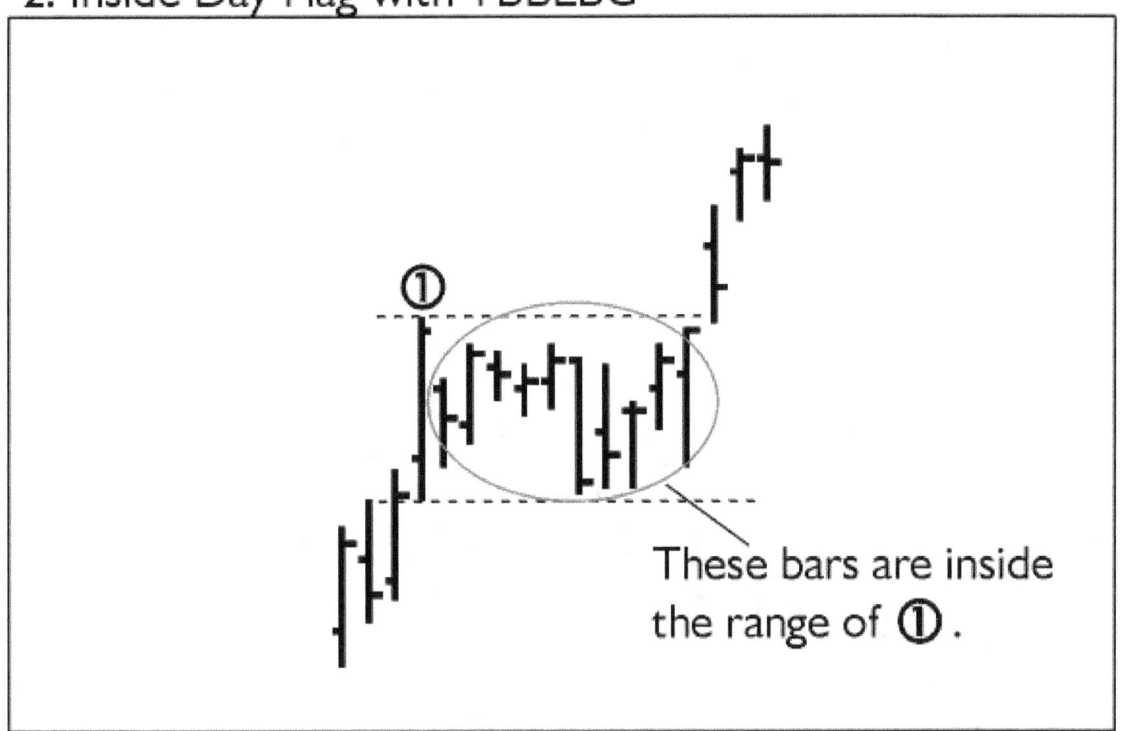

These bars are inside the range of ①.

3. Triangle with TBBLBG

TBBLBG

A triangle is a consolidation pattern where, again it does not retrace more than 38% of the preceding move. Here, prices move into a narrow and narrower range before finally breaking out on a gap, lap, or thrust.

A pennant consolidates into an expanding range. A breakout occurs when the trendline connecting the highs is broken by a TBBLBG

4. Pennant with TBBLBG

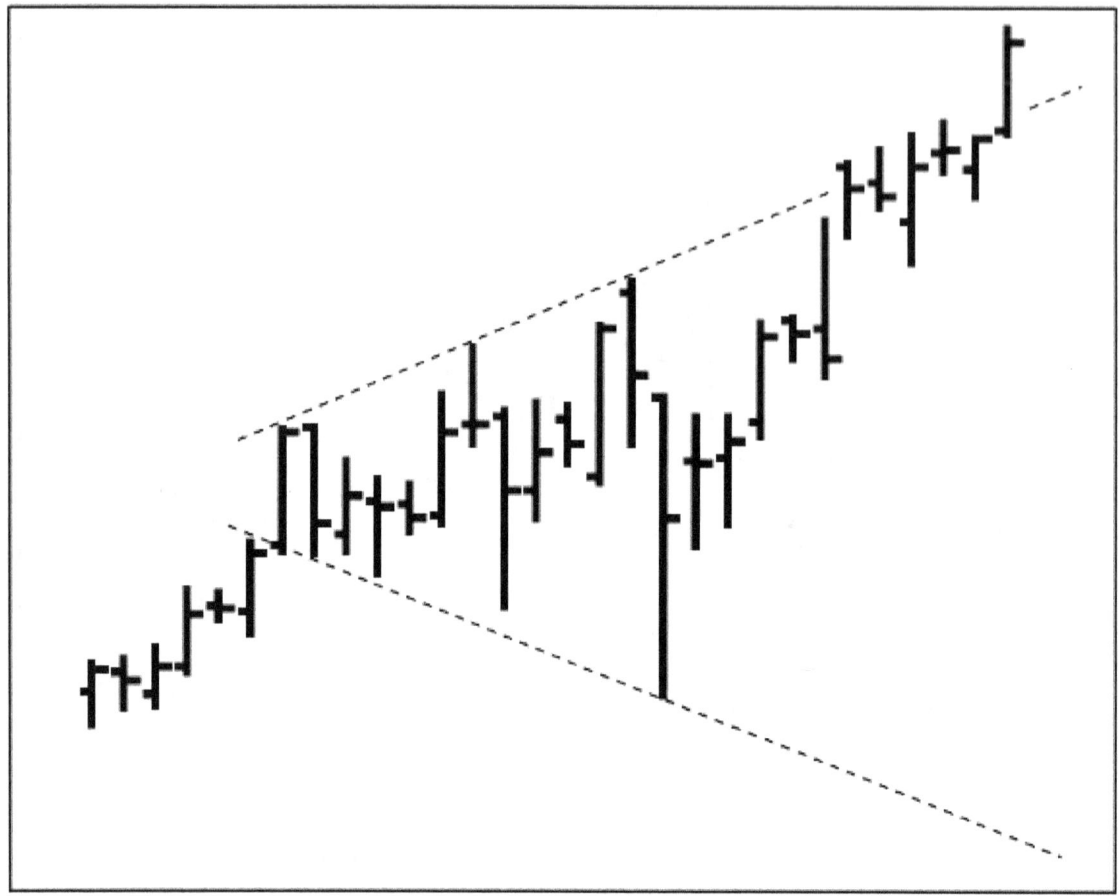

5. 2-3 Day Sharp Reaction with TBBLBG

Two sharp down days are all this strong market can muster against the trend. New highs are made on a TBBLBG.

6. Multiple Inside Day Combination with TBBLBG

7. Tight Trading Range Consolidation with TBBLBG

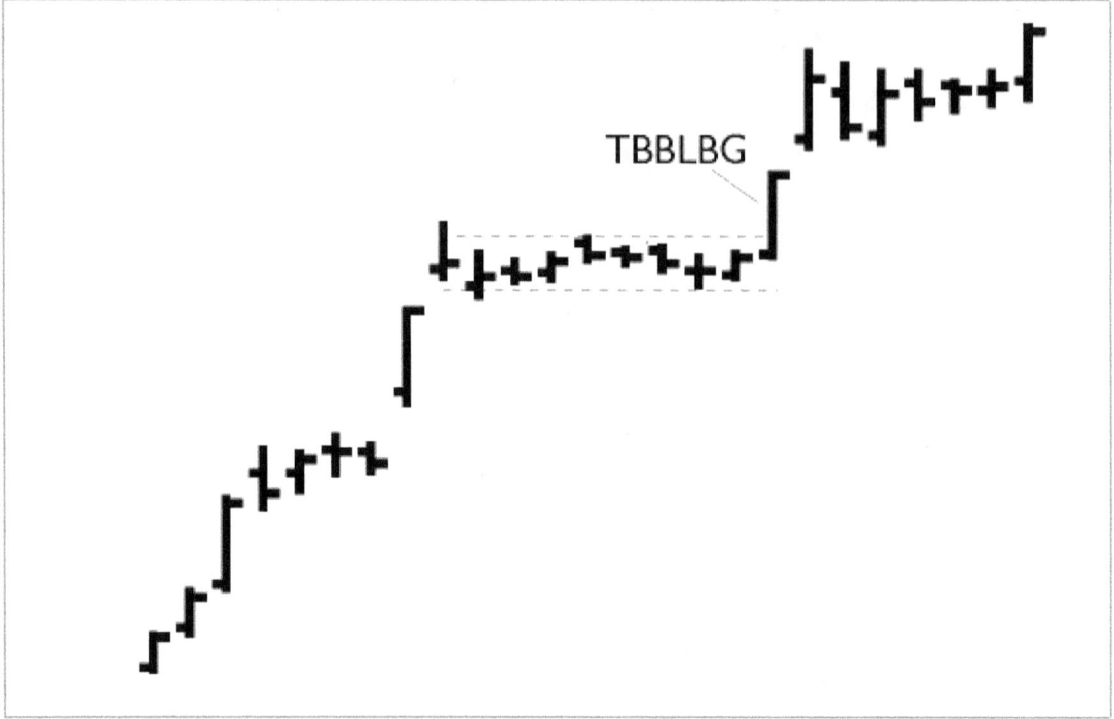

A breakout from a very tight trading range on a TBBLBG is not only very bullish, but it also has very low risk and high reward potential.

8. Swing Breakout on TBBLBG

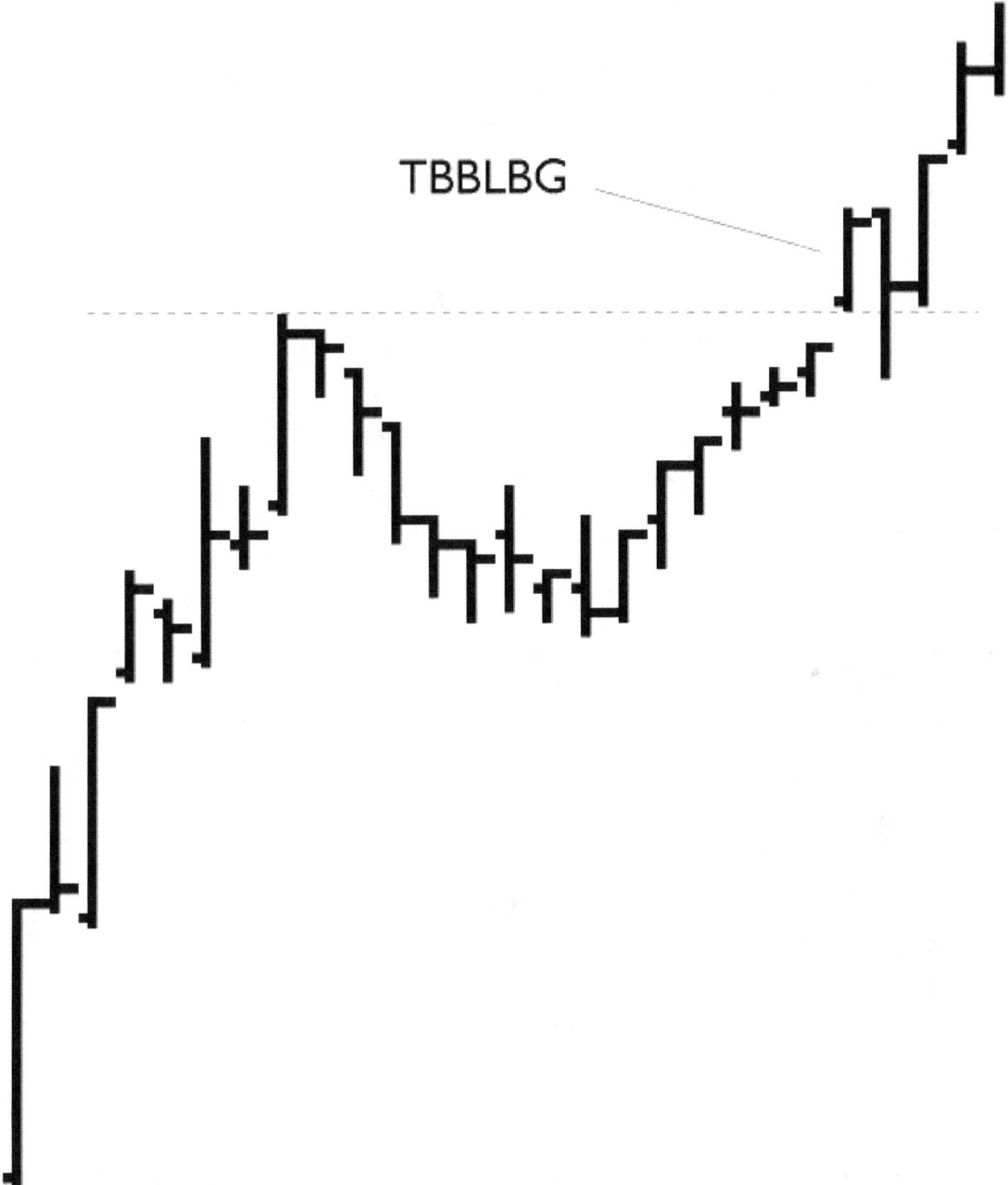

A "swing down" occurs when the low of the high day is broken. Following a swing down, prices reverse back up to break out to new highs on a TBBLBG.

9. 5-day runs

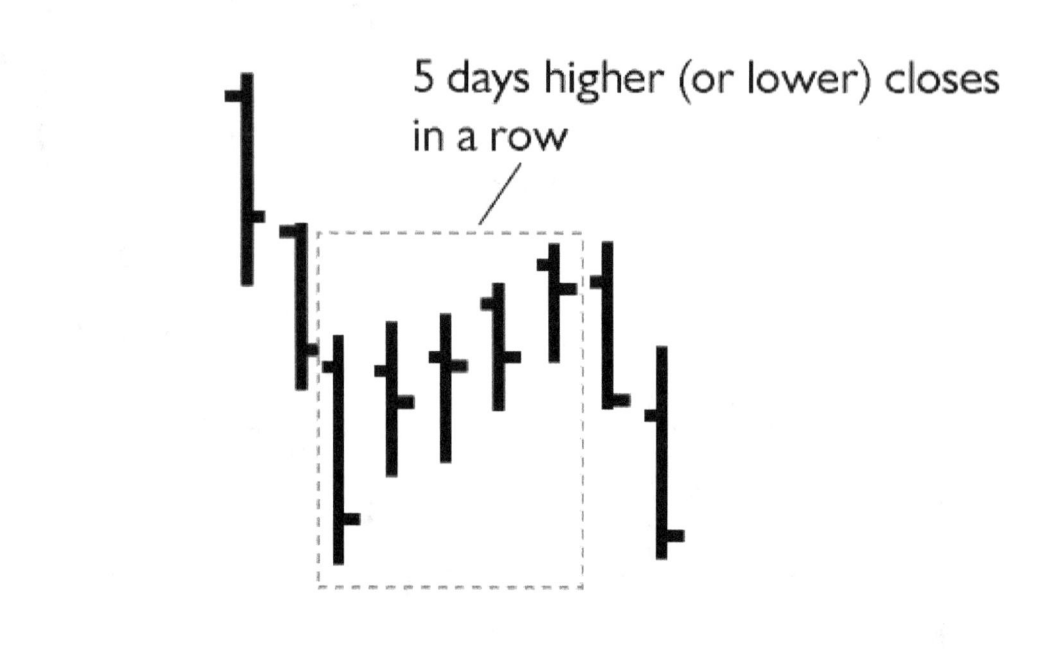

5 days higher (or lower) closes in a row

9. 5-Day Tails

5 days higher with higher highs, lows, and closes
or
5 days lower with lower highs, lows, and closes

11. Thrusts

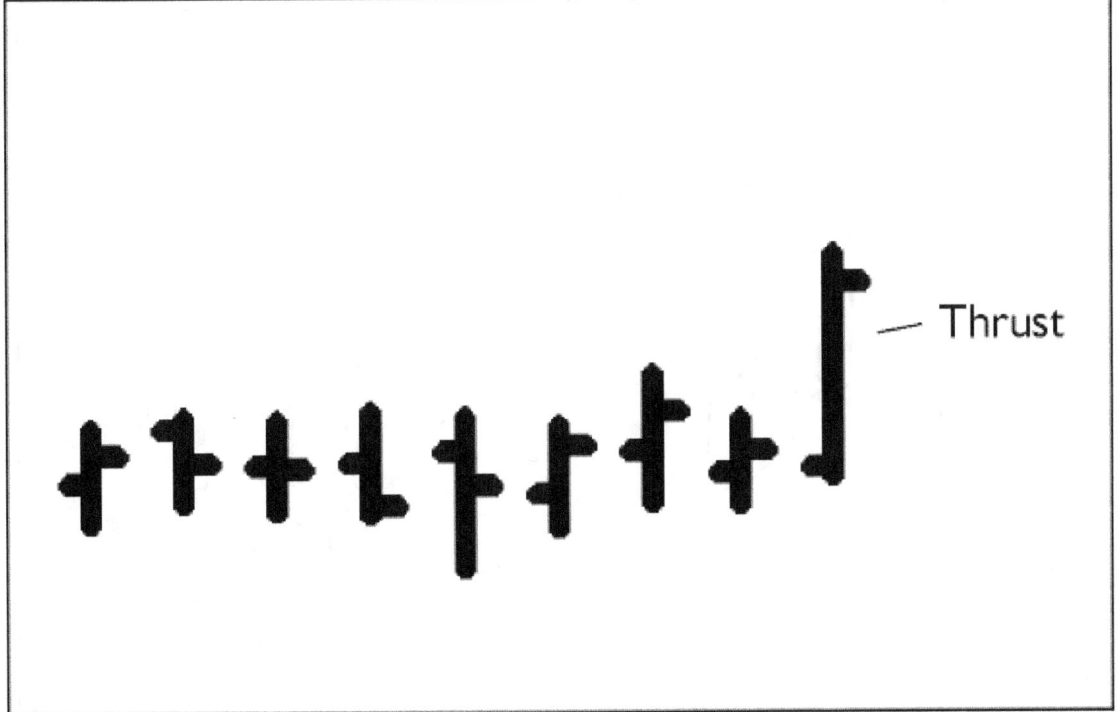

Remember that a thrust pattern is simply a day in which the range (high-low) is two or more times the average range of the preceding 20 bars; the volume is higher than the volume of the prior day; and the close is in the top 1/3 of the day's range

Finally, we have the **Corrective Patterns**

An "N" correction is another name of an ABC correction where C is lower than A.

1. "N" Corrections with TBBLBG

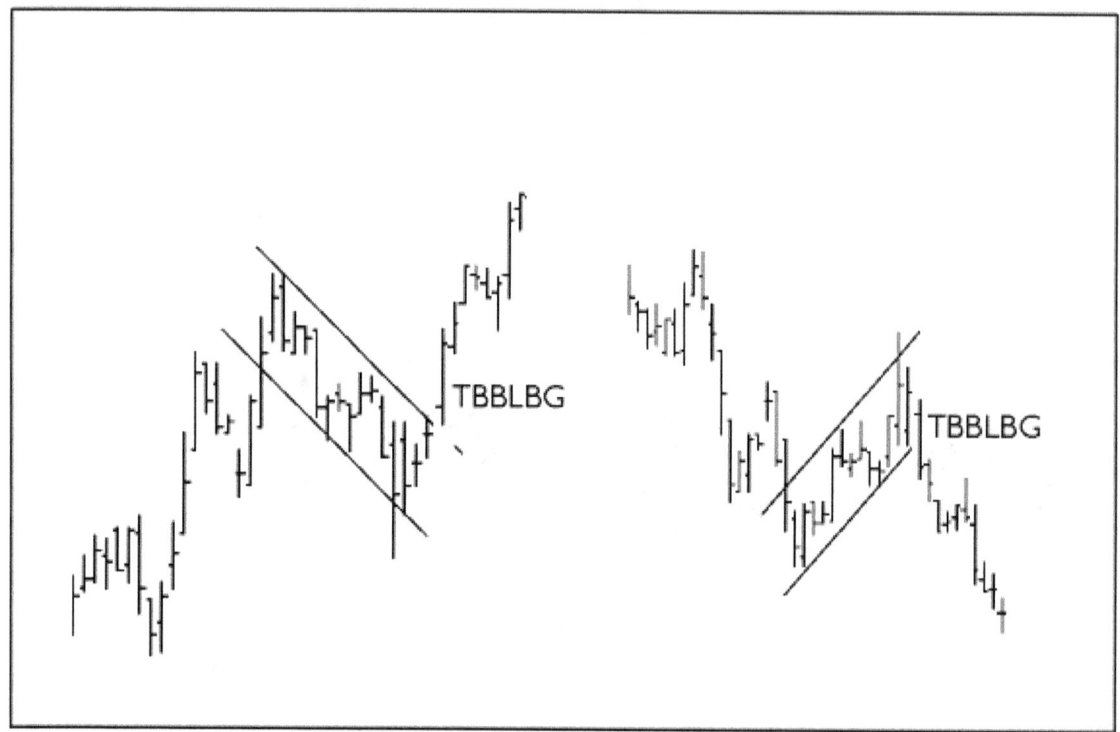

2. Staircases

Prices make a series of 2 or more consolidations with each consolidation climbing higher to levels not seen before.

3. Overlapping Staircases

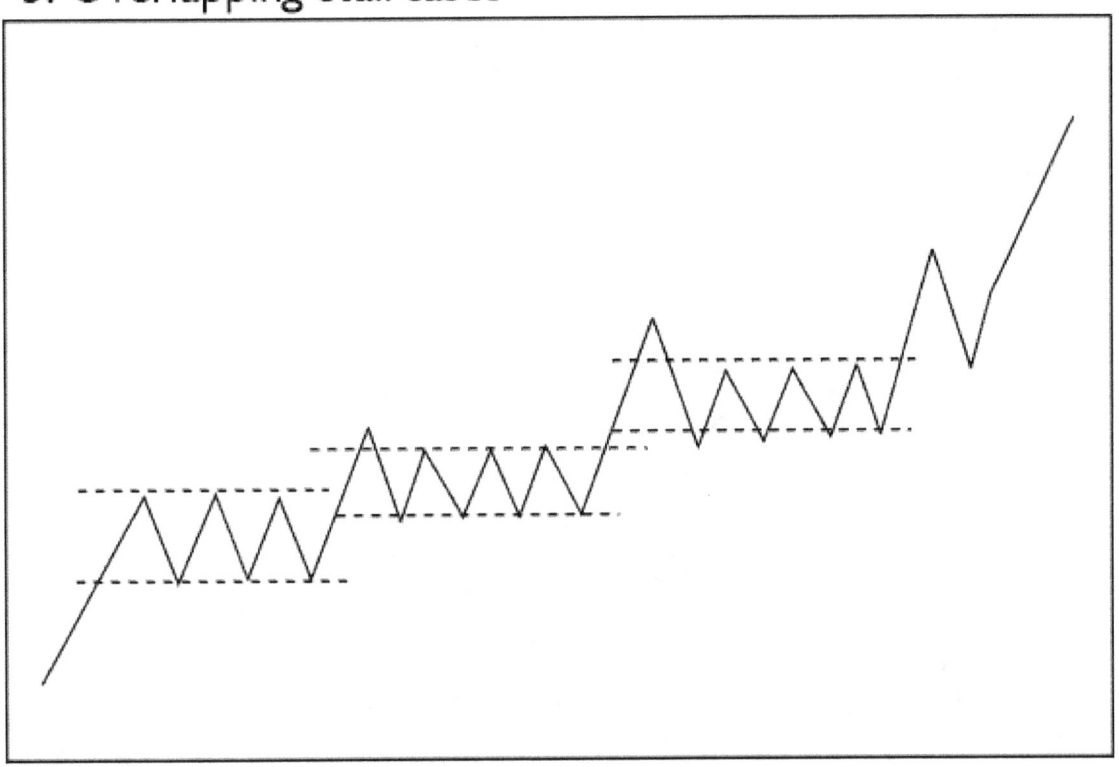

Prices consolidate, breakout, and then immediately consolidate again. In this case, the consolidation levels overlap.

Corrective Patterns

4. Normal Trading Range Correction

Now--perhaps you're wondering of what the **practical use** of all the preceding patterns are. In the following section I'll explain:

The 5/21 Method of Identifying Runaway Markets

Here is a simple way in which you can identify <u>Runaway Markets</u> in stocks and futures. Here's how it works:

Based on my research, **70 percent of all runaway moves have at least 5 days that exhibit Runaway characteristics out of a 21-day period** sometime in the initial third of their move. These include any combination of <u>laps, gaps, thrusts</u>, or any of the <u>Runaway Market Patterns</u> I showed you on the previous pages.

> **Therefore, when you see a market that has 5 or more Runaway Characteristics within any 21-bar period during the course of a move in a particular direction, you can count it as a runaway trend as long as that**

trend is still in force. The strength of the argument is especially strong if there are 10 or more Runaway Characteristics in a 21 bar period.

If the stock or futures market you're looking at has at least 5 Runaway Chracteristics also has fuel, then you have a viable vehicle in which to look for trading opportunities.

Let me now show you a few examples of how this works.

Examples of Markets with 5 or More Runaway Market Patterns
Example 1: FWRD

To get a feel for this, look at the Runaway Characteristics, 1, 2, and 3. On the chart it may seem to be one unified pattern, but I separated it into:

1. Breakout from consolidation.
2. Gap
3. Thrust (a large range day accompanied by volume that is greater than the previous day's volume)

Runaway Characteristics 6 and 7 are:

1. Breakout from consolidation
2. Lap

This may take some getting use to. I have looked at thousands of charts so it's second nature to me. You may need to spend several days to several weeks looking at many charts to get the hang of it.

Also, keep in mind that all the charts I'm showing have more Runaway Characteristics than just the one's I've pointed out. You may want to use them as an opportunity to get some practice.

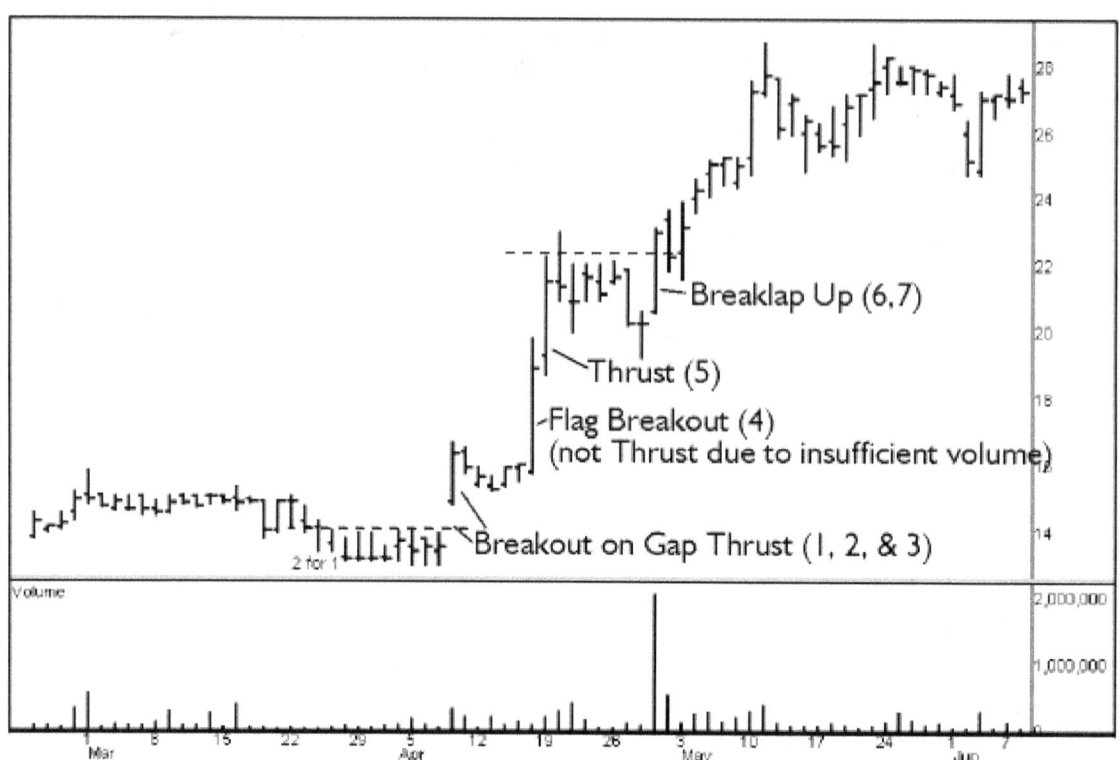

Examples of Markets with 5 or More Runaway Market Patterns
Example 2: MTW

Notice how Runaway Characteristics 5 and 7 are borderline Laps. That is, their lows are at about the same level as the highs of the previous bars. If they were slightly higher, they'd be Gaps

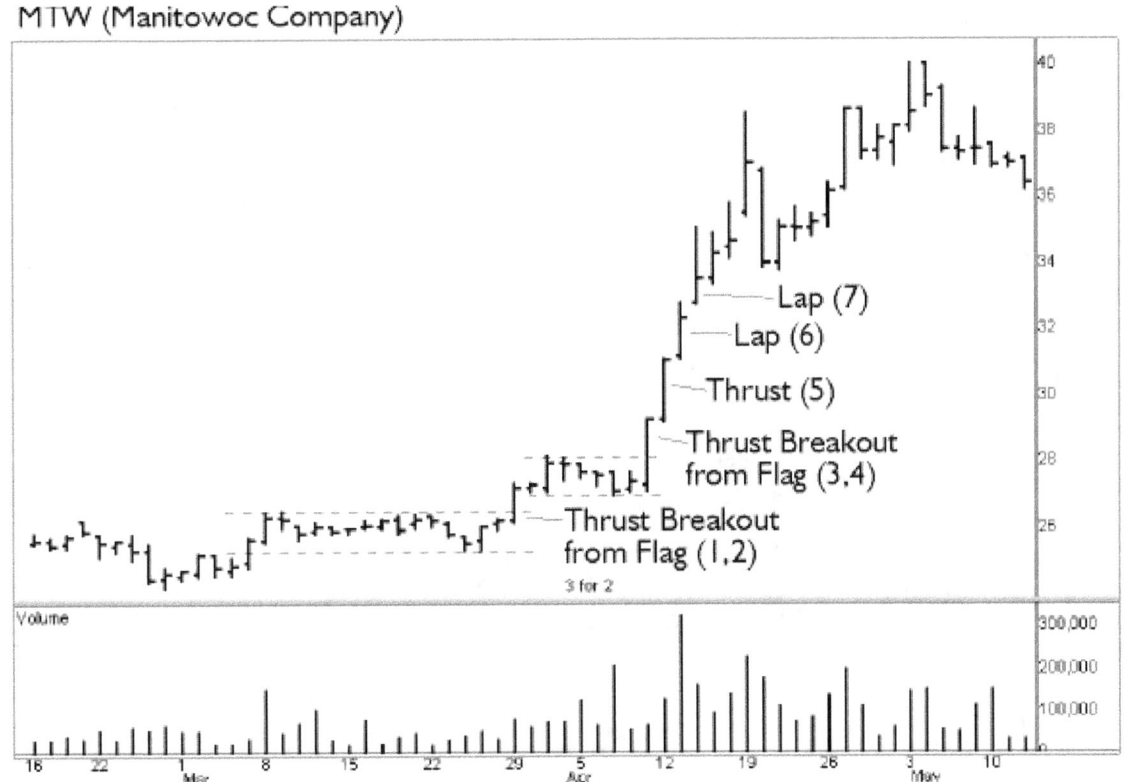

Examples of Markets with 5 or More Runaway Market Patterns
Example 3: FAE

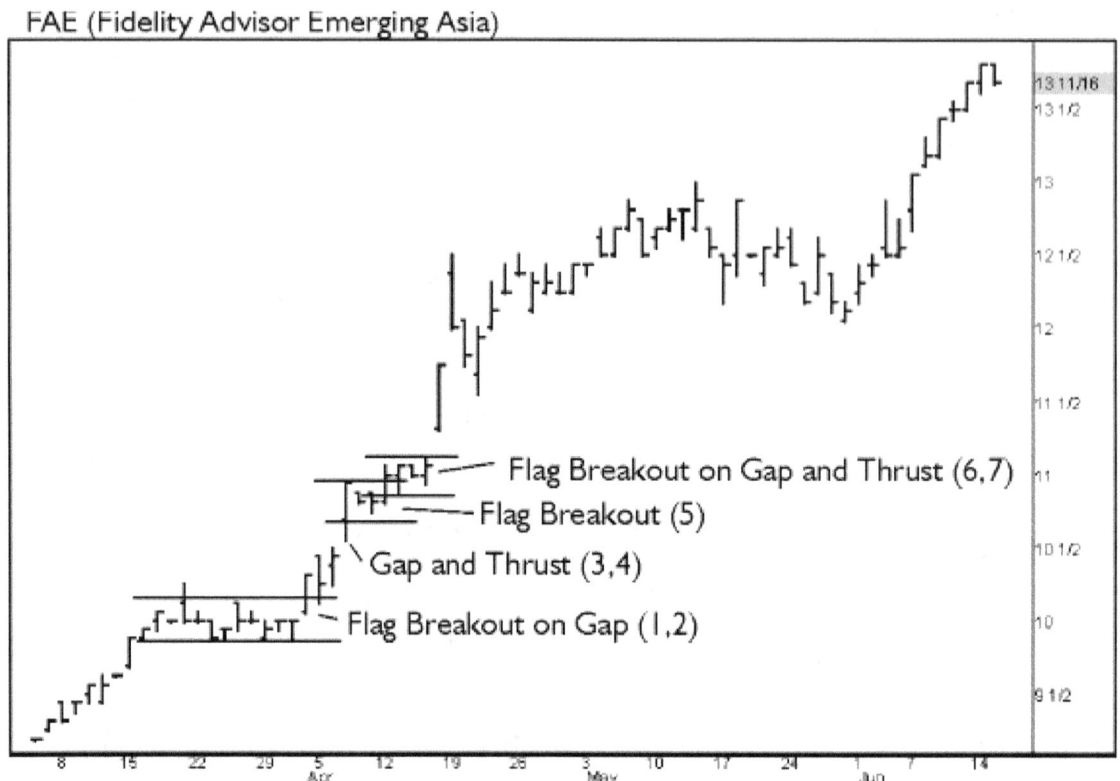

Examples of Markets with 5 or More Runaway Market Patterns
Example

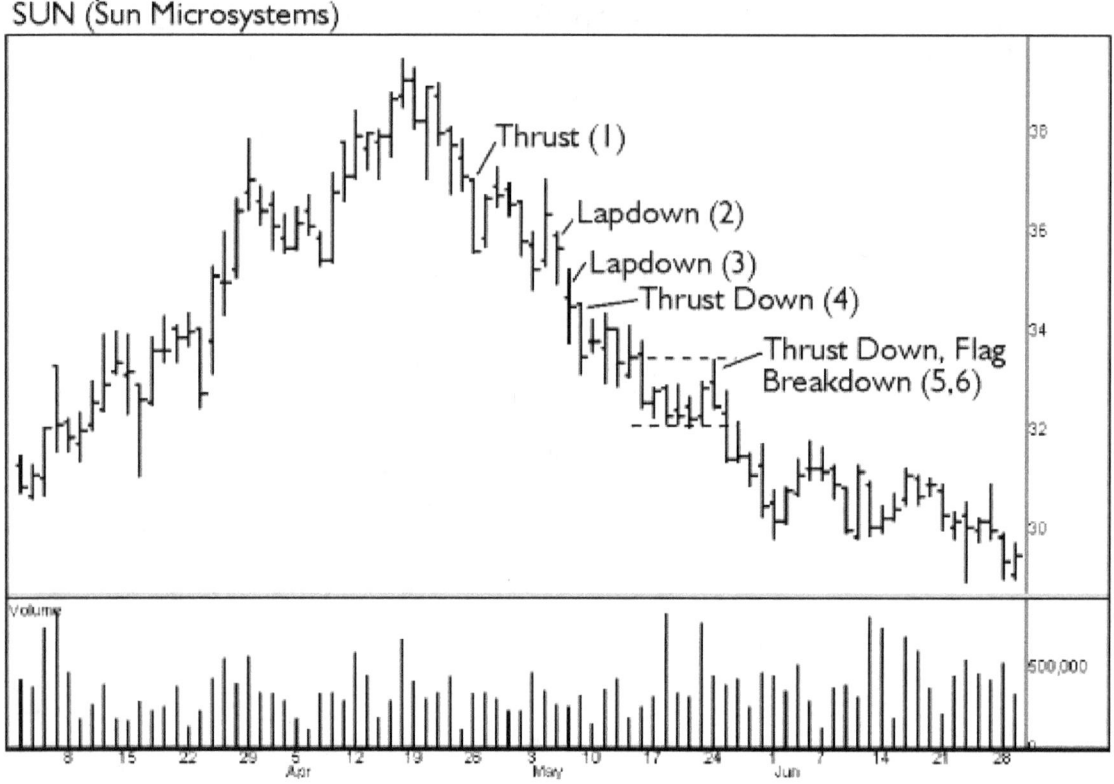

Examples of Markets with 5 or More Runaway Market Patterns
Example 5: TEN

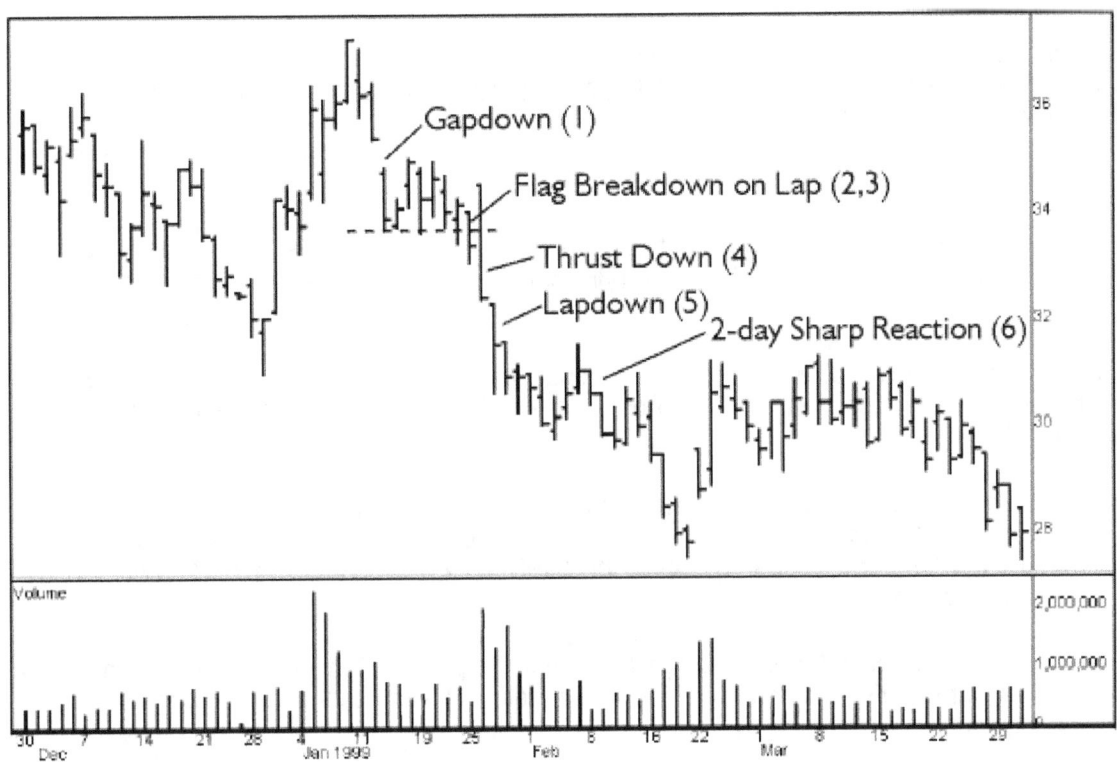

Now let's take a look at **one of the trading strategies that I most often use** in order to exploit Runaway Markets

Price Breakouts Preceded by Volume Accumulation Indicator Breakouts

Let's say I have visually scanned through thousands of stocks and found 50 with runaway market characteristics. Then I narrow the list down some more and find 25 of those that have the fuel with which to make a sustained move. With all these factors in their favor, you might think that statistically speaking, a viable strategy would be to just buy all 25 stocks and wait a few weeks to collect my windfall profits.

The truth, however, is that **I would never buy a stock unless I saw some sort of technical buy signal**. While I've done my homework to identify the right vehicle, I still want to optimize my entry into that vehicle by getting in when the risk is the least and the potential reward is the greatest. So, I will sit and wait patiently for the right technical patterns to develop.

Breakout Patterns: Pulling the Rug Out from Optimization

Breakout Patterns have gotten a bad rap of in recent years. During the early years of the personal computer, many off-the-shelf mechanical trading systems that were developed incorporated different variations on the breakout theme. Unfortunately, most of these systems were over optimized and not very robust over time. That is, they were designed to show good returns on the basis of segment of historical market data. But since the character of the market changes continually, the systems **simply disintegrated** after people bought them and so did trading accounts of the purchasers.

However, there's **a twist** that should not only make intuitive sense, but, in reality **makes Breakouts one of the most powerful techniques you can use.**

According to our research most stocks and futures spend more than **1/2 of the time in congestion patterns**. In other words, the lion's share of any move happens in a very short period of time, while most of the time a stock or future is in congestion, in a correction, or in a very slow moving situation. Most stocks and futures make this sharp, quick movement after a **breakout above or below congestion or resistance or support.**

However, while the attraction of breakout patterns is that they occur at periods of the greatest explosive movement in a stock or future, **applied globally, their reliability falls short of excellence.**

The twist I have in mind is not to apply breakout patterns globally across all market conditions, but rather to identify those market conditions under which breakout patterns are super-reliable. In other words:

> **Rather than optimizing a breakout system that tries in vain to work under all market conditions, we limit ourselves to applying breakout patterns to the market conditions that breakout patterns, by nature, tend to work most reliably under.**

We found in our research that Breakout patterns, when applied to Runaway Markets during a new phase of rapid movement up or down alone with certain indicator actions, really kicked some proverbial butt.

On the next few pages, I will show you an approach that I apply frequently to stocks and futures markets that pass the test for Runaway Market Patterns and Fuel.

The Method

Here are the conditions that must be in place for this to work:

1) **Has fuel; maximum fuel is better.** Fuel parameters can be found at the beginning of this week's topic.

2) **Has at least 5 runaway patterns within 21 days.**

3) **Has a flag pattern.** A flag pattern consists of a sharp run up (or down) followed by a tight consolidation. The consolidation should have at least four bars (time periods like days or weeks depending on the time frame you're watching). The flag cannot correct 37% or more of the previous move from a significant low or high.

The Trade:

4) The pattern is triggered when an accumulation indicator such as On-balance Volume (or other volume accumulation indicator such as WAD, SWAD, or VOLAC) **breaks out to new highs before price breaks out above (or below) the flag highs (or lows).**

5) **Enter a buy stop** a few ticks above the flag high with an OPS a few ticks below the flag low.

Examples

Example 1: FWRD

Notice how the breakout from the consolidation in OBV occurs **2 days prior** to the breakout in price

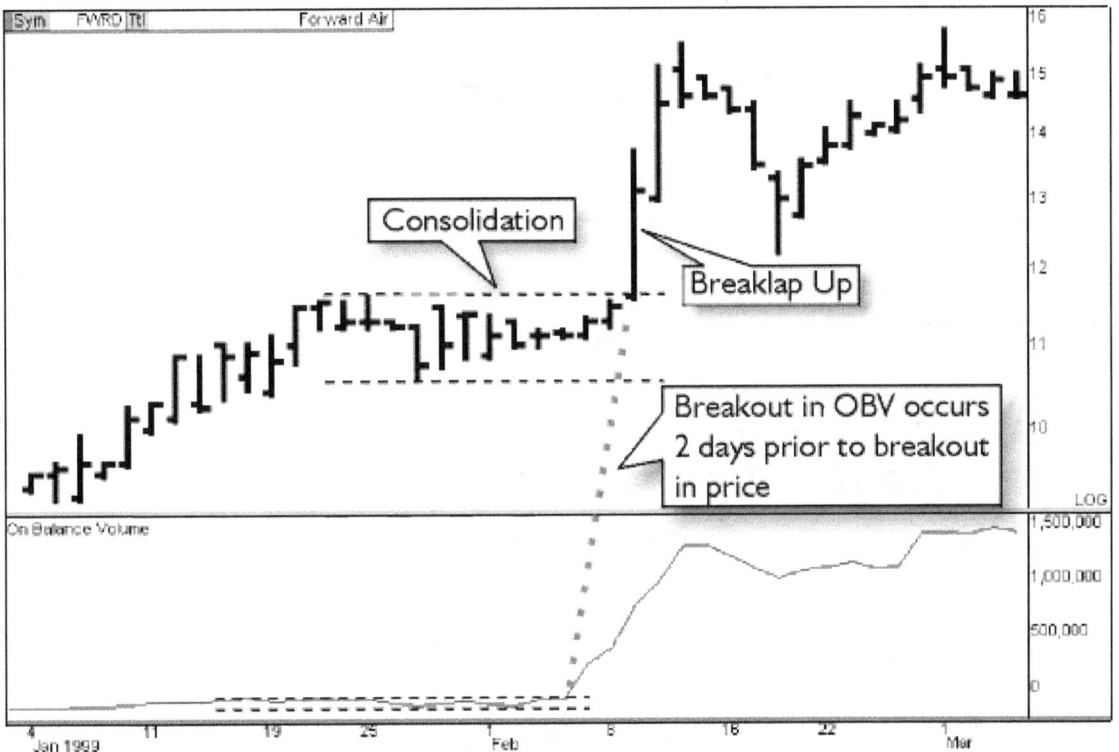

Example 2: JAKK

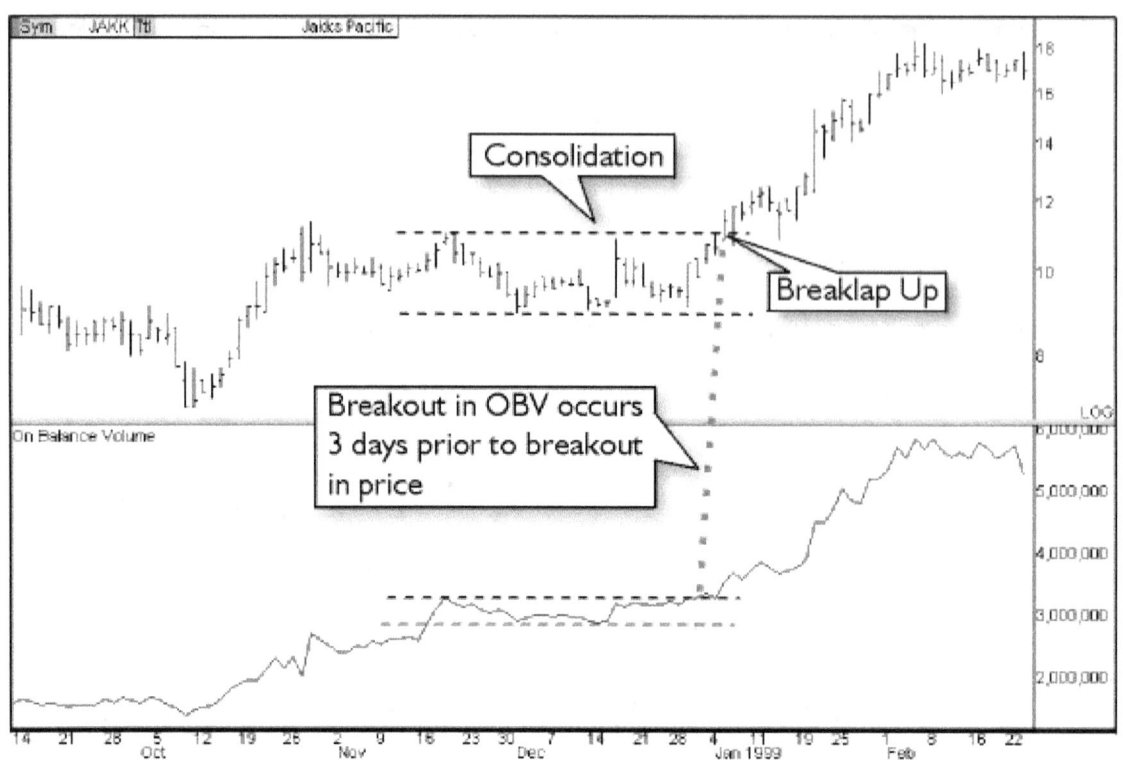

Example 3: RUSH

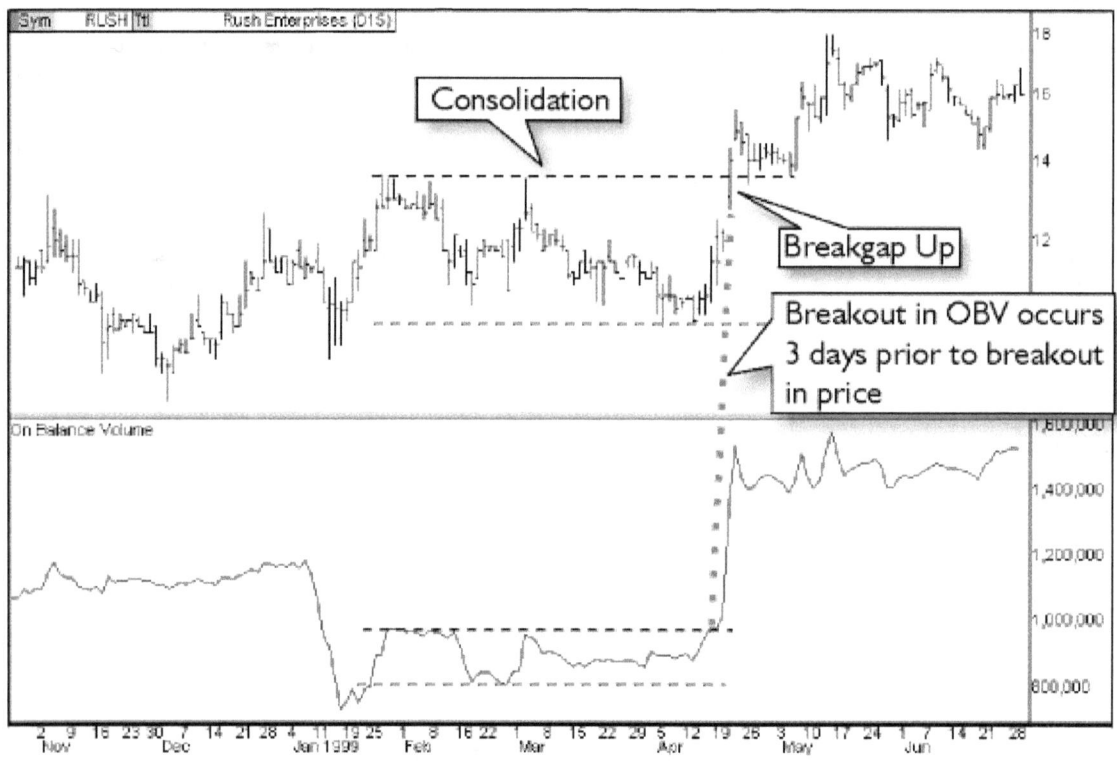

Example 4: VISX

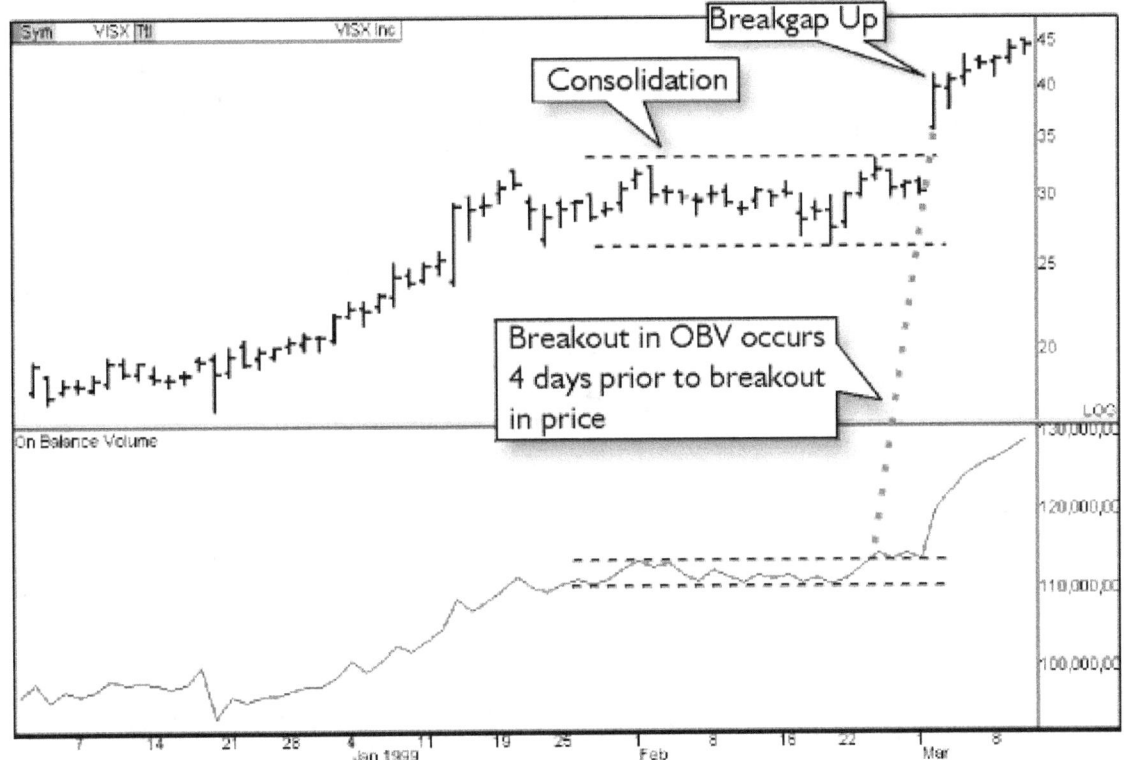

Example 5: ADSK

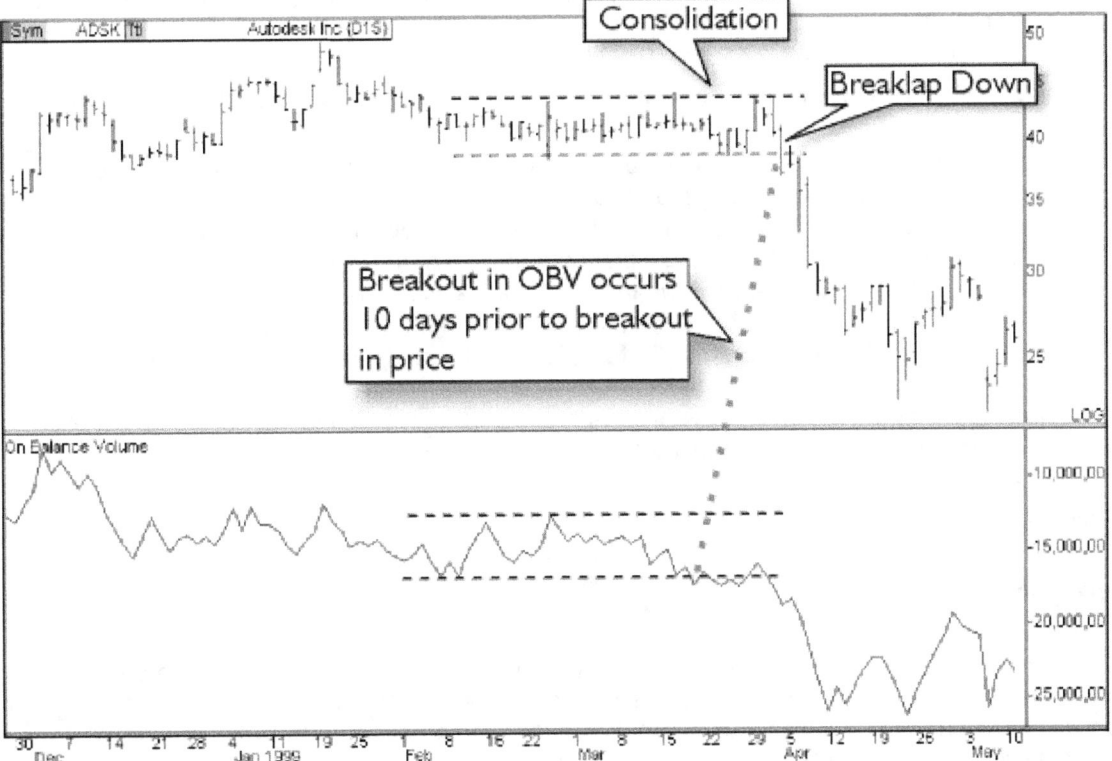

Example 6: G

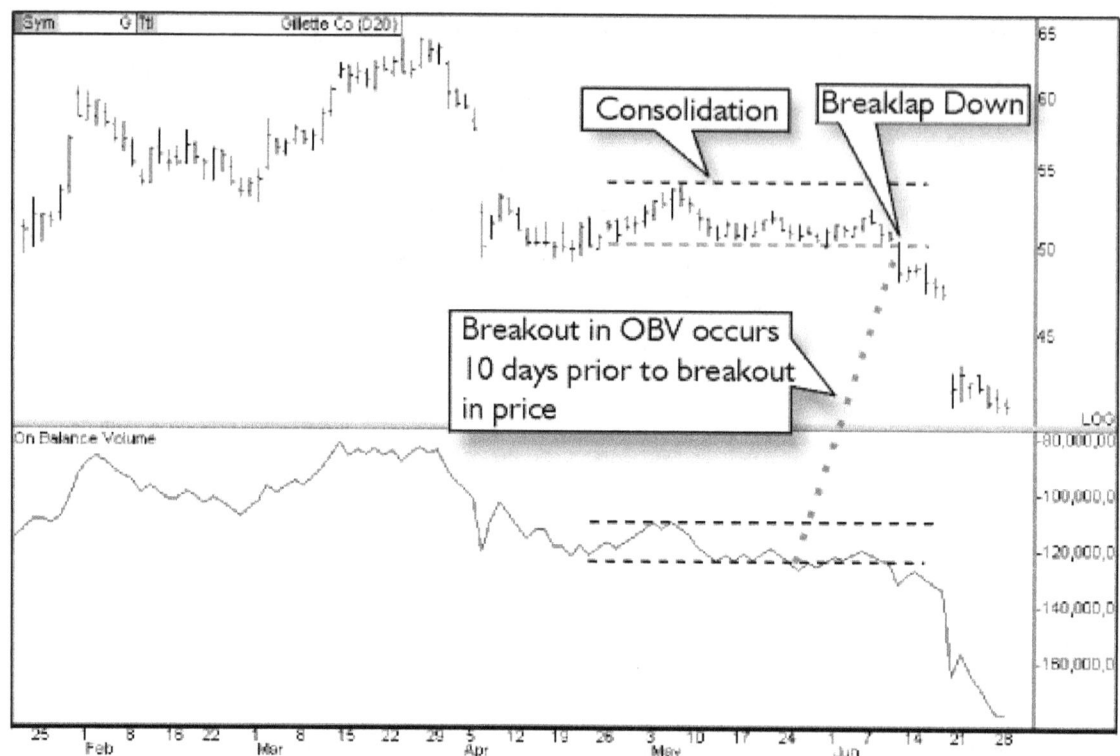

Closing Remarks

The biggest secret I've found toward achieving consistent, reliable, and substantial profits is this: **Go where the oil is.**

In trading, that means go where the strong trends are. How do we find the strongest trends?

- **Look at Relative Strength and Runaway Characteristics** and find stocks that are in the extreme ranges of strength or weakness.
- **Make sure the stock has fuel** (or lack thereof for a downtrend stock)—and then wait for a valid breakout from a consolidation in order to enter the trend with low risk.
- **Use the technical indicators** we talked about last week as long as you focus only use them on most powerful relative strength/runaway market vehicles in the market.
- **Apply all of the above on a solid foundation** of sound money management principles.

Don't try to predict the markets or catch tops or bottom—simply listen to the market **when it speaks very loudly and try to follow its lead with low risk.**

Simple—but not easy!

Next Week's Topic

To become a true market master, one must truly understand the markets. It seems pretty straightforward, but the problem arises when traders think they can achieve this mastery by using one system or method. That, in my opinion, is like learning only one strategy for playing competitive chess against Gary Kasparov.

Next week, I'm going to show you yet another one of the piece of the puzzle, Pattern Recognition. As you've seen, there are certain patterns that I consider to be my family jewels; these are the TBBLBG consolidation breakouts I've been discussing. But, you will greatly deepen your understanding of the markets by grasping pattern recognition in general. There are many patterns I see in the charts plastered all over my walls (and ceiling) which are crucial to my market analysis; but I don't necessarily use all of them to generate buy and sell signals. Rather, they are important for understanding the state of the markets and how fertile the soil may be for good trades.

Understanding pattern recognition will help you to "smell something fishy" even when a methodology you're using is screaming at you to "buy!" It will also help you to boldly ease into positions even when the news is bleak.

If you want to be a Gary Kasparov type trader, tune in next week for my discussion of Pattern Recognition.

Best regards,

Mark Boucher

TradingMarkets.com Members, Welcome Back to the Course:

We've all seen the old Western movies in which a sheriff and his Indian sidekick are hot on the trail of a gang of bank robbers. At first they can follow a trail of dust, then that disappears. But they can still rely on hoof prints. But then they disappear. Soon the trail itself ends and they are standing at the threshold of a vast prairie where all the obvious clues as to the direction of the armed bandits have blown into the wind.

The sheriff takes off his hat and wipes the sweat off his brow as he contemplates heading back into town empty handed. But the Indian gets off his horse and puts his ear to the ground. He paces back and forth looking at broken twigs and tossed dirt. He sniffs the wind. And then he points in a particular direction toward the horizon. A few days later, they capture the bandits.

What did the Indian have that the sheriff did not?

In my mind, the Indian had an understanding of all the **subtle patterns in the environment and was able to assimilate those details to draw a coherent conclusion: "They went that-a-way."** While every cowboy or mere farmhand could follow obvious footprints, it took an individual with a masterful understanding of patterns to determine the right course of action.

As with chasing bank robbers across the prairie, so too do we need a higher level of understanding in the financial markets to be successful traders. This is not just my opinion; this is reality. I have had the opportunity to meet many traders of varying skill levels and backgrounds and I always found that those who actually made money over the long haul had a level of understanding that rendered them independent of any single methodology, technique or software program. I do not want to downplay the importance of having the right tools. Believe me, I do use many of these high-tech tools. But I believe there are a lot of vendors who are selling you a dream when they tell you that a methodology alone can make you rich. The reality is that you **have to work hard to become an expert in the markets and gain as deep a level of understanding as you'd have if you were to become proficient in any profession.**

At the tail end of last week's session, I mentioned to you I wouldn't have much of a chance of beating Gary Kasparov at chess, if I just learned one strategy from a book. I know I couldn't. That's because Gary has a true understanding of chess whereas I don't.

One of the many pieces of the puzzle that will help you increase understanding is Pattern Recognition. Let me explain this now.

Enter Week 7: Pattern Recognition

Introduction to Pattern Recognition

Trading successfully is not a matter of merely finding buy and sell signals. That's because whatever system or methodology you employ, it will tend to work well under certain circumstances and very poorly under others. If you do not have a handle on this, your trading account will surely self-destruct. As I told you in our session on Money Management, people somehow forget that when your trading account sustains a lot of damage, it takes much longer to rebuild the account (if that's possible) than it took to wreak the damage in the first place, because you have far less trading capital to work with.

You may be the proud owner of a shiny new trading system, but it is of paramount importance to understand the circumstances that you are presented with each and every trading day so that you know the context in which your buy and sell signals occur.

Understanding the patterns that unfold in a standard bar chart is one of the keys to knowing this context. When you understand patterns, you will be able to intelligently second guess your trading system and survive and thrive in any kind of market environment. In my case, however, I don't think those times at which I ignore a textbook TBBLBG breakout from a consolidation as second guessing--it's just that my strategy is bigger and more all-encompassing that just that one little setup.

The Dirtiest Word in Technical Analysis

There is probably no other form of technical analysis that is more criticized for being "hocus pocus" than pattern recognition. **The operative dirty word is "subjectivity."** Many technical analysis books and courses expose beginning traders to classical chart analysis and then move on to approaches that are more mechanical and objective with the implication being that chart patterns are from the old school of thinking. Having subjected many systems and techniques to computerized analysis and seen how my results are improved through knowledge of chart patterns, my conclusion is that pattern recognition is quite relevant to today's high-tech trader.

The challenge for us this week will be to reconcile the usefulness of pattern recognition with the apparent discomfort that many traders have with using their 'ol noggin to interpret something that seems, on the face of it, to be random noise.

To do this **I will show you a way of viewing a bar chart that objectifies the pivot and swing relationships** that are the building blocks of patterns. Once you can see pivots and swings and the relationships between them, recognizing complex patterns becomes more of an **objective process.**

With practice, you'll be able to look at any chart and see important patterns that have direct bearing on any trading opportunity you may be contemplating. You'll be able to sniff out reasons to be cautious as well as those times when you can trade more confidently.

I want you to become like that Indian who can look at a few broken twigs and figure out where the bank robbers have gone.

How to Make Sense Out of the Nonsense

When you look at an ordinary bar chart, it's easy to see patterns of different sorts just a child might see elephants and giraffes looking at clouds. What is difficult is to define parameters that separate patterns that are useful and those that are not.

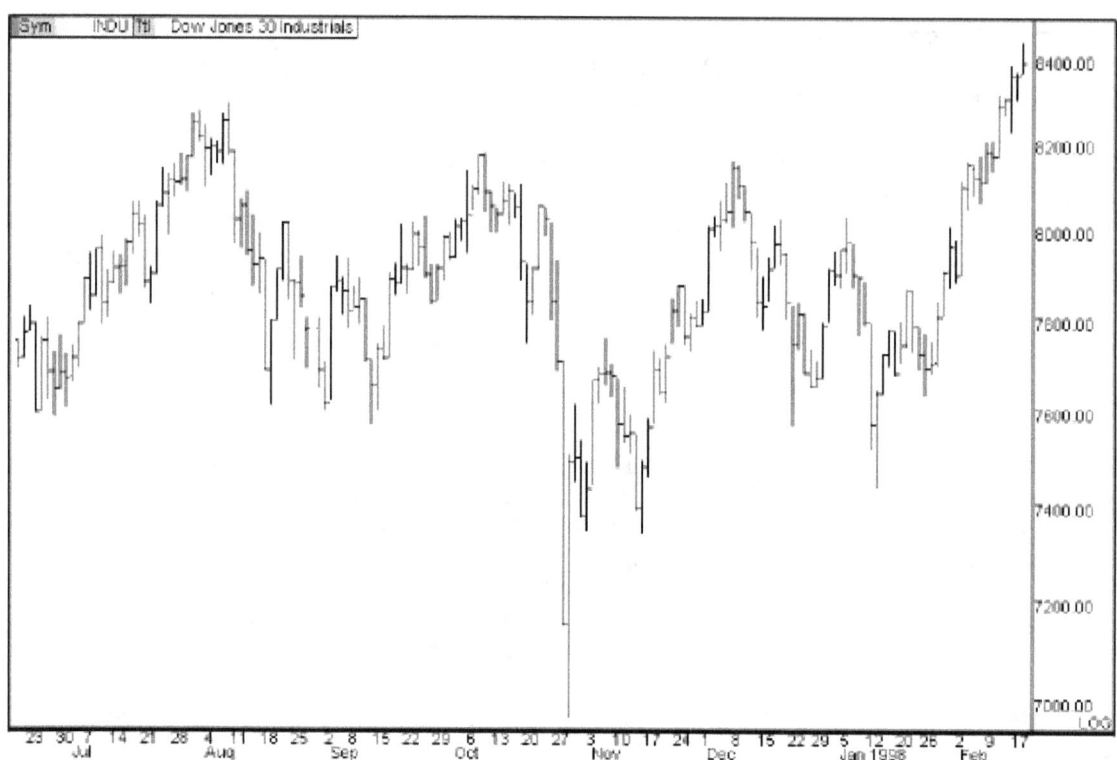

To find patterns objectively, we need a system that removes enough subjectivity to allow different people to arrive at the same interpretation independently of each one another. Doing this, we will steer clear of one the pitfalls that frequently causes people to poke fun at Elliott Wave analysis, i.e., that no two Elliotticians ever come up with same wave interpretation.

The solution is to draw what's called a Swing Chart according to objective rules. By applying consistent rules, everyone who looks at a given bar chart should be able to draw the same swing chart.

How to Draw a Swing Chart

A swing chart is comprised of two components, pivots and swings.

The pivots are the points at which price changes direction. When price goes up and then changes direction to the downside, a high is made. When price goes down and changes direction back to the upside, a low is made. The definition of pivot highs and pivot lows in the creation of a proper swing chart is as follows:

- A **pivot high** occurs when prices are advancing and the low of the highest bar is penetrated on downside. At that point in time the high of the highest day of the advance becomes the pivot high and you begin looking for the next pivot low.
- A **pivot low** occurs when prices are declining and the high of the lowest bar is penetrated on the upside. At that point, the low of the lowest bar of the decline becomes the pivot low and one begins you begin looking for the next pivot high
- Once you have figured out where each pivot is, **you draw the swings, which connect the pivots.**

A swing chart simply connects each pivot high to the next pivot low and each pivot low to the next pivot high.

Below you'll see a swing chart of the chart shown at the beginning of this page.

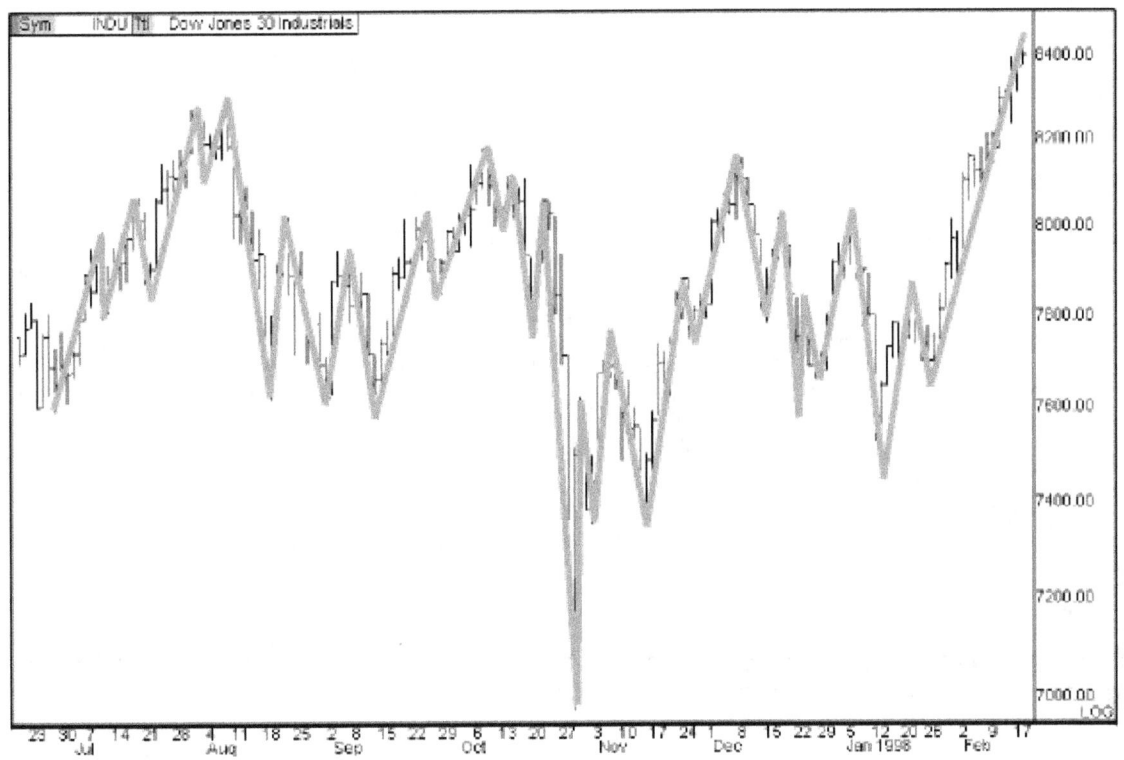

Swing Chart Practice, Example 1

Here is a chart of DELL. Print out the chart and try draw the pivots and swings according to the rules we've discussed.

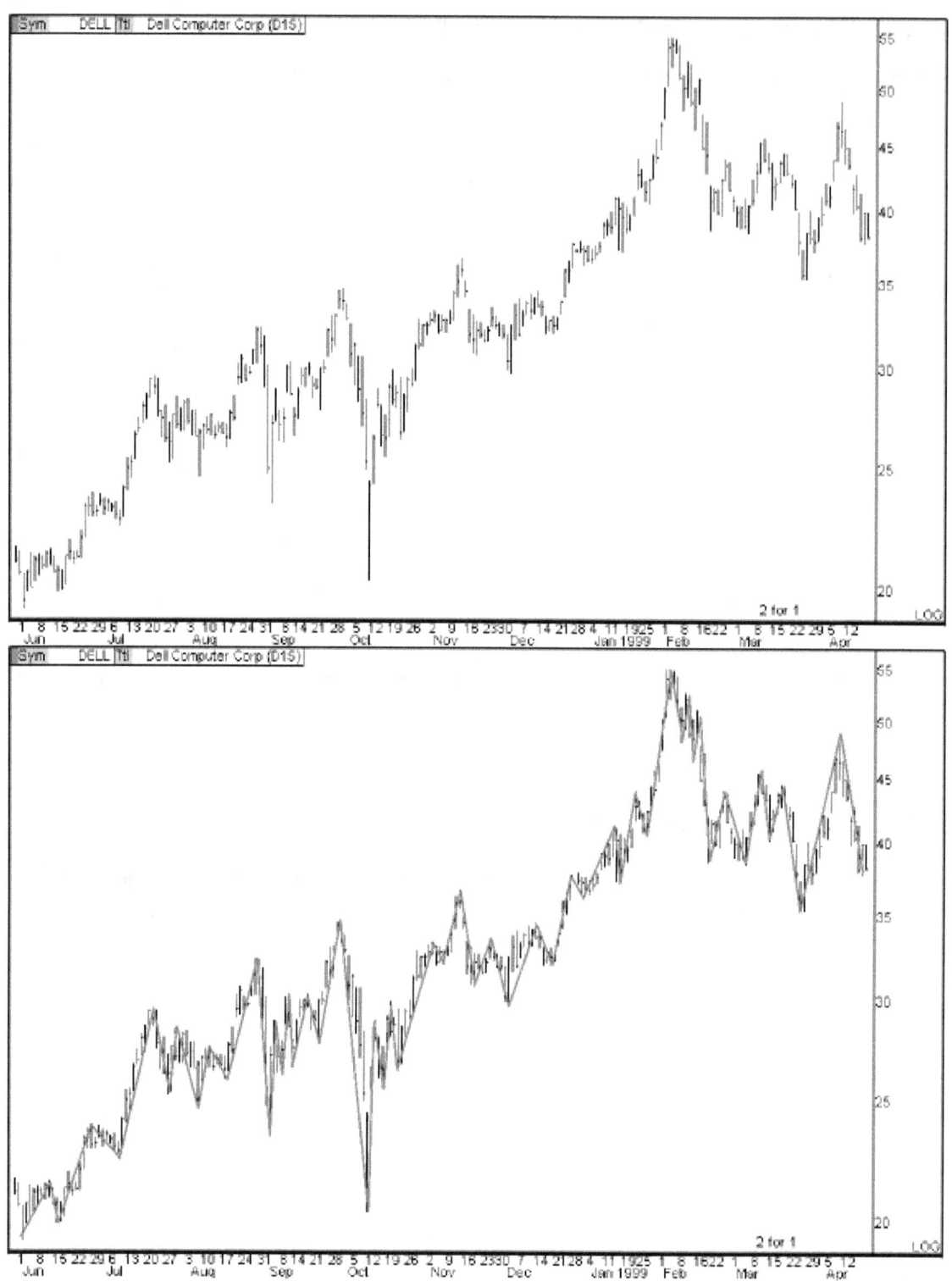

Major Pivots and Major Swings

Now let's switch gears and work on longer-term pivots and swings.

- A major pivot high is a pivot high that has a lower pivot high before it and a lower pivot high after it.
- A major pivot low is a pivot low that has a higher pivot low before it and a higher pivot low after it.

A major swing chart connects each major pivot low to the next corresponding major pivot high and each major pivot high to the next corresponding major pivot low.

Major Swing Chart Practice, Example 1

Here is a chart of the Dow Jones Industrial Averages. Print it out and draw the major swings.

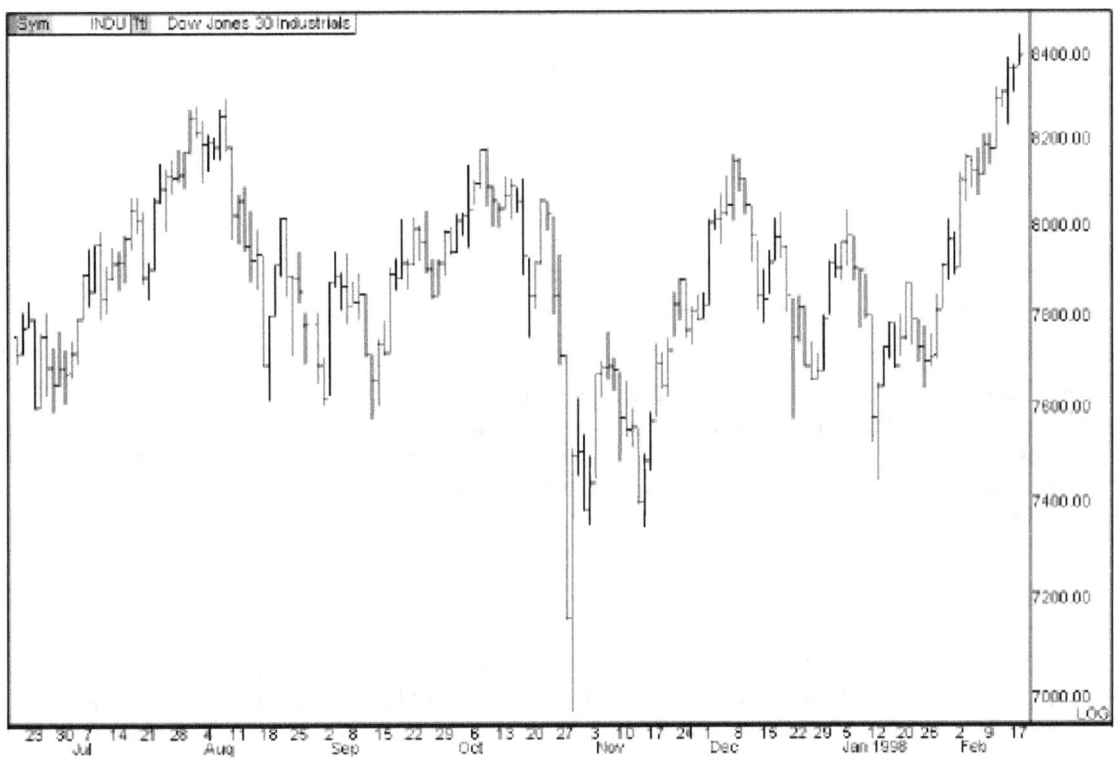

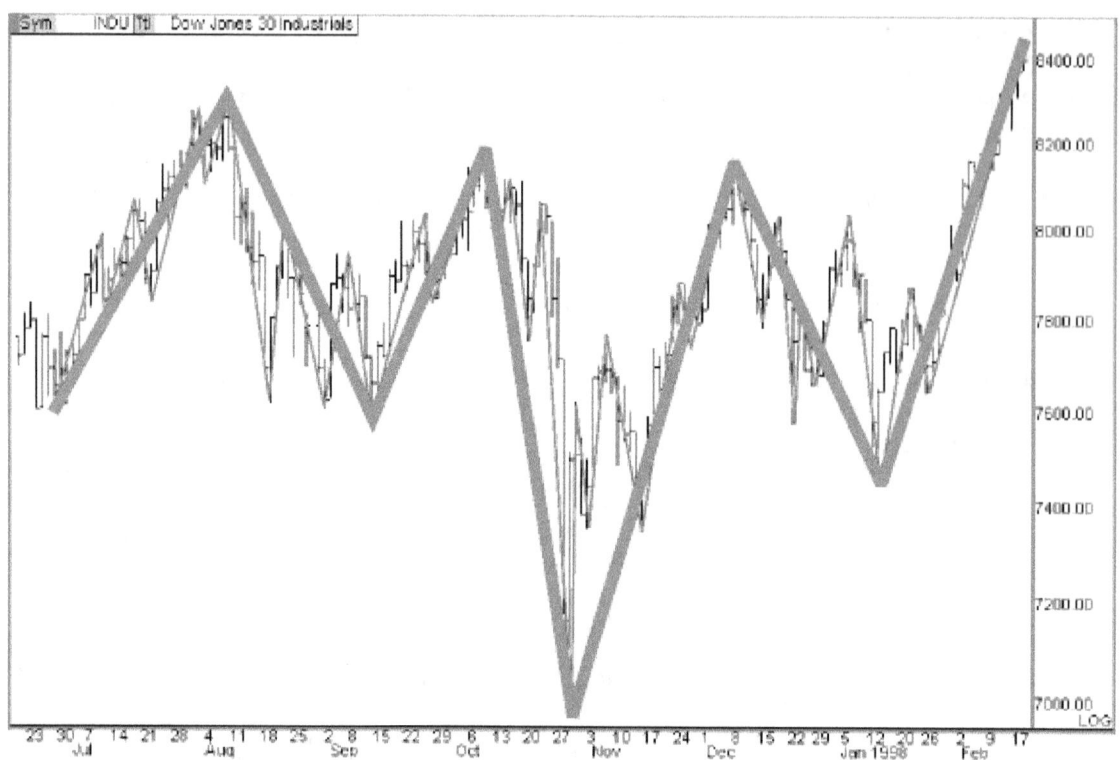

I realize I've breezed through this topic of Swing Charts pretty rapidly. But I think you'll find this technique pretty easy and intuitive when you look at different charts on your own. Plus, once their usefulness becomes more apparent in the following pages, they'll probably be even easier for you to draw. In fact, I'm not really advocating that you draw them in actual practice. It's enough to be aware of swings and to be able to visualize them when you see a chart.

Classical Chart Patterns

For the past several weeks I've been talking about how important certain chart patterns are in helping me select the right market in which to search for low-risk, high-reward trading opportunities. Using these patterns, I'm able to:

1. identify runaway markets
2. identify good trading opportunities in runaway markets

If you review our discussions on Liquidity Cycles, Relative Strength, Runaway Markets and Market Selection, you'll see that once I've drilled down from the Macro to the Micro perspective, patterns take on critical importance. They are the key to getting into the right markets at the right times and getting out at the right times.

Now, unless you've had previous exposure to pattern recognition, the use of chart patterns to help you trade profitably may be foreign to you. For this reason, as well as the way in which patterns allow me to see the big picture context in which actual trading signals may occur, my discussion this week starts with **classical chart patterns.**

Back in the 1930s and 40s, descriptions of chart patterns were first trickled out to the public by Richard W. Schabacker in his widely sought after, but hard-to-get limited publication books. Later, **Edwards and Magee**, brought classical chart analysis into the mainstream with their book Technical Analysis of Stock Trends. The pioneering works by these market masters remain extremely important today, despite their popularity having been circumvented by computerized approaches.

The Importance of Swing Charts

When you look at the charts on the following pages, you'll recognize the **importance of the swing charts** I taught you to draw in the preceding section. By extracting the pivots and swings from standard bar charts, you remove the noise. By removing the noise, you are left with a bare structure which, after a little practice, will help you to see chart patterns sticking out like sore thumbs.

On the following pages, I'm going to show you some of the common key classical patterns I see when I look at my charts. I don't ordinarily take trades on these patterns, but they serve as critical added confirmation that my trades are going with the dominant trend. If you would like to learn more about classical chart patterns, a good introduction is Technical Analysis of Stock Trends by Robert Edwards and John Magee. Advanced students of charting may want to check out a new re-release of Richard W. Schabacker's classic Technical Analysis and Stock Market Profits: The Real Bible of Technical Analysis.

Classical Chart Patterns
Double Bottoms

A Double Bottom or "W" bottom as it's often called, looks like the following diagram on a major swing chart:

Double Bottom

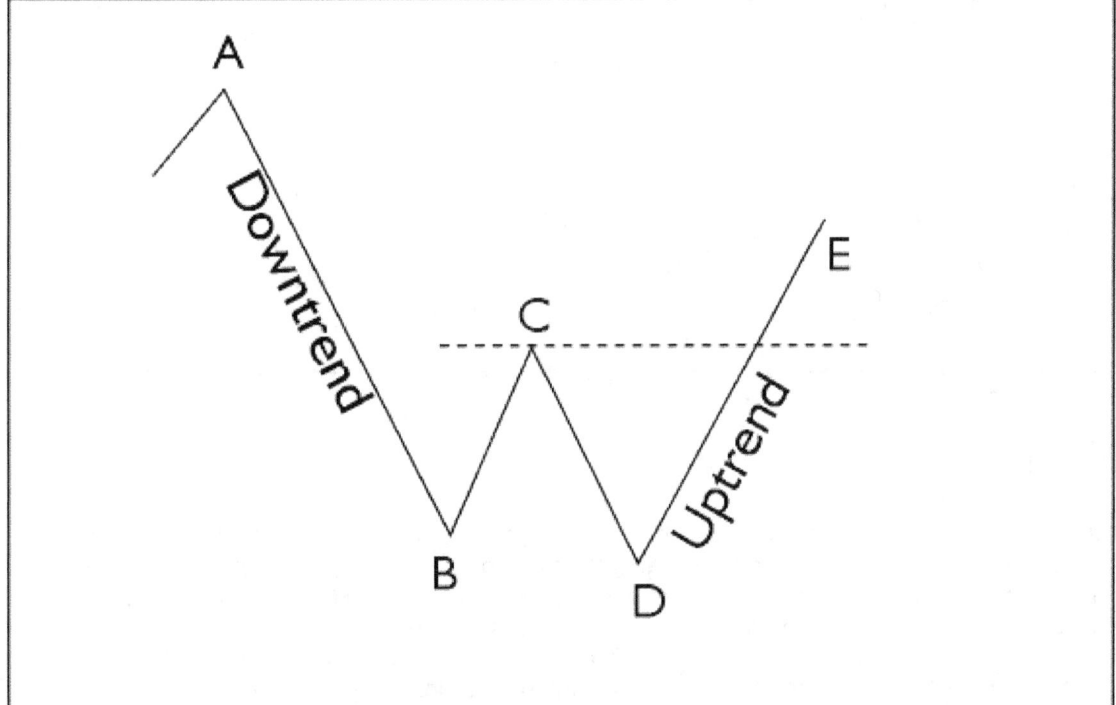

- where A > C

- there is not a greater than 20% difference between the distance from B to C and from C to D.
- the upswing E goes above C

The thing that makes some chart patterns such as Double Bottoms important is that they're frequently **telling you something important if they occur in conjunction with Runaway Markets** where my TBBLBG Breakouts occur. When I see a stock that has 5--or even, better 10--Runaway Characteristics together with extremely favorable Relative Strength and Fuel, you can bet that I'm even more delighted to see a Double Bottom pattern preceding it.

In fact, many powerful Runaway Markets I see are initiated by Double Bottom Patterns. You can see that in MTW shown below. This is one of the hot Runaway Markets I've been following recently. If you recall the Runaway Patterns I taught you in Week 6, you'll see several of them in this chart in addition to the Double Bottom pattern shown (you'll probably need to pull MTW up on your own charting software to see them, however). What we have, in essence, is a Runaway Market that kicked-off with a Double Pattern.

Watch for Synchronicity

Want to know one the of the best tricks for identifying high-probability turns in the stock market as well as individual sectors and groups? Watch for many of the same classical patterns to show up simultaneously in large numbers of stocks at crucial junctures. If you had scanned through many stocks in late 1994, you would have noticed many classical chart patterns forming bottoms at that time. Similarly, there were many Double Bottoms in individual stocks in late 1998 that alerted me to a strong possibility of a move that would take the broad market up much higher. When you scroll ahead a few pages, you'll see the Double Bottom formation in the S & P 500 index itself

Classical Chart Patterns
Double Tops

A Double Top or "M" top as it's often called, looks like the following diagram on a major swing chart

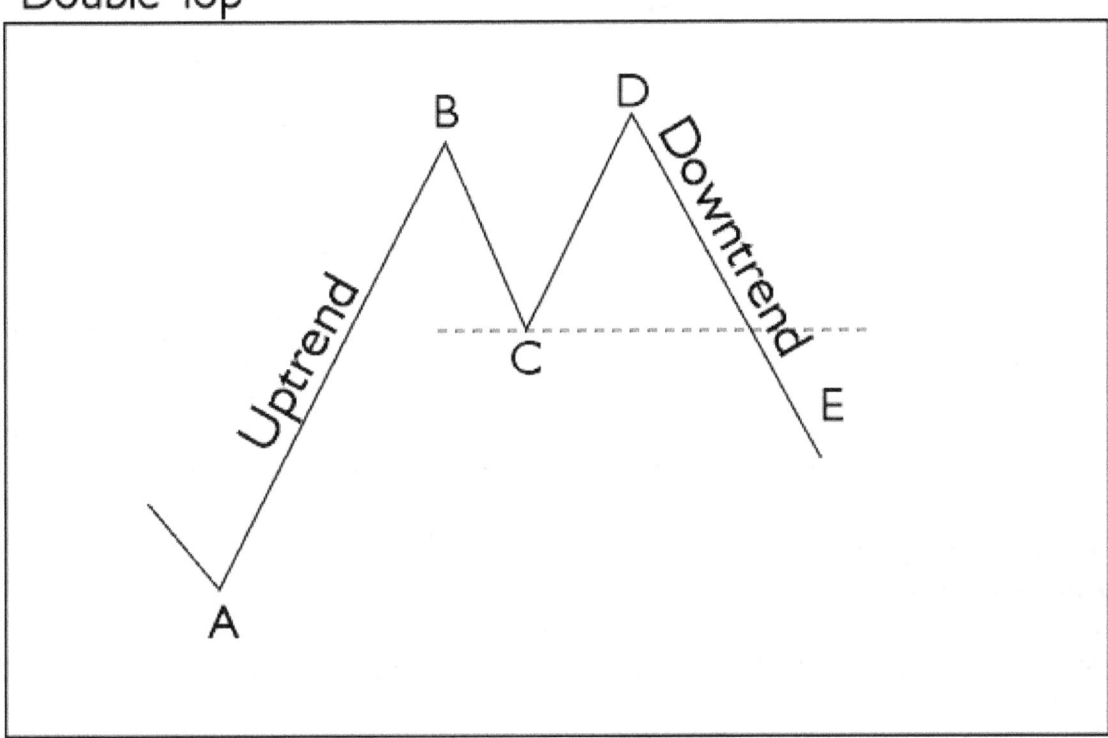

- where A < C
- there is not more than 20% difference in the distance between B to C and D to E.
- downtrend E goes below C

Here is an example in Pfizer, Inc.

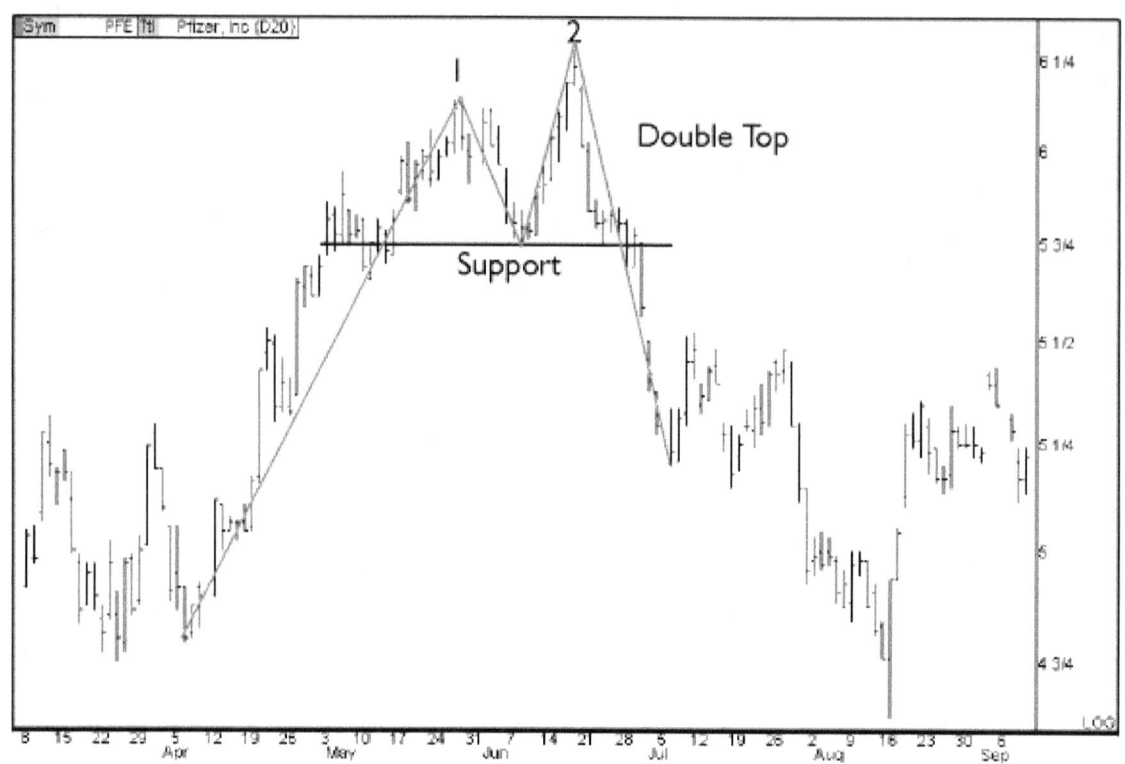

Classical Chart Patterns
Head and Shoulders Tops

A Head and Shoulders Top looks like the following diagram on a major swing chart

Head and Shoulders Top

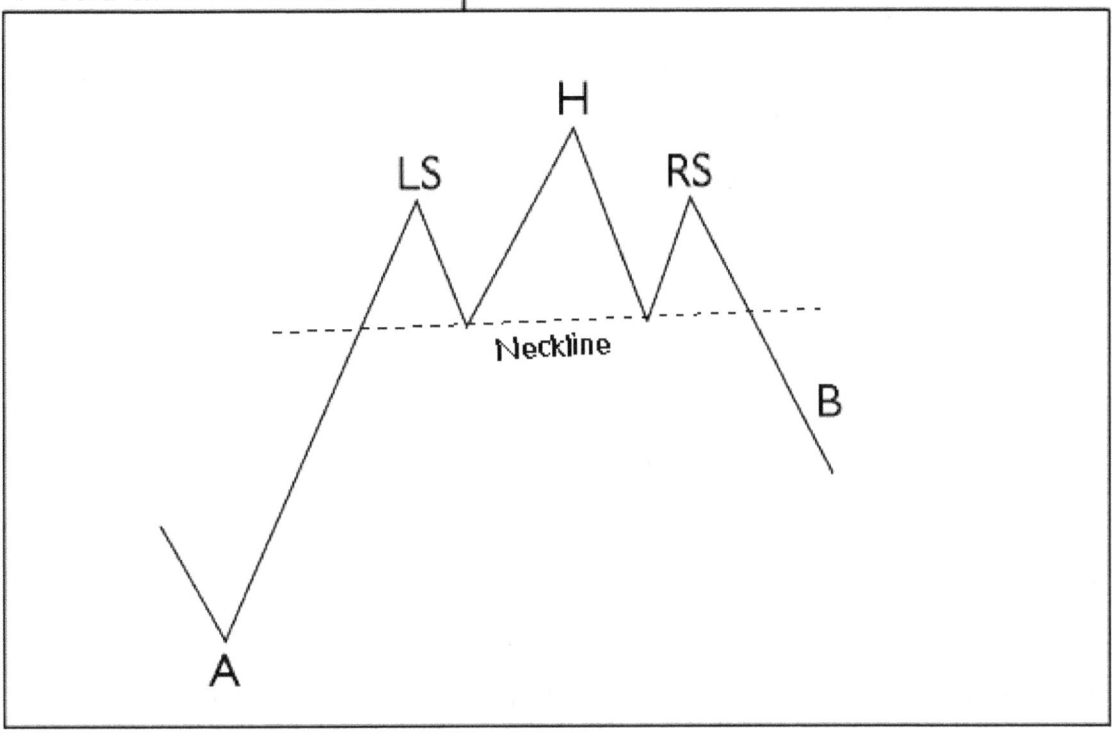

- where A < the Left Shoulder, Head, and Right Shoulder
- both the Left shoulder and Right Shoulder are < the Head
- the price at the Left Shoulder and price at the Right Shoulder are within 20% of each other. In other words, they should be in rough balance with each other.
- the downswing B goes below the Neckline

Here is a Head and Shoulders Top in IBM.

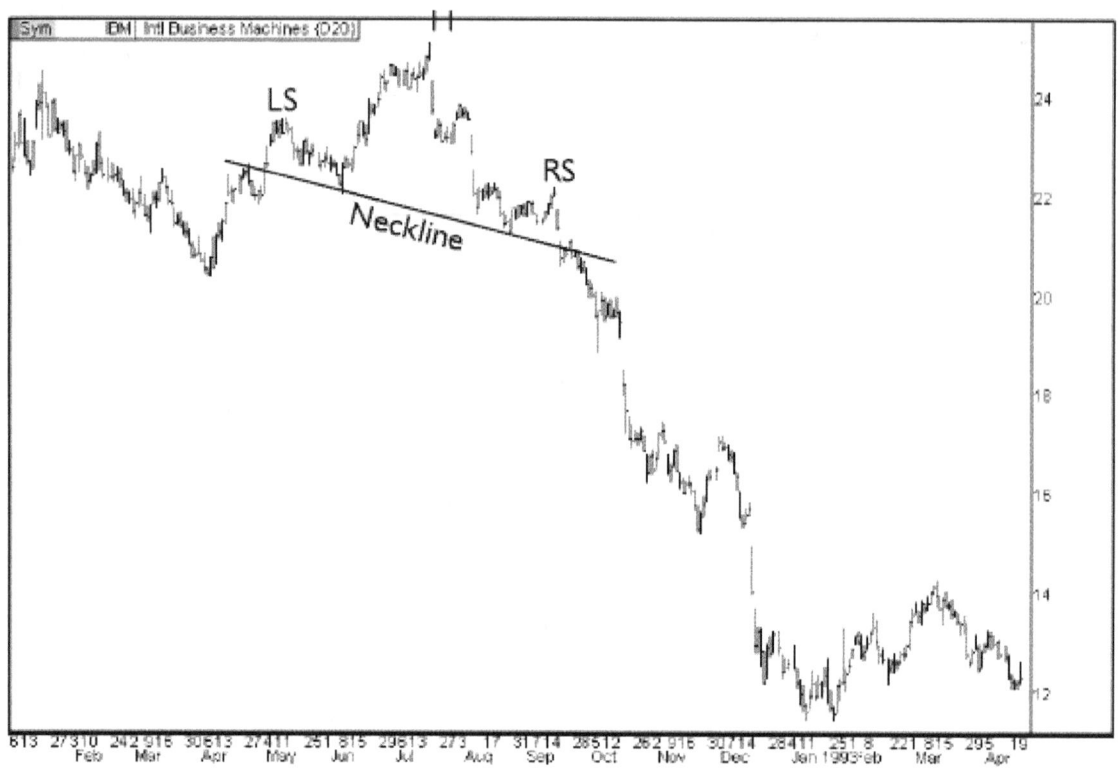

Classical Chart Patterns
Multiple Patterns

It is the rule, rather than the exception to see multiple patterns within a single chart. This is as true of classical patterns as it is of Runaway Characteristics.

When you see a market, such as JAKK, in which you can identify several patterns, and the market behaves as it's supposed to in conjunction with each pattern, you develop that **deeper level of understanding** I've been preaching about. When the pieces of the puzzle fit together well, you'll able to trade more confidently when the buy signals eventually come.

In this case, a Head and Shoulders top coincides with the expected behavior--the price plummets after the neckline is penetrated. The market then culminates with a solid bottom that is confirmed by a Double Bottom formation. Once the Double Bottom is complete, JAKK exhibits a large number of Runaway Characteristics and becomes a prime trading candidate whenever breakout signals arise

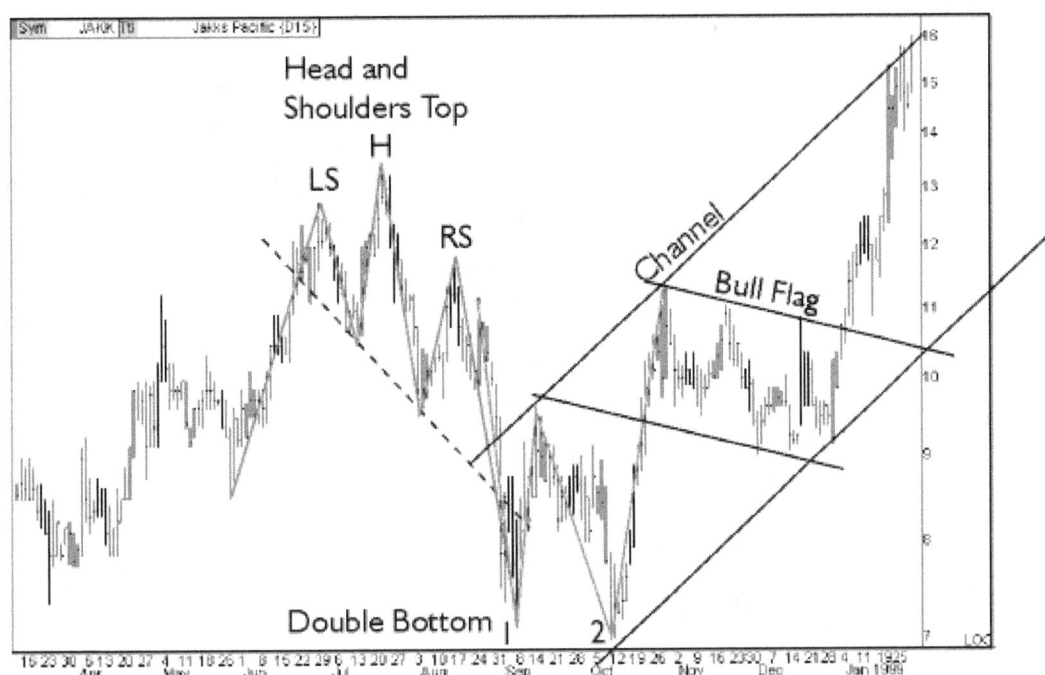

Here are a few more charts that show how different patterns serve as a way of understanding the markets better

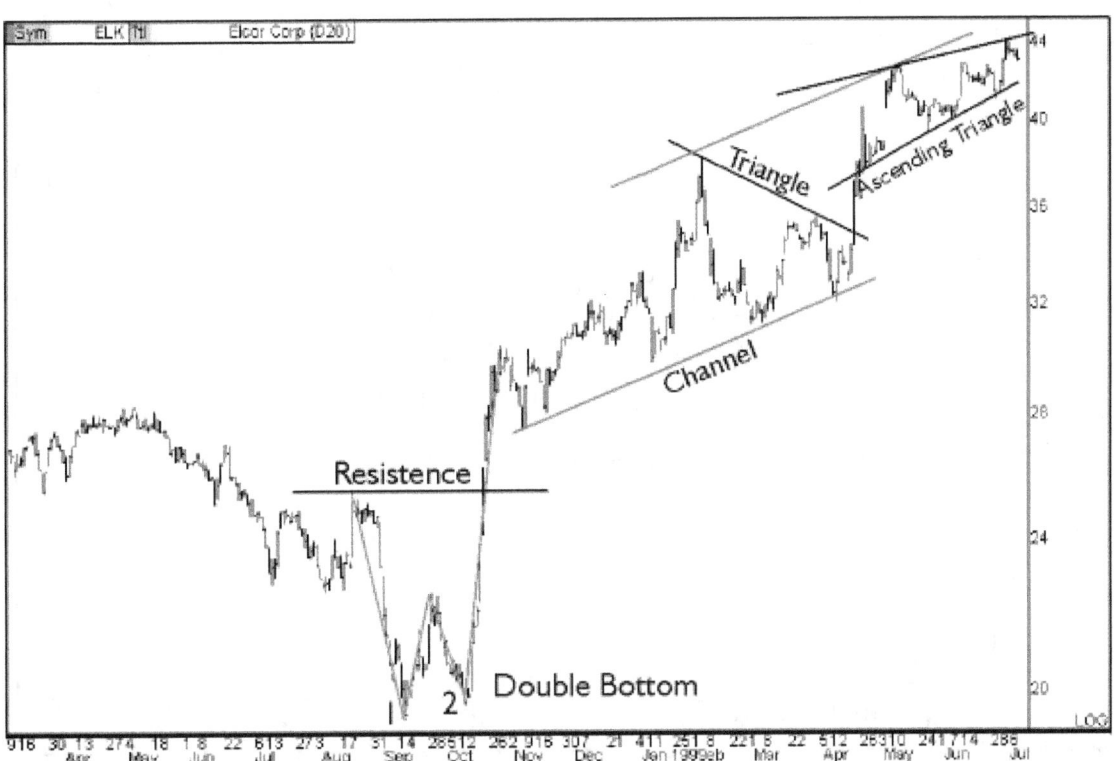

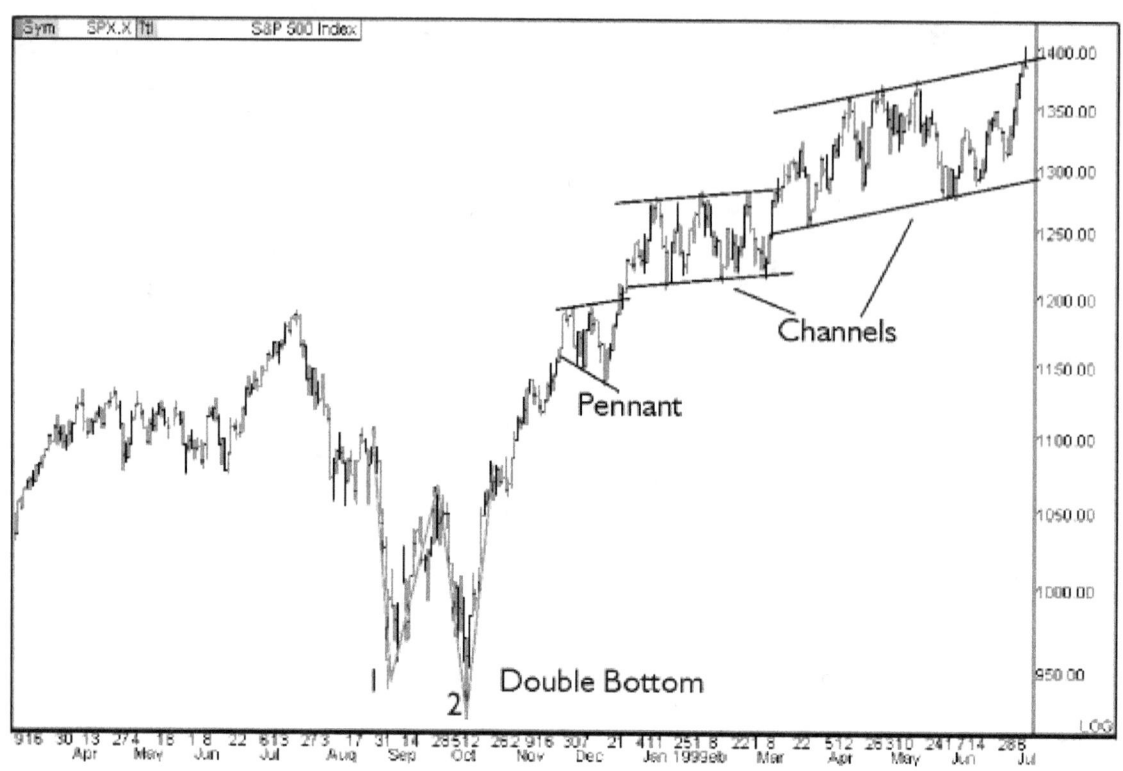

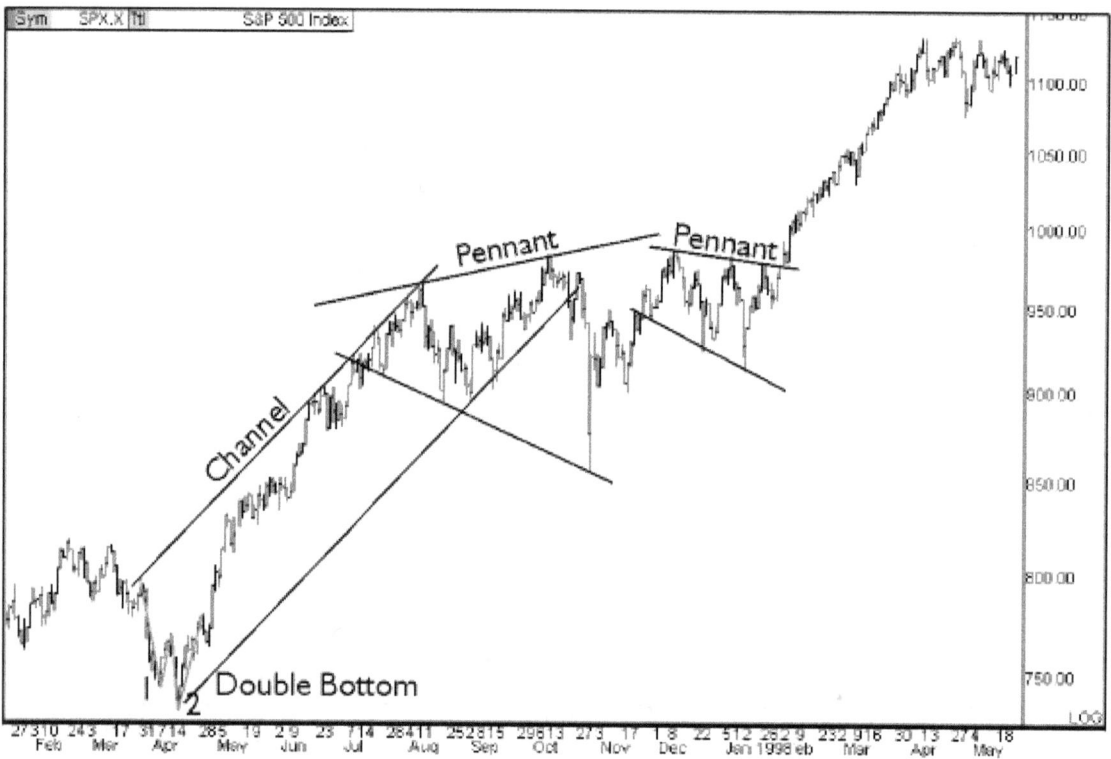

In them, I show some other patterns in addition to Double Bottoms and Head and Shoulders. If you're already an experienced trader, you may be familiar with these patterns. If not, it's probably best for me to not deviate too much from my own course agenda by going into detailed descriptions of channels, pennants, trendlines. There are already some good books available that do a fine job of describing these types of patterns. Let me just state that traders sometimes look at these old classic tools and doubt their usefulness because there are so many high-tech approaches now. But remember, being proficient in chart patterns is not necessarily intended to help to find specific trading opportunities. Rather, they just increase your awareness of what a market is doing. This factor alone can mean the difference between being a market master and a weekend hack.

In the vast scheme of all the indicators I use, patterns such as these play an important role. When I look at a chart and see patterns support the evidence I've gathered for a Runaway Market, I have more information to work with when I make trading decisions whenever breakouts with TBBLBG occur.

Reaction Patterns

Most traders make the mistake of trying to catch major market bottoms and tops. In fact, our research has shown that catching market tops and bottom with any degree of reliability or even profitability is a very difficult task. If I, a hedge-fund manager with access to the best trading knowledge base in the world, cannot make money doing this, then **it stands to reason that the more typical trader has a better chance of winning in Vegas than trading market tops and bottoms profitably.**

In trying to locate high-probability, high-profit trades that work consistently throughout our data history, we have found two main situations to capitalize on:

1) **breakouts or breakdowns** in price to new highs or lows,

2) **corrections (or reactions)** within a verified and strong trend.

My favorite approach is to use flag pattern breakouts with TBBLBG. I talked about these patterns in Week 3's Runaway Markets, Week 5's Indicators, and Week 6's Market Selection.

Many short-term traders have great success, however, focusing on correction or reaction strategies (Jeff Cooper calls them pullbacks). In fact, some of them will tell you that they prefer correction strategies because **there is something a little unnerving about buying a stock right after an explosive move has already started--as I regularly do.** These traders prefer to find situations where they can buy right before the explosive move starts. I have used different patterns real time since the mid-1980s and have done historical research on them extending back to the late 1800s. Overall, the flag pattern within a runaway market context is better and more reliable than a correction pattern. Yet, it's important to discuss correction patterns because you may find a host of factors that favor a powerful and sustained runaway move in a given market, but you might not see any breakout patterns that allow a low-risk entry. When pullbacks present themselves in such situations **they present you with an alternative means of seizing upon low-risk/high-reward trading opportunities.**

The following patterns will objectively define correction patterns that will allow you to catch correction lows and highs with very low risk and yet high potential and high historical reliability.

Before proceeding, if you are unfamiliar with bar relationship patterns, I suggestion you review the definitions in Week 3's Topic, Runaway Markets

Reaction Pattern 1
Key Island Reversal Reaction Low

This pattern has exceptional reliability and profitability, but you won't find it very often. In a study I did of the pattern, **85% of them were profitable**. A similar statistic was found for the mirror-image of this pattern, the Key Island Reversal Reaction High.

Before you start getting too excited, however, remember that I'm not just looking for standard Island Reversal Lows alone. I'm also looking for a number of other factors to coincide that make it a valid Reaction Low, as opposed an occurrence at any arbitrary point within stock's trading pattern.

All these criteria make the supply of needles in the haystack considerably more scarce.

Let's take a closer look. In the following example, we have a Key Island Reversal Low in a bar chart that is accompanied by a stochastic indicator is 5 and SD is 3.

The definition of a Key Island Reversal Low is:

- Day 2's high is < day 1's low and day 3's low.
- Pattern is completed on day 3.

However, for me to want to trade this, it must be a Key Island Reversal Reaction Low in which:

- The major trend is up and the last rally was 20% or more in a stochastic or major pivot cycle.
- A reaction occurs retracing less than 62% of the previous rally.

Either as the reaction is making a new low or after the reaction low appears, a key island reversal occurs while SD has fallen below 30.

Strategy:

Buy on the open of day 4 with a stop-loss one point below day 2's low.

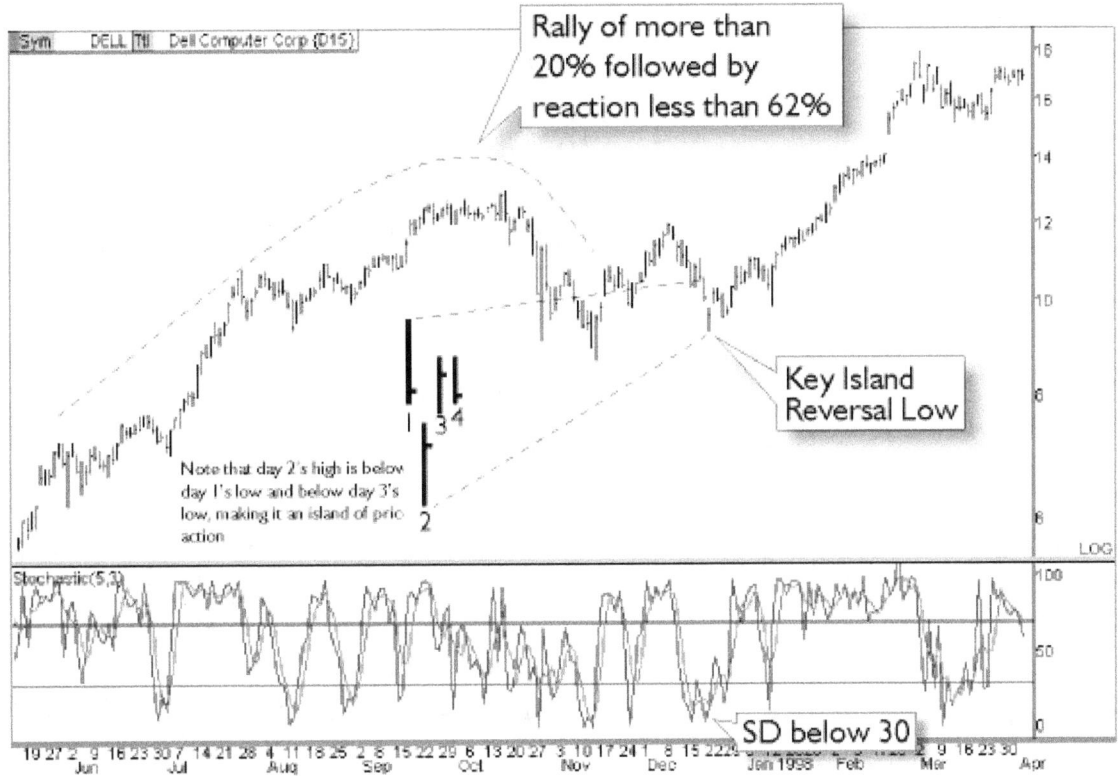

Reaction Pattern 2
Close Gap CPR Up with SD 5 < 30 on Swing Low Day

On its own, this simple pattern has an amazing amount of statistical reliability. Of all the Close Gap CPR Ups I found in a study I did, 62% of them would have reached my profit objectives.

A Close Gap CPR occurs when:

- The low of day 2 is a swing low.
- The close of day 2 is below the close of day 1.
- The low of day 3 is above the close of day 2.
- The close of day 3 is above the high of day 2 (this relationship is called a CPR).

It is essentially a swing low followed by a lap up day that closes above the high of the swing day.

To qualify as trading opportunity, the pattern I've just described must occur while SD is below 30 on the day of the swing low (day 2), and is divergent with the reaction occurring against a runaway trend.

Strategy:

The basic strategy is to buy the next day's open and use an OPS below the low of day 2.

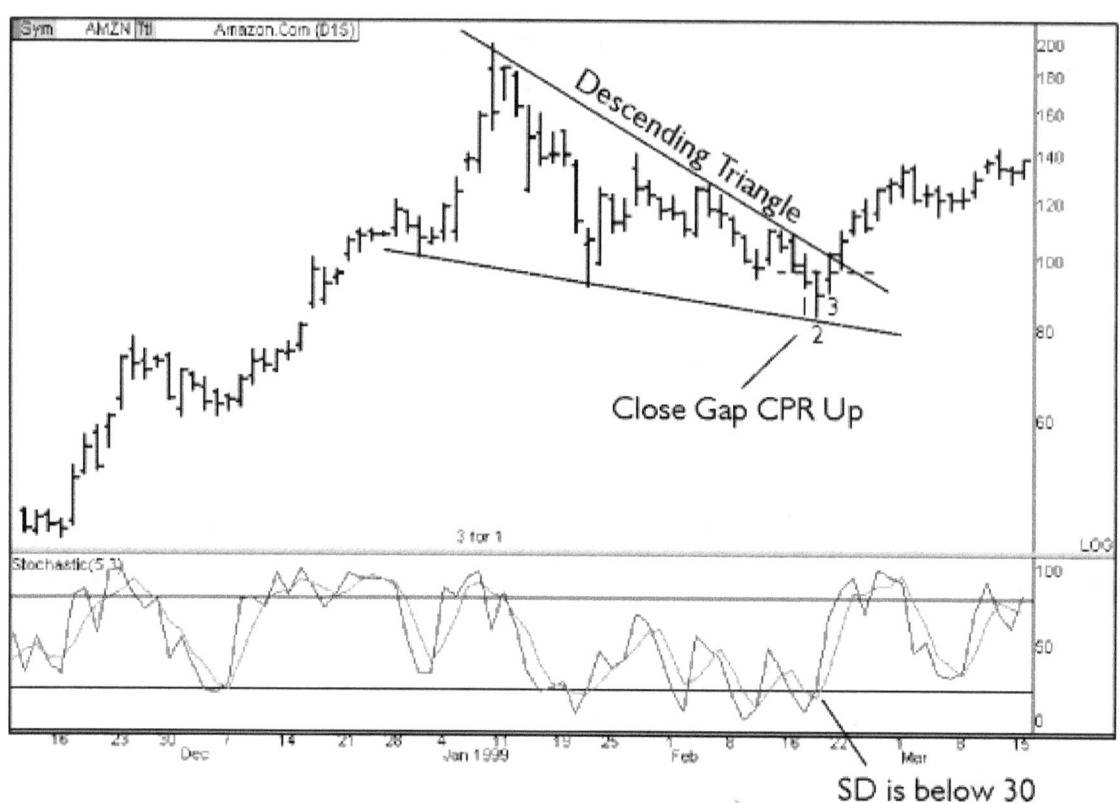

Reaction Pattern 3
Close Gap CPR Down with SD 5 > 70 on Swing High Day

A Close Gap CPR Down occurs when:

- The high of day 2 is a swing high.
- The close of day 2 is above day 1's close
- The high of day 3 is below the close of day 2
- The close of day 3 is below the low of day 2.

It is essentially a swing high followed by a lap down day that closes below the low of the swing high day.

To qualify as a trading opportunity, I'd want to see this pattern occur while SD is above 70 on the day of the swing high, and is divergent with the reaction against a runaway trend. I analyzed thousands of these patterns and found that 63% of them would have reached my profit objectives.

Strategy:

The basic strategy is to sell short the next day's open and use an OPS above the high of day 2.

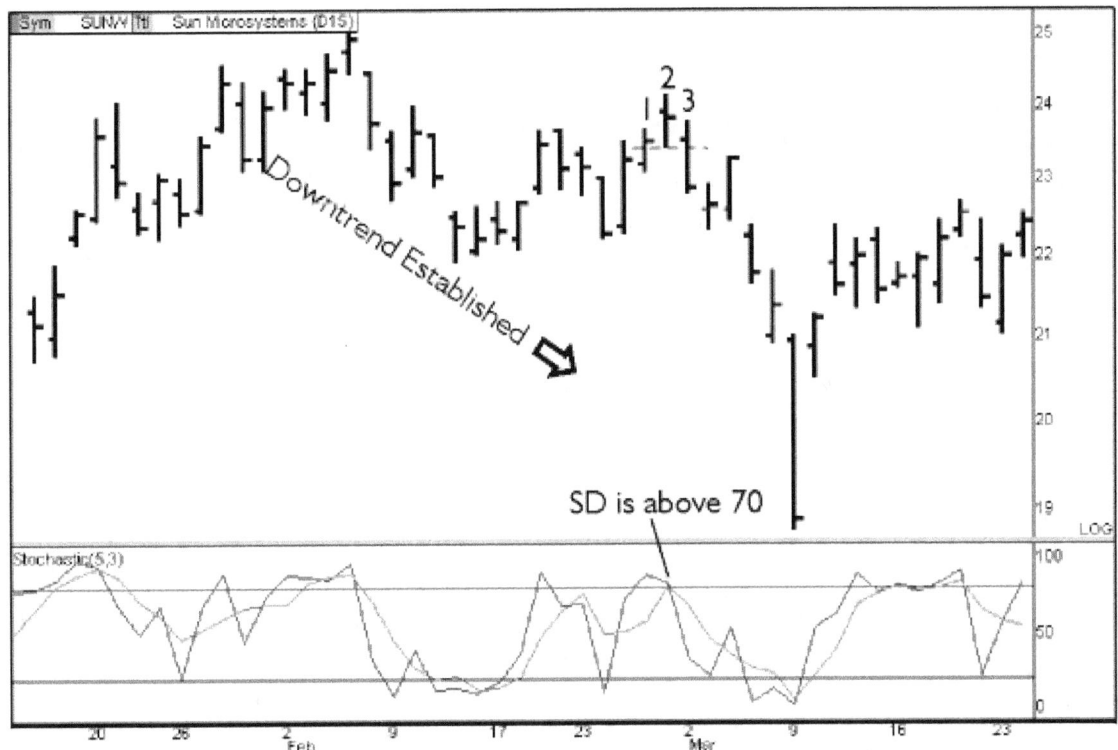

Reaction Pattern 4
Outside Day Up with Stochastic Divergence at the Low

In a generic Outside Day Up, the following occurs:

- The high is higher than the previous day's high.
- The low is lower than the previous day's low.
- The close is above the previous day's close.

In other words, the trading range of the Outside day is outside the trading range of the previous day.

A trading opportunity presents itself when the low of the Outside Day is a swing low and it diverges with SD at the same time, with the reaction being against a runaway trend.

Strategy:

Buy on a stop one tick above the high of the outside day, with an OPS one point below the low of the Outside Day. In my research, I found that 59% of these setups would have been profitable in the stocks that tested.

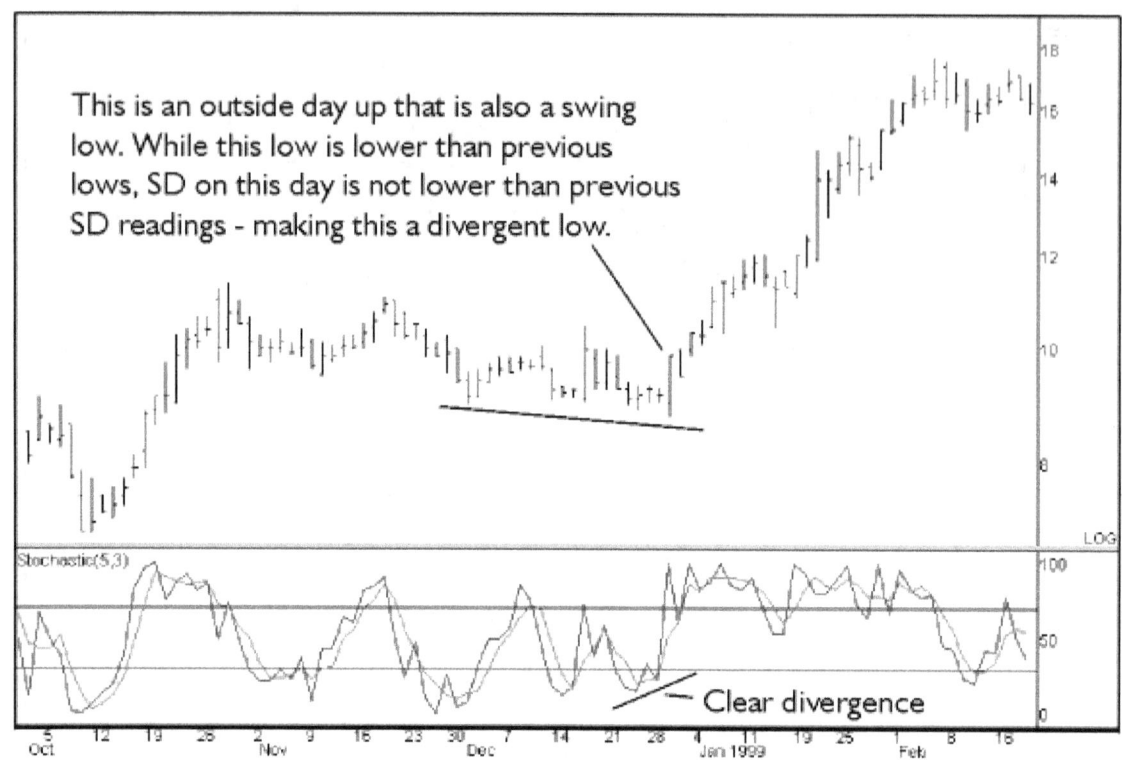

Reaction Pattern 5
Outside Day Down with Stochastic Divergence at the High

This is a simple pattern in which:

1. The high is higher than the previous high.
2. The low is lower than the previous low (making it an Outside Day)
3. The close is lower than the previous close.

The trade occurs when an Outside Day Down occurs where the high of the Outside Day is a swing high and it is divergent with SD at this time with the reaction being against a runaway trend. In my work, 61% of these patterns in the stocks I studied would have been profitable.

Strategy:

Sell short on a stop one tick below the low of the Outside Day, and use an OPS one point above the high of the Outside Day.

Reaction Pattern 6
Inside Day High Downward Breakout with SD Divergence

An Inside Day High Breakout occurs when:

- The market is in a correction against a runaway trend and makes a new correction high followed by an inside day (high of that day is lower than or equal to the high of the previous day and the low of that day is higher than or equal the low of the low of previous day)
- On a later day, the market moves below the low of day 1 before it has moved above the high of day 1, breaking out of the range of the "outside prior day" to the downside. Keep in mind that there can be several "inside" days prior to the breakout and not only one as shown below.
- This action must occur while SD is divergent with day 1 of the pattern. As long as the main trend is not down and is in a runaway market down, this pattern is valid for short-term traders.

Strategy:

Sell on a stop one tick below day 1's low with an OPS one point above day 1's high.

I found that 58% of instances of this pattern I found would have produced trading profits.

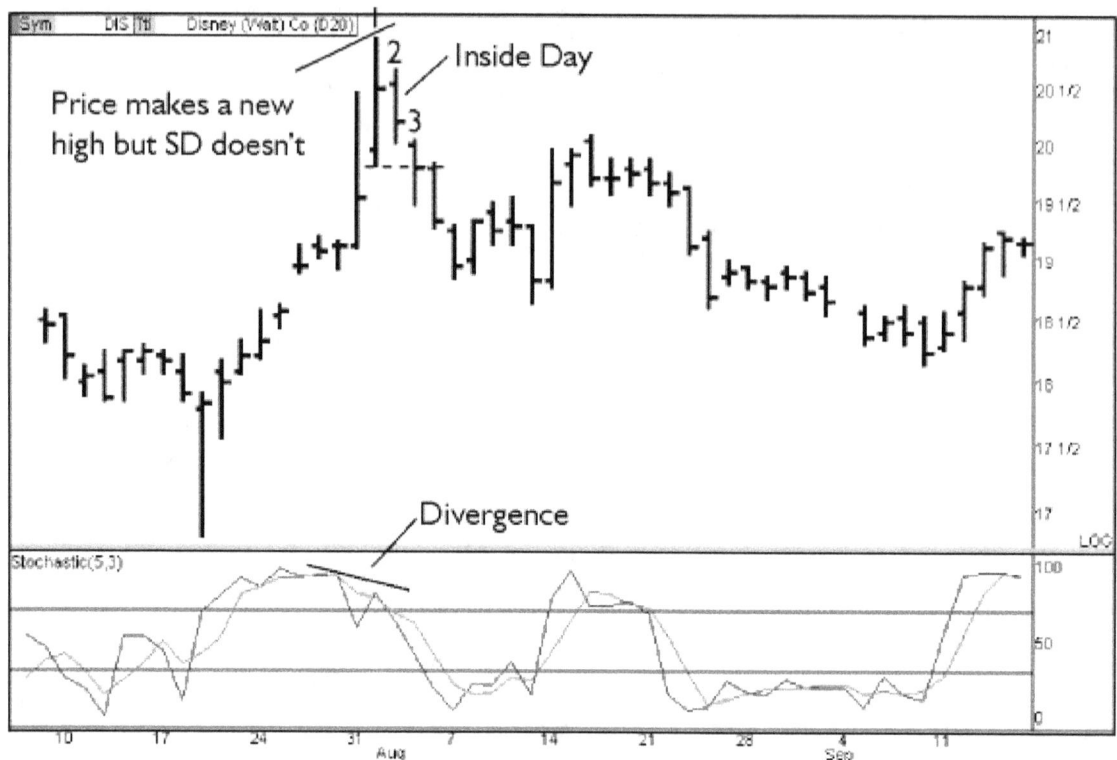

Reaction Pattern 7
Inside Day Low Upward Breakout with SD Divergence

An Inside Day Low Upward Breakout occurs when:

- A market makes new lows in a correction against a runaway trend and makes a low day followed by an Inside Day.
- The market moves above the high of day 1 prior to moving below the low of day 1.
- The Inside Day low occurs at a time when SD has not confirmed the low made the previous day. As long as the main trend is a runaway up market, this pattern is valid for short-term traders.

Strategy:

Buy on a stop one tick above the high of Day 1 with an OPS one point below the low of Day 1.

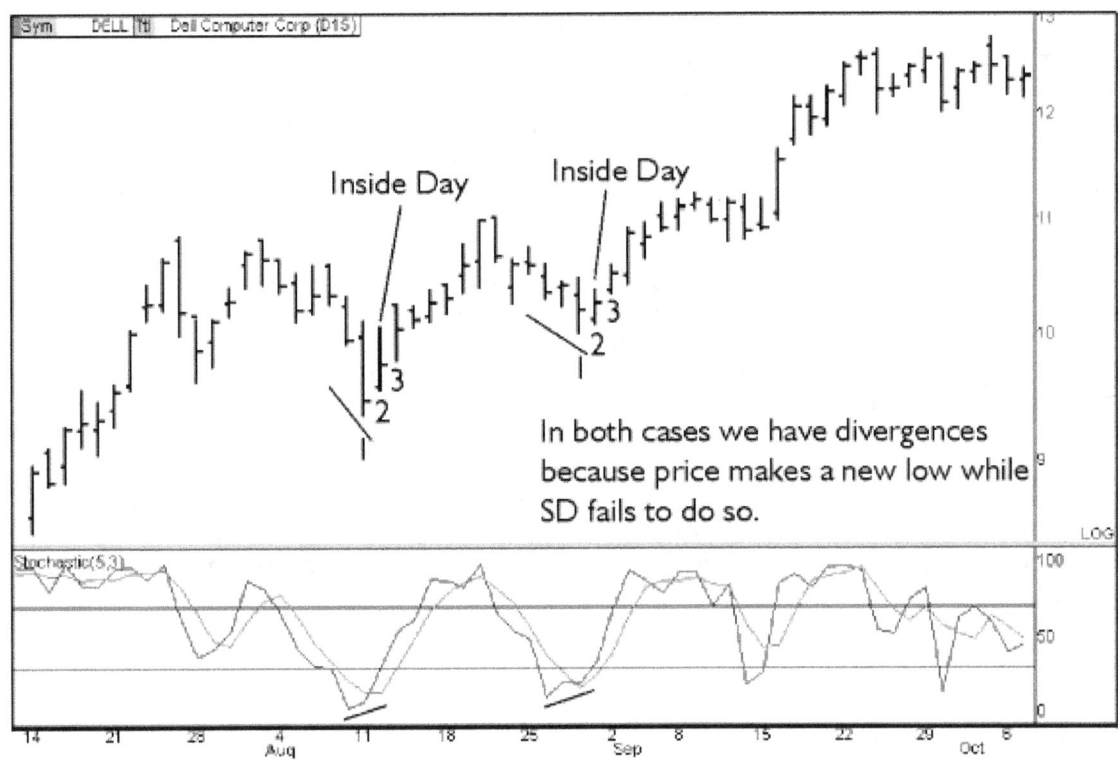

Closing Remarks:

In his book Flow: The Psychology of Optimal Experience, author Mihaly Csikszentmihalyi describes the process by which optimal performance happens. He says that athletes, musicians, artists, business people, and **people like us traders** do our very best when we achieve a state of "Flow." Flow happens when:

- You become completely absorbed in your work
- You forget about yourself completely
- You enjoy present moment
- Complete absence of fear of the future and worry about the past
- You lose your sense of time
- Nothing else seems to matter

The mental state described above allows you to achieve your **absolute best performance.**

In trading, I don't think you can achieve a state of flow unless you understand cause and effect in the markets. When events seem to cause shock waves in the markets, everybody else panics—but you just continue going with the flow.

This week I've given you an introduction to pattern recognition. It's a huge topic which I hope you'll study further on your own because so much of the moment-by-moment experience of trading comes from looking at stock charts. I surround myself with these charts and I believe that having the ability to spot the many patterns therein adds another important dimension to that broad understanding of the underlying causes of market behavior that I so very highly covet. The foundation I hope all this provides you with will enable you to look at a chart and be able to read the mind of the market.

Every single time you trade, you should have a sense of how the trade fits within numerous bits of disparate information that you've pieced together from the stock's fundamentals, the current state of the Liquidity Cycle, where the stock ranks in relative strength, the stock's Runaway Characteristics, and the chart patterns which precede your buy signal. But you won't be doing this in a deliberate or mechanical fashion because the fruit of all your intensive study will enable you to process these things without thinking, the way a top quarterback doesn't have to think before throwing a winning pass--just as he is about to get sacked.

Remember that a major part of studying patterns is so that you can begin to develop skills of reading what the collective markets are saying. When many stocks and commodity futures all breakout of or form valid patterns with a short period of time, the markets are very likely to be making a significant move in the indicated direction. Reading the markets in this way is a critical skill for a trader to develop.

Also remember not to get too hung up on entry patterns and to focus most of your time and effort on market selection first. Occasionally, a reaction pattern may allow you to enter a runaway stock you were itching to get into for a long time. Usually, you should wait for a consolidation breakout, but now you at least have the flexibility to make an intelligent judgment based on a wide host of factors.

Next Week's Topic

Perhaps I've been preaching money management, relative strength, market selection, and liquidity cycles to the point where you're blue the face thinking "this guy must pay not attention whatsoever to market timing!"

Well, it's certainly true that I don't focus on what the rest of the world focuses on. That's because I've tested every methodology in existence and have concluded that approaches that are superficially appealing often don't work as well as those which are counterintuitive. I do pay attention to market timing--lots of it. It is plays an indispensable role in my trading, but market timing in and of itself does not = trading profits.

Next week, I'll show you what my favorite market timing approaches are as well as how you can use them to reduce risk and increase the profit potential of every trade you get into.

TRADINGMARKETS MEMBERS, Welcome Back to Mark Boucher's Trading Course:

One of the fantasy trips that novice traders go through is to sit down with a calculator and see how quickly **$1000 becomes $1,000,000** when you repeatedly double all your money--each time reinvesting all your profits.

I think market timing advisory services and the whole range of stock market newsletters aimed at predicting market bottoms and tops cater to peoples' tendency to indulge in these types of fantasies. The best way to do this is to look at big historical moves and ask people to picture how much money they would have made if they had traded them. In fact, if I had a penny for every market timing service that claimed they had predicted the 1987 top or the bull market leg that started in 1994, I certainly would far richer than if I actually listened to their advice.

The truth, my fellow traders, is that steady returns can only be yours if you're willing to invest the time to learn every aspect of trading and market analysis from M to Z. M, of course, stands for Money Management. From a Money Management perspective, you are able to deal with the reality that you'll get into losing trades 30%-50% of the time as well as the occasional unexpected catastrophes that occur in the markets that tend to purge traders who got lucky for one to ten years using a highly optimized system, one-way bull market only system, or newsletter writer's advice.

It is with these happy sentiments that I begin this week's talk on Market Timing, which probably would have been the topic of Week 1 for anyone else's ten week course.

Enter Week 8: Market Timing

In all thy getting, get understanding
--Malcolm Forbes

The purpose of market timing is to **help you trade in sync with the markets** when you identify legitimate buy and sell signals using the pattern setups I showed you in previous weeks. In my opinion, market timing tools in themselves do not provide you a viable path to impressive trading profits. Let me elaborate on this now.

First of all, I think it is literally impossible to time the markets with an adequate degree of precision or accuracy using cyclical analysis. This includes the use of tools such as standard cycles, Fibonacci, Gann, and Elliott Wave. I do, however, feel that these can be valuable tools once you understand the underlying economic reasons that cause markets to move the way they do. It just seems so commonsensical that if you're studying the financial markets, which are a manifestation of business and economic activity, that you should focus on business and economics, not the pyramids of Giza. **Otherwise, you are driving a car by using your rear view mirror.**

The tools that are proven to be useful for market timing are derived from economic, monetary, technical, and other variables that our research shows are robust over time. Traders following these models more or less mechanically will do better than buying and holding, but hardly well enough to write home about. To use them more effectively, however, you must simply understand the way economies work.

Understanding the way economies work consists of:

- determine which variables statistically correlate well with certain market behaviors
- be able to determine what the economic environment (phase in the Liquidity Cycle) is currently by monitoring these variables
- know what needs to happen in order for the current economic environment to change (to the next phase in the Liquidity Cycle)

If you can do the above, you're a market master who can read the pulse of the economy and figure out its relevance to every buy and sell order you place. If you can't, then you're just guessing; you are less likely to be able to incorporate this information into your trading.

An Example to Clarify

Theoretically, if you looked at charts of the following three indicators...

- Wage Inflation Pressures
- Factory Capacity Utilization
- Leading Index of Inflation

...you would see that every time all the indicators were at certain levels, the market either was flat or declined.

- 90-day T-Bill
- Trade-weighted dollar

...just prior to the major declines in 1972 and 1987, you would see a pattern that appeared useful in predicting future crashes.

What is incredibly interesting is that lots of technical indicators lined up perfectly to strongly suggest that a crash was imminent in early 1995. During this time, how many famous market timers were saying that their indicators and lined up perfectly for the "final top" to occur that would usher in a multi-year bear market? Being wrong will be a way of life if you are a market timer who simply interprets indicators mechanically--any kind of indicator, be it economic, liquidity, or technical.

However, life in the markets is not so simple that we can say, for example, that three discount rate hikes are bad for the market while two are okay. It's just not that simple. Perhaps this can be a decent rule of thumb that alerts you to monitor the situation closely, but that's about it.

Understanding the big picture would allow you to interpret the positioning of the above indicators in 1995 completely differently because while the rules of thumb were triggered, the reasons that made rules of thumb work in the past were not in place during 1995. Let me explain this briefly for you fans of macro-economics.

In January and February of 1995 while the above indicators were screaming a crash scenario:

- there was little evidence of C.P.I. increases that would force further rate hikes
- the bond and T-bill markets were rallying sharply
- the yield curve had come down from a record slope and had flattened somewhat, but did not indicate tight sharpening

Further, you can't compare apples to oranges. The market environments of 1972-73 and 1987 were different from that of 1995.

- In 1973, global inflation was taking off like a rocket and the Fed was literally forced into creating an inverted yield curve to try and stem the tied of exploding inflationary pressure, which was also leading to a rapidly declining dollar. Interest rates were exploding and monetary policy was extremely tight, which drained liquidity and forced financial markets lower.
- Similarly in 1987, bond and T-bill prices had been declining rapidly for months prior to the market crash. Again global inflation was on a milder upturn, and the dollar was plummeting, as were bonds.

1995 was different from both these environments, however. Inflation, as reflected by the CPI, had turned down since 1994, as had commodities. T-bond and T-bills and bottomed following 1994's carnage. Some who understood this might have understood that equities were safer than at any time since 1993.

When will the next bear market occur? When bonds and T-bills begin to decline in earnest again, and evidence mounts that further Fed tightening will be required in 2004. And please. . .don't even take what I say at face value. The moral is:

> *Don't just use the timing models and variables mechanically. They are just rules of thumb. Learn to understand how and why variables work and you'll gain greater insight and profits.*

Timing Models I Use

In the following section, I will present **my favorite timing models** and tools for U.S. stocks. The models are based on data from two relatively inexpensive services:

1. **Barron's Market Lab.** Barron's is available weekly at any newsstand.
2. **Media Logic's Business Cycle Indicators SCB series data bank**, which dates back to 1945 and is available for only $129 (call 1 800 305-7575 to order).

You should also consider the **Bank Credit Analyst Research Group.** I highly recommend that you explore their website at: http://www.bankcreditanalyst.com. While their data and models are not cheap, they are worth the price.

Some of the models are presented as full-blown trading systems, but are useful mainly as general guides for those trading mutual funds. Others are presented as green-light/red-light indicators, with information about how the market has performed when the indicator is in different phases. In all instances, the information gained is likely to be helpful either in aiding exact entry and exit, or allowing one to find favorable points to add to positions, institute leverage, or increase exposure at low-risk/high-reward junctures. We will explain uses of these techniques in the course of the discussion.

Our stock market indicators are based on:

- **Monetary Gauges**
- **Economic Gauges**
- **Seasonality**
- **Sentiment**
- **Breadth**

Please note that credit for the original work and ideas these indicators are based on go to the following pioneers: Marty Zweig, Ned Davis, Dan Sullivan, Edson Gould, Gerald Appel, Nelson Freeburg, John Hussman, Stephan Leeb, Martin Pring, Edward Renshaw, Larry Williams, Jake Berstein, Richard Eakle, Joe Kalish, William Omaha, Norman Fosback, and many others.

Monetary and Economic Indicators

Since this week's discussion on market timing is very closely tied to understand the Liquidity Cycle, this page will serve as a review and summary of some material I already covered in Week 4.

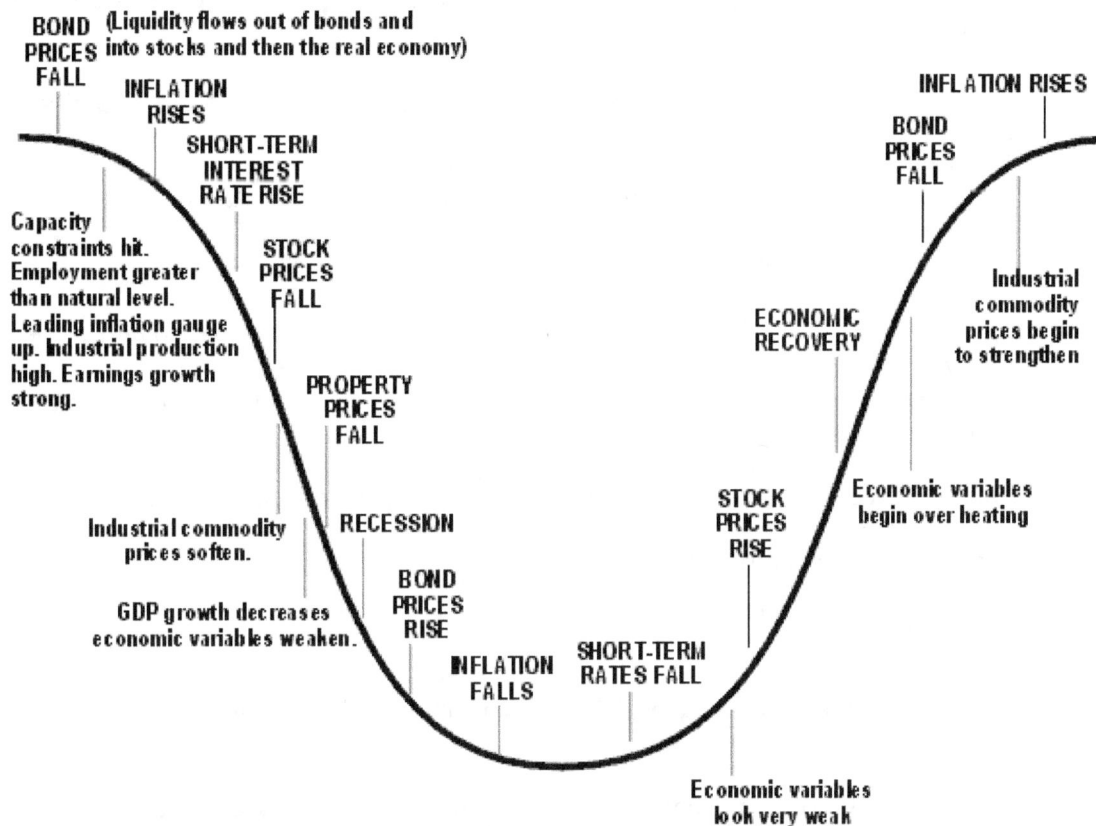

General Rules for Using the Liquidity Cycle in Trading

Here is a brief summary of what I look for in various monetary and economic gauges in order to figure out where we are in the Liquidity Cycle at any given time. I have developed and tested systems which help me to know whether it is safe to be stocks. A quantitative description and formula for each system is beyond the scope of this 10-Week Course, but you can get that more in-depth view from my book "Hedge Fund Edge" (1999, John Wiley & Sons, NY).

Monetary Gauges

Let's say we're looking for an environment in which stocks perform well. This is what I need to see:

1. T-Bill rates rising at a slow rate or preferably falling.
2. Corporate bonds are moving up or flat.
3. The yield curve steepens (the ratio of 30-Year Treasure Bonds to 90-day Treasure Bills increases).
4. Bond prices are rising.

I have quantified each of the above gauges into spreadsheets that make it make it easy to monitor all these variables and conceptualize the big picture. Here are two examples of the inputs I used and the projected annual returns.

1) 3-Month T-Bill Yield Rate of Change (ROC) < or = to 6% ("T-Bill rates rising at a slow rate or preferably falling")

- System Description: Buy S&P when the 12-month rate of change of 3-Month T-Bill Yield is < or = to 6.0%. Exit when > 6.0%.
- Significance: When T-Bill rates aren't rising rapidly, stocks rise nicely.
- Data Used: Monthly close of 3-Month T-Bills and monthly close of S&P 500.
- Test Period: 1/29/43 to 12/31/97
- Annual Rate of Return: 18.8%

2) Dow Jones 20 Bond Index Close ROC > -1.5% ("Corporate bonds are moving up or flat")

- System Description: Buy S&P when the 12-month rate of change of the Dow Jones 20 bond Index close is > -1.5%. Exit when < or = -1.5%.
- Significance: When corporate bonds are moving up or flat, stocks perform very well.
- Data Used: Monthly close of Dow Jones 20 Bond Index and monthly close of S&P 500.
- Test Period: 1/29/43 to 12/31/97
- Annual Rate of Return: 17.4%

Economic Gauges

In addition to the above monetary gauges, I look at confirmation in the following economic gauges:

1. The economy is not overheated as shown in lower Capacity Utilization Rates
2. Industrial production growth is not high as reflected in Industrial Production Index.
3. Unemployment is increasing or not going lower swiftly.
4. When Inflation and Gross Domestic Product growth are not moving up at too fast a pace.

I have quantified each of the above gauges, just like I did with Monetary Gauges. Here is an example:

1) Capacity Utilization < or = 81.5% ("The economy is not overheated as shown in lower Capacity Utilization Rates")

- System Description: Buy S&P when the Capacity Utilization Rate < = 81.%. Exit when > 81.5%
- Significance: When the economy slows down, stocks perform well.
- Data Used: Monthly Capacity Utilization Rate and monthly close of S&P 500.
- Test Period: 1/29/43 to 12/31/97
- Annual Rate of Return: 20.4%

Putting the Pieces of the Liquidity Cycle Puzzle Together

The Liquidity Curve is a basic model that tells us what to expect and watch for as we move from one phase of the cycle to another.

One of the trickiest aspects of the Liquidity Curve is that it leads economic statistics. **Economic statistics are lagging indicators** that help economists to gauge the relative health of the economy. Since the stock and bond markets are the first to feel the effects of new money printing, they will be strangely **ahead of** what you hear economists and journalists talking about in the news media.

Normally, people think that the worst time to buy stocks is during a recession when economic statistics look horrible. However, what we've learned about the Liquidity Cycle makes this view **incorrect and even dangerous.**

In actuality, when economic variables are weak and the Fed begins lowering rates and stocks start responding by rallying, that is the best time to get into stocks and bonds. As we said earlier, the effects of lowered interest rates are typically not seen in the economy for 6 to 18 months. In the face of continued bad news about the economy, stock market prices can start moving up much sooner. If you were watching the markets in 1982, 1992, and 1995 and late 2002 this will have a familiar ring.

Conversely, the riskiest time to invest in equities, or to be heavily biased toward long positions if you're a trader, is when the economy looks good but the bond market is beginning to head lower (which is a reflection of a rise in interest rates).

Breadth Indicators

Breadth indicators typically measure the number of stocks that are **advancing and declining** at any given time and compare them in a way that tells you the internal strength of any given market.

The public is usually fixated on the Dow Industrial Average and news as the principle way of gauging the health of the stock market. When the Dow moves up, people become excited and optimistic. When the Dow goes down, people get depressed.

Often, however, you'll get a better idea of the **true strength or weakness** of the market by looking at the number of advancing and declining stocks and comparing them in some meaningful way. That's what breadth indicators do.

OTC Index 7.9 Percent Momentum Model

Simply keep track of daily over-the-counter (OTC) index closes.

- When a close drops 7.9 percent or more from a peak close, a sell signal is given.
- Conversely, when a close is 7.9 percent or more above a trough daily close, a buy signal is given.

This is so simple, and yet, it beats a buy and hold approach even when transaction costs are considered. Since 1963, buy and hold has returned 11.76 percent compound annual rate with a 59.5 percent drawdown in the NASDAQ OTC index. This simple momentum model has returned an astonishing **18.2 percent compound annual rate of return since 1963** with a **22.4 percent maximum drawdown** (which is a bit too high for us to just use the system "as is"). This system's trades were profitable 61 percent of the time. The NASDAQ index was profitable 70 percent of the years tracked while this system was profitable 91 percent of the years tracked, although it had back-to-back losses in 1993 and 1994. Traders willing to risk drawdowns should consider this system as a whole or component of an aggressive trading strategy. Both shorts and longs were profitable.

Five-Day Moving Average of Advancing Volume over Five-Day Moving Average of Total Volume

Here is yet another example of how simple a powerful marketing timing model can be:

- Take the five-day moving average of advancing volume and dividing it by the five-day moving average of total volume.
- Whenever the five-day moving average of advancing volume is 77 percent or more of the five-day moving average of total volume, an extremely strong breadth situation is developing into a very strong buy signal.

Three months later, the S&P is up an average annual rate of 25.3 percent--this is the time to get aggressively long.

Eleven-Day A/D Ratio

Here's one that uses data from advances and declines:

- Take the 11-day moving average of advances and divide it by the 11-day moving average of declines.
- This gets bullish on moves over 1.9.

Three months later, the S&P is up at an average annual rate of 29.2 percent. This is another breadth signal that tells you when to get aggressively bullish.

New Highs / New Lows T-bill dividend Ratio

This model produced a 16.1% gain per annum versus 10.6% buy and hold with statistical risk 30% less than buy and hold.

Compute an 8-day moving average of:

- new highs
- new lows
- new highs + new lows

Let--

- NH = 8 day Moving Average New Highs
- NL = 8 day Moving Average of New Lows
- SUM = d day Moving Average of New Highs + New Lows
- T = 90 day T-bill yield/S&P dividend ratio
- A = 0.58; B = .79; C = .66; D = 2.13
- P = Price at close
- M = 18 day Moving Average of close

Buy when NH > ((T * A) - B) * SUM and P > M

Exit when NL > ((T * (-C)) + D) * SUM and P < M

Sentiment Indicators

Sentiment Indicators

Sentiment indicators usually measure the degree of optimism or pessimism among traders and investors. The idea behind this is that the market tends to turn down when market participants become extremely optimistic and tends to turn up when they become extremely pessimistic

Most market technicians and traders are aware of the importance of sentiment, but sometimes these indicators are ascribed magical properties and get over-used. Therefore, you have some market timing services for whom sentiment is the only focus. Many of these timing services have gotten soundly pummeled during this present bull market because a number of popularly followed sentiment measures had flashed numerous sell signals between 1995 and 1998. The rule of thumb, once again, is to understand the overall structure of the markets. Use sentiment indicators only when they flash critical extreme readings, and distribute the weight of your interpretation appropriately among your other economic, monetary, breadth, and other technical timing tools.

- When economic, monetary, and technical models are bullish, look for overly negative sentiment to confirm that it's the right time to be long. Be cautious if sentiment is overly optimistic.
- Conversely, when indicators are clearly telling you to short the market, look for overly optimistic sentiment readings for confirmation. Be cautious of sentiment that is too pessimistic.

It is interesting to note that many of the best sentiment indicators tie in directly with critical junctures within the Liquidity Cycle. When the Fed artificially stimulates the economy through the lowering of interest rates, money flows into the economy and ultimately demand for goods and services increases because people have more confidence about their financial future. Companies misallocate their resources into increased production capacity to meet that artificial demand. Once the demand dries up, that production capacity becomes excess and thousands of people get laid off. Consumer pessimism sweeps in. Money flows into and out of the stock market as a function of what phase of the Liquidity Cycle we're in.

So when people talk about optimism and pessimism among traders and investors, they're really talking about a manifestation of the manic-depressive behavior of the economy induced by the Liquidity Cycle.

Consumer Sentiment Index

The more confidence that consumers have about the stability of their jobs and the health of the economy, the more money they are willing to spend when they go shopping. This is reflected in the Consumer Sentiment Index.

- When this index of consumer confidence goes to a euphoric level above 99.5, the S&P has moved down at a -2.5 percent annual rate.
- When the consumer sentiment index is below or equal to 99.5, however, the S&P has moved up at a 14.2 percent annual rate.

Share of Household Assets in Stocks

One of the old gems of Wall Street wisdom says to start lightening up your positions when your taxicab driver or the guy that changes your oil starts talking about how much money he's made in the stock market.

In other words, when the mainstream public begins to love the stock market, it may be time to shift away from the stock market into another asset class. When a market gets frothy, many people who ordinarily don't typically play the markets begin to pile in. Because they shoot from the hip, usually on the basis of the advice of "experts," they panic and mass liquidate when the market takes a hit.

The rule of thumb:

- Whenever the share of household assets in stocks moves over 50% and then turns down, stocks failed to beat T-bill returns over the next three years.

Stock Mutual Fund Net Sales/Market Cap

If you take the ratio of stock mutual fund net sales to market cap and it's less than 5%, the S & P has yielded an average of +24.4% annualized return.

- When that ratio is greater than 5% and rising, the S & P has yielded an average of +11.6 annualized return.
- When the ratio is greater than 5%, but falling, the S & P has fallen, yielding an average of -10.6 annualized return.

Five Day Average Put/Call Ratio

The least sophisticated traders in the markets are options buyers. Many people get lured by the prospect of making a huge fortune with only a small amount working capital, which is made possible by huge leverage afforded by options, particularly those that are out-of-the-money. The excitement of vast overnight riches blinds these people to the fact that the odds are almost always heavily stacked against the options buyer due to time decay and the zero intrinsic value of out-of-the-money options that results in an option being worthless at expiration. To make money, an options buyer's timing has be nearly perfect.

The Five-Day Average Put/Call Ratio indicator is fairly popular among short-term traders.

- When the ratio is below 40, the S & P declines, generating an average -15.4% annualized return.
- When the ratio is above 64, however, the S & P has yielded an average 29.9% annualized return.

Seasonality

There are certain dates of the month that are surprisingly profitable buy and sell days in both stocks and bonds. Here is a summary the most powerful that Larry Williams found in his work. My recommendation is to use these as confirmation tools which either strengthen or weaken your confidence when you're considering a combination of factors in any given trade.

BOND FUTURES BUY DAYS AND RULES:

- 11th - exit next day or take $2,000 profit whichever 1st.
- 25th - exit six days later or $2,000 profit whichever 1st.
- 30th - exit four days later or $2,000 profit.

BOND FUTURES SELL DAYS AND RULES:

- 18th - exit in six days or $2,000 profit

- 22nd - exit in four days or $2,000 profit

S & P FUTURES BUY DATES AND RULES:

- 1st, 28th, - exit next day or $2,000 profit
- 5th, 26th - exit in four days or $2,000 profit
- 29TH - exit in 6 days or $2,000 profit

S & P FUTURES SELL DAYS AND RULES:

- 2nd - exit in six days or $2,000 profit.
- 13th - exit in four days or $2,000 profit.

If you combine all days and trades, only taking trades when the exact date is a trading day, you get a $202,000 profit on a $12,330 max drawdown with 81% of trades profitable over the last 10 years in S & P and T-bond futures. When you are using different kinds of trading techniques note the date that you're entering and try not to fight these dates.

The Real Synergy of Systems - Combining Their Force

I once visited a little village in Columbia that had a small airport. While I was there one night at around 2 am, the town bell went off sixteen rings. Everyone jumped into action. "A plane is coming," my exasperated host informed me, "com'on we must hurry!" Every single villager with a car or truck drove to a designated parking spot surrounding the runway and turned his/her headlights on. My host explained to me that the airport did not have runaway lights. "Each point of light illuminates more," he explained to me. "No one light could make this runaway visible, but by putting together small lights from different vantage points we can make this landing zone safely lit." **Market timing systems are much the same way**.

You want a combination of systems to point in the direction of your trade-and the more systems (based on independently reliable factors) that point toward a market heading up or down, the more likely it is that that trend will take force.

Let me give you some examples. In our section on breadth systems we disclosed "Up volume > 77% of Total Volume" breadth thrust as well as our "11-day Advance/Decline Ratio > 1.9" breadth thrust. And in our monetary systems section we disclosed our "Monetary Composite" system which looks for certain readings in corporate bonds, T-bill rates, and bond rates. What do you think the market would do if both monetary and breadth models were positive?

If an investor waited for both the monetary composite and one of the breadth models to be positive, and stayed bullish until neither breadth model nor the monetary composite was bullish, he would only have been long nine times since 1949, and only 20% of the time. Yet an investor shifting from T-bills to the S&P only during these times would have actually beaten the total return of the S&P since WWII, and with a maximum drawdown of only 13% versus a 50% drawdown for the S&P itself. And this while being in risk-free cash nearly 80% of the time. Each of the nine bullish monetary and breadth periods was profitable.

A more aggressive investor could leverage 50% by buying Spiders on margin, by buying a leveraged Profund or Rydex fund, or by using futures. On margin, an investor could have more than double the return of the S&P buying via the above rules, with half the drawdown of the S&P! The bottom-line is that when both breadth and monetary variables are clearly positive it is a very safe and profitable time to be aggressive.

Similarly, if we take these three models and simply buy only when any one of them is bullish and exit when all three are not, we trade more frequently (about 45% of the time we're in the market), but with similar market-beating results. 32 out of 40 (80%) of such signals are profitable, the worst drawdown is around 15%, and simply shifting into cash T-bills when no model is bullish and into the S&P when any one model is bullish allowed an investor to beat the total return of the S&P by 1 ½ times. An investor could use this combo model for timing entry and exit into mutual funds, for example, for a relatively easy way of beating the market on both a risk and reward basis.

The point is that by combining reliable methods that are based on totally different factors, we can locate highly profitable and highly reliable periods in which to invest. Clearly, when monetary variables and breadth variables line up, traders can be more aggressive with relative safety.

In this 10 Week Trading Course, it's impractical to show you more than a sampling of the models we watch based on sentiment, breadth, momentum, monetary, economic, and seasonal factors. In my book, The Hedge Fund Edge, and in my course, The Science of Trading, I outline more than 50 such models that investors can use and combine to locate many more highly reliable periods to invest more aggressively.

In my own money management I do use several combinations of such models to enter/exit the market for a portion of our portfolio. While this is a viable strategy for investors for a portion of their portfolios, my main point here is that there is substantial value to be gained by monitoring a number of reliable models, based on different factors. You must watch for periods in which several models are positive or negative on the market because these periods are likely to be particularly profitable or risky.

If enough TradingMarkets.com members express their interest in market timing, we will post several combination timing systems updated daily with track records, for traders and investors to use in their own investing.

Closing Remarks

We've taken a look at the whole battery of market timing indicators that I keep an eye on constantly. Market timing is a way of determining which way the wind is blowing. No matter how good any trading setup might be, I'll always want to trade in the direction the wind is blowing. It may sound like a cliché, but when you look at the mathematics of money management--

The best offense in trading is defense

Market timing falls into the defense category more than do many of the strategies I've been talking about because I do not use market timing to find specific trading opportunities. Rather, it is another bit of evidence that either helps to build a case for or against taking any given trading opportunity.

So I may find many Runaway Characteristics in a high relative strength stock that has fuel, but if my market timing indicators are weak, I'm going to stand on sidelines.

One thing that might be somewhat disconcerting about the market timing indicators I've shared is that there are so many bits of information that you have to input into these arcane formulas. For the most part, we're dealing with simple calculations, but there are many of them. You might want to try keeping track of these calculations by building tables in spreadsheets so that all you have to do is input the variables from the Barron's Market Laboratory and have the spreadsheet do all the calculations automatically. I know this may sound crude in a world of slick system testing and artificial intelligence software, but many times, the market analysis tools that are the least marketable for software vendors are also among the best ones.

What's in Store for Next Week?

Trading psychology is a popular topic these days. Many fine books and seminars are available on this topic although many of them are written by non-traders. Well, here's my chance to say my piece. Next week, I will have the pleasure showing you the strategies I use maintain my trading discipline. Nothing I've taught you so far means anything unless you have the discipline to do them and this will be my focus when we get together again.

How do I make myself do what I have to do in order to be successful as a trader?

If you have been trading for a while, you already know that it is often easy to do the wrong thing and hardest to do the right thing. I know this from first hand experience. The techniques I'll show you have helped me tremendously. They include:

- Trading Journal
- Daily Action Plan
- Visualization
- Mental Trading Account (which I talked about in my my live forum with Larry Connors on TradingMarkets.com)

I hope you'll join me in this session because I truly believe that anyone can shape their own destiny by being conscious of their own thoughts and applying techniques which eliminate self-sabotage. Many traders with the right aptitude still shoot themselves in the foot because their emotions cause them to deviate from their trading strategy.

Find out next week how to end this problem.

TradingMarkets.com Members, welcome back to the course!

In the previous 8 weeks, I've revealed to you to the essence of what I use in order to make my living as a hedge fund manager and trader. Don't kid yourself, though, into thinking that your path to understanding ends with this 10 Week Course. In terms of methodology, I think I've pretty much covered my crown jewels. But in terms of making money with them, there is one critical component to trading success around which everything thing I've talked about from Week 1 to Week 10 revolves. That component is YOU.

Let me illustrate this with the following story:

> There was a 10-year-old boy who decided to study judo despite the fact that he had lost his left arm in a devastating car accident. The boy began lessons with an old Japanese judo master. The boy was doing well, so he couldn't understand why, after three months of training, the master had taught him only one move. "Sensei," the boy finally said, "shouldn't I be learning more moves?"
>
> "This is the only move you know, but this is the only move you'll ever need to know," the sensei replied.
>
> Not quite understanding, but believing in his teacher, the boy kept training. Several months later, the sensei took the boy to his first tournament. Surprising himself, the boy easily won his first two matches.
>
> The third match proved to be more difficult, but after some time, his opponent became impatient and charged; the boy deftly used his one move to win the match. Still amazed by his success, the boy was now in the finals.
>
> This time, his opponent was bigger, stronger, and more experienced. For a while, the boy appeared to be overmatched. Concerned that the boy might get hurt, the referee called a time-out. He was about to stop the match when the sensei intervened.
>
> "No," the sensei insisted, "Let him continue."
>
> Soon after the match resumed, his opponent made a critical mistake: he dropped his guard. Instantly, the boy used his move to pin him. The boy had won the match and the tournament.
>
> He was the champion.
>
> On the way home, the boy and sensei reviewed every move in each and every match. Then the boy summoned the courage to ask what was really on his mind.
>
> "Sensei, how did I win the tournament with only one move?"
>
> "You won for two reasons," the sensei answered. "First, you've almost mastered one of the most difficult throws in all of judo. Second, the only known defense for that move is for your opponent to grab your left arm."
>
> The boy's biggest weakness had become his biggest strength.

--Unknown author

In trading every single methodology you use has strengths and weakness. The patterns I most strongly advocate only meet my risk and reward criteria in markets that pass the Runaway Markets test. In the above story, the boy doubted himself when he faced an opponent that was bigger, stronger, and more experienced. He didn't understand the strategy he was using, just as most traders do not understand the strategies they apply in their trading; therefore, he froze. **The sensei who had true understanding knew that the circumstances were ripe for victory and advised his young student accordingly. Victory was theirs for the taking.**

I've already made the point many times that you have to understand the markets before you can trade them successfully over the long haul, as opposed to just a lucky winning streak. This story illustrates that perfectly. But also notice what this "understanding" did for the sensei. When the odds seemed stacked up against his young one-armed student--when it even seemed as though he could get injured by continuing the match, the sensei **calmly** proceeded with his strategy. The act of doing what was most difficult at that time happened to be the only way to win, but he had no hesitation about proceeding down that path. Think about this: Wouldn't it have been perfectly reasonable for the sensei, in spite of his superior understanding, to still have let fear overwhelm him and call for an end to the match?

Here's my point from a trader's perspective:

You might be a master at managing your money, have the best techniques in the world, and have a true understanding of the markets, but you must have the **mental hardness and discipline to carry it all out.**

How to Attain the Character and Discipline Needed for Successful Trading

How to Attain the Character and Discipline Needed to for Successful Trading

What you can do or dream you can do, begin it. Boldness has genius, power, and magic in it.
-Johann Wolfgang Goethe

There is a huge wealth of material available in bookstores and through seminars about how people can maximize there ability to succeed in life. These range from the old classics such as Think and Grow Rich by Napoleon Hill to new insights from Anthony Robbins in his book Awaken the Giant Within. I consider the dedicated study of these ideas to be essential for traders, because unlike other professions, there is no system of accountability in which someone (like a boss or supervisor) is telling you what to do or not to do. Even if you run your own company, you still have to answer to the needs of your customers. In trading, you alone are responsible for your decisions every moment of every trading day. **You will only reap the rewards of these decisions if you can be brutally honest about your mistakes and take whatever steps are necessary to correct them.** Further, maintaining discipline is a never-ending battle because your mind will always try to fool you into judging your performance in a favorable light.

After studying the ideas of experts in the self-improvement field and combining that with what I've learned through my own experiences, I have arrived at my own strategy for developing and maintaining trading discipline. I will share this strategy in the following pages. While I realize that different individuals have different temperaments and hang-ups, I've talked to enough traders to know that there is a lot of commonality between the techniques I use for myself and those in use by other traders I'd consider to be successful. So, if you think you have a good trading strategy, but are still searching for tactics which will strengthen your discipline to carry it out, I hope you'll receive some benefit from what I have to say.

Keep a Journal

Recently, when Larry Connors interviewed me in a live forum on TradingMarkets.com, I pointed out the importance of maintaining a **trading journal** and doing so religiously. In fact, I'd go as far as to say you should be something of a fanatic about it.

Most novice traders have heard something about the importance keeping a trading journal and they see this as a text-only diary in which they record the rationale they had for entering a trade and their emotional state at the time. Actually, that approach only scratches the surface of the more hard-core approach that I put to use in my trading.

When I tell you to keep a "journal" I mean that for every single trade that you get into:

1. Print out a chart of the market you traded.
2. Draw arrows pointing to entry point and protective stop.
3. Write onto the chart or on a separate piece of paper, all the reasons you had for making the trade, as well as any other information that you feel is relevant.
4. Draw lines and arrows as necessary in order to describe visually any technical patterns and Runaway Characteristics that describe your trading setup.
5. Every time you move your protective stop, print out another chart with the updated price action and add your new protective stop.
6. When you exit the trade, print out another chart and draw an arrow pointing to your exit point.
7. In full detail, add any other notes you may feel are pertinent.

In essence, you are creating for yourself, a "how to" book that you can refer back to in the future-- but you are refining what "how to" means as you progress in your trading. Depending on what your trading time frame is, refer back to your past trades and learn from your mistakes by adjusting your strategy as necessary in order do better next time.

As you can see, the trading journal I create for every trade is detailed and in my opinion vastly better than the little namby-pamby diary that I've heard that many traders keep. Remember that the purpose of a religious journal is not to merely gush out your mental state or your innermost thoughts, but rather to **create a ladder for you to steadily climb upwards to the ultimate goal of trading success. Each time you trade you'll be adding to your knowledgebase of dos and don'ts which become the rungs of the ladder you climb.**

Outline of My Daily Action Plan

As I inferred earlier, maintaining one's trading discipline is a battle that **you must fight constantly** because everyday little situations crop up which tempt you to do the wrong thing. In order to keep yourself on that narrow path to consistent trading profits, you must have a daily strategy which helps you to stay focused on the goals you've set and keep doing the things that will get you there.

Below I've outlined my **Daily Action Plan for Successful Trading**. Even if you've read about some of these ideas before, I encourage you to click on each link anyway because everything I described is framed in the context of trading--after all, you are not training to be an astronaut or salesman. There are particular insights I want to share with you that may help you as you explore each one of these Action Plan components.

A Word About the Mental Trading Account

I want to especially highlight my excitement about a strategy that I **consider essential** to maintaining my trading discipline. It's called the **Mental Trading Account.** It is modeled after the Mental Bank Course, which has helped thousands of people to successfully execute the steps they needed in order to achieve their goals. I truly believe that this one tool, along with the kinds of strategies I've already outlined in the course, **will revolutionize the way you trade and the way you live in general.**

Click on each link to read a detailed description of each component of the outline.

Daily Action Plan for Successful Trading.

1. Statement of Purpose

2. Sensory Goal Statement

3. Photographs and Pictures of Achievement

4. List of 10 rewards for achieving your goal and vision

5. Daily visualization of achievement of goal with rich sensory images

6. Evening Review of the Day in Light of Your Goal

7. Evening visualization of the achievement of your goal

8. Recording Entries Into Your Mental Trading Account

    Mental Trading Account Contract

    Value Events (examples)

    Mental Trading Account Passbook

    Mental Trading Account Passbook Events and Assertions

9. Review the Following Ten Traits of a Self-disciplined Person

CLOSING REMARKS

1. Statement of Purpose

Your Statement of Purpose is your goal or reason for your wanting to trade successfully. To help you collect your thoughts, here are some questions to ponder:

- **Why have you been studying this 10 Week Course?** (Presumably you want to make more money in the markets and do so consistently).

- **Do you have a specific goal** for what your trading profits will be used for?
- Why is that goal **important to you?**
- What do you want out of life, and **how will improving your trading give it to you?**

Remember, reasons are more compelling and powerful than even goals themselves. If you have a powerful reason for wanting to achieve a goal write it down, and you will persevere until the goal is yours. Finally, incorporate your reasons and goals into a statement of purpose, which is stated as a general long-term goal. Here's an example:

"I want to earn millions of dollars; be happy, free, loving, and continuously grow by trading the markets; and help all men become prosperous, happy, and free by living up to their full potential."

Now would be a good time to write your own personal statement of purpose.

2. Sensory Goal Statement

Dreams are a dime a dozen, everyone's got dreams. It's not dreams, but their execution that counts."
--Theodore Roosevelt

Here you will transform your purpose into a specific shorter-term **process-oriented goal** that you want to achieve in both your trading and life in general. Focus on the specific process that will give you **consistent and continuous improvement**, rather than a numerical goal, because the process is what allows you to realize concrete goals. What are the steps involved in achieving your goal? Write them down. Whatever trading success means to you, incorporate this into your sensory goal; this is a first step toward achieving your larger purpose.

Here's an example of a Sensory Goal Statement:

Beginning immediately and for the next six weeks, I will:

- **record my trading journal** and account daily
- **do a thorough analysis** of each and every trading decision
- stick to my **written trading plan**
- **apply the discipline** of only entering or exiting a trade when patterns or pre-written strategy events develop

Write your personal sensory goal statement now.

3. Photographs, Images, and Pictures of Achievement

Seek out from magazines, books, art pictures, photographs, or any other source you can think of which show **images of successes similar to the ones you're trying to achieve.** If you have a photo of yourself at a time you realized a big achievement, look at it daily and imagine yourself there again so you can feel, see, and taste it. Use your imagination to walk yourself from where you were today through to the full achievement of your goal—and then revel in your success and celebrate it. Seek out triumphant pictures of sports or other heroes feeling the thrill of victory. Andre Agassi pictured himself winning Wilmbledon every day of his life for many years so that by the time he finally won it in real life he had to pinch himself to be sure it was for real. Remember that the imagination of man is the most powerful force on earth. And remember that the subconscious cannot fully distinguish the difference between vivid dreams and reality. **If you picture yourself working towards and reaching your goal often enough, you will eventually convince your brain that you have already achieved it—and you will become the type of person who achieves the goals you have set for yourself. So right now, do some brainstorming!**

- Think of the sources of pictures that **exemplify the type of success you want to achieve** and start gathering them. The Internet is a great place to start.

- List the times in your life when you **experienced victory and relive the feelings on a daily basis.**

- Picture yourself making continual progress toward success and **repeat this again and again** to achieve your goal.

4. List of 10 Rewards for Achieving Your Goal

This is a compilation of all the **reasons** you seek the goal you do. Why do you seek your goal? What will your true rewards be? Picture and fully associate yourself with your goal in hand—what's better about your life? **List the top 10 changes that accomplishing your goal will make in your life.**

Here's an example:

1. Freedom and independence
2. Stronger self-confidence and sense of purpose
3. Respect and admiration of peers
4. Ability to own or buy any house or luxury good I want
5. New sense of ability to tackle any new goal I set
6. Potential to travel, learn, and grow continuously
7. Time to enjoy family, friends, and loved ones
8. Enhanced ability to contribute and help others achieve their potential
9. Increase influence to empower others to help change the world for the better
10. Enhanced feeling of inner peace, resolve, and connection to others

Think carefully of ten rewards your goal will mean to you and write them down. Remember that to fulfill our basic needs we need to feel a sense of certainty, love and connection, variety, significance, growth, and contribution—make sure these six human needs are covered in your ten rewards.

5. Daily Visualization of Achievement of Goal with Rich Sensory Images

Once you've establish what your goal is, you'll want to develop a **clear picture** of what success will be like in your mind's eye. Assume you have achieved your goal.

What picture can you produce in your mind that will sum up the exhilaration and feeling of happiness and success you will feel? **What does success taste like, sound like, feel like, and smell like?** Perhaps you've having a "first million" party. Perhaps you're winning a tennis match on your tennis court that is part of your new luxury home. Picture how the achievement of your goal will transform your life. Burn these images into your brain so that you'll feel yourself already in possession the rewards your goal has to offer.

Now write down a detailed description of that picture with impressions you will experience when your goal is reached with regard to sight, sound, touch, taste, smell, and emotion. Make this picture **clear and vivid** in every detail and visit it daily until it is real.

6. Evening Review of the Day in Light of Your Goal

Make a small journal entry every evening in which you review your day **in light of the progress you made toward your goal.** Emphasize the positive aspects of the day. When you make a mistake, record it and make a plan of how you will avoid repeating it again in the future. Also spend five minutes brain-storming about how you can achieve your goal more efficiently, and about any new impulses or ideas you might have. Thomas Edison did this religiously, and felt that it was one of his most important activities. Did you make a trading error, or take a profit too soon? Write down the circumstances in intricate detail. If you tend to make the same mistakes repeatedly, writing it into your journal will allow you to more easily document it and find a solution to it. Bernard Baruch kept a daily trading journal religiously.

7. Evening Visualization of Achievement of Your Goal

Each day spend **four or five minutes seeing, hearing, and feeling yourself in possession of your goa**l. Fully associate with being the type of person that regularly achieves such goals. Look around, and drink in the atmosphere. Use your imagination and add new aspects to the picture so that you are continually developing it into finer detail.

For my own use and now yours, I have created an adaptation of what is taught in the Mental Bank course called the **"Mental Trading Account Passbook."** This is shown in detail on the next several pages. The concept is simple and takes only about 5 minutes per day, but it has an **incredible impact on your subconscious and helps you to change your behaviors rapidly.**

What I like about this approach is that it goes beyond just the mere mental activity of imagining success and forces you to **take action and create success**. Many times, people want success and they just sit around daydreaming, thinking that this alone will conjure it up in reality. But to become a successful trader you absolutely must work hard and have the discipline to follow your trading plan. You may initially find that much of what you need to do is boring or unpleasant. **The Mental Trading Account will attach a positive mental reward to every important daily task you have and ensure that you'll be chipping away at the accomplishment of your goal.**

The Mental Trading Account works by assigning an imaginary dollar value per hour that you spend doing each task that is required for you to ultimately achieve your goal. Every time you perform the task you calculate the number of hours you spent doing it, and pay yourself in these imaginary dollars. Money is such a powerful motivater that the subconscious cannot tell the difference between these imaginary dollars and real ones.

Now let me show you how this is done:

MENTAL TRADING ACCOUNT CONTRACT

The first thing you have to do is make a contract with yourself that signifies your commitment to maintaining the Mental Trading Account. This clearly delineates a beginning to the whole process and greatly increases the chances that you're taking it seriously.

On this day of _____, 19 ____, I_____
hereby agree to rewrite my mental script to arrive at an annual trading income of

$_____, or an account with a value of $_____. I will arrive at this amount by assigning a hourly dollar value for the "value events" I've listed which will assure that I will achieve this goal. These dollar values will be paid in "mental" money according to the time I spend doing each value event.

_____   _____
Signature   Date

VALUE EVENTS (examples):

Here are some examples of what Value Events look like. To make up your own list ask yourself: What actions, done every day, would guarantee success?

VALUE EVENT	RATE/HR.
1. Keep up Gann charts and angles on runaway stocks	$500
2. Make and keep my daily journal, giving reasons for each action taken, the pattern upon which entries are taken, and the plan for every possible exit opportunity in the markets.	$500
3. Work on Mental Trading Account	$6,000
4. Do daily discipline plan	$1,000
5. Do daily computer scans and find all runaway markets and all patterns on the stocks I'm watching	$500
6. Half-hour review of historical data using techniques learned in Mark Boucher's 10 Week Trading Course and verified validity to build confidence in these techniques	$500
7. Read a new book or course or attended a new seminar. Apply learned techniques to historical data first, and then upon proof of viability, apply techniques to improve my own trading and trading methodology.	$500

MENTAL TRADING ACCOUNT PASSBOOK

Here is the "**control center**" of the Mental Trading Account technique. This is where you transform yourself into a **winning trader.**

There is powerful leverage in the few minutes you spend keeping the passbook updated because, without expending any more time and effort than just what's involved in logging the amount of time your spend engaged in your value events, you are generating a considerable amount of motivation toward doing what you must do in order to become a **successful trader**. What's great about this technique is that you don't have to use a lot of willpower or mental gymnastics in stay disciplined. **If you have done this properly, the changes will begin to take place automatically.**

Tips and Tricks

1. **Give yourself a $1,000 bonus for having a "perfect day."** That is a day in which you did everything in carrying out your trading plan and discipline. Note that this may not necessarily be a day in which you made money, but theoretically, if you stive to make everyday a perfect day, you'll make the big bucks in the long run.

2. **Every time you have more then 10 consecutive perfect days reward yourself** with some frivolous, but enticing gift. It could be a visit to your local Baskin-Robbins, or some electronic gadget. Whatever the case, make the process of doing the right things fun.

3. **Assign a high value to "high leverage" activities.** That is, give a higher hourly rate to those activties that give you the most return for the time invested.

4. **When you make real money in trading, subtract that from the Mental Trading Account Balance.** By doing this, you are in effect buying real money using the imaginary money you've accumulated. This creates a real perception of value for each Value Event and establishes this concrete relationship in your subsconscious:

Doing the right things consistently earns you real money.

As you can see, the Mental trading account goal of $1,000,000 is not play money!

5. **Adjust your the hourly rates for your Value Events** accordingly if make so much in trading profits that your Mental Trading Account Passbook is always in the negative. Keep raising the bar of excellence.

Mental trading account goal: $1,000,000

DATE	VALUE EVENT	RATE	HOURS	DEPOSITS	REAL YIELD	ACCT. BALANCE
7/30	1. Gann Charts	$500	1 hr.	$500	$0	$500
7/30	2. Journal	500	1/2 hr.	250	0	750
7/30	3. Mental Trading Acct.	6,000	5 min.	500	0	1250
7/30	4. Discipline plan	1,000	1 hr.	1,000	0	2250
7/30	5. Scan patterns	1,000	1 hr.	1,000	0	3250
7/30	6. Accounting	500	15 min.	125	0	3375
7/30	7. Historical data review	500	1/2 hr.	250	0	3625
7/30	8. Read new book	500	15 min.	125	0	3750
7/30	9. PERFECT DAY!	1,000		1,000	0	4750
8/2	3. Mental Trading Acct.	6,000	5 min.	500	0	5250
8/2	4. Discipline plan	1,000	1 hr.	1,000	0	6250
8/2	TRADING PROFITS -- JAKK				$4275	1975

MENTAL TRADING ACCOUNT PASSBOOK EVENTS AND ASSERTIONS

Because the Mental Trading Account, when done properly, will be a **driving force pushing you to do the right things**, it's important to stay motivated doing it. To keep myself from slacking off, I maintain a concise diary of positive events and continually write down "Mental Trading Account Assertions."

Here's how it works:

DATE	POSITIVE EVENTS

8/2	My first perfect day!! I did something in every value event!
8/2	I ignored buying a stock today because the trade had too much risk for my account size and I felt good about it even though the stock went up 12 points today!
8/2	I felt more confident than ever in entering orders
8/2	I took my first big profit since the seminar! It felt quite groovy!

MENTAL TRADING ACCOUNT ASSERTIONS

I am become a better stock and commodity trader all the time and my account size is growing rapidly

I am a disciplined trader and my discipline and success in trading are spilling over into all other aspects of my life, making me more successful and happier than I ever imagined possible.

9. Review the Following Ten Traits of a Self-disciplined Person

"A trading system is only a tool - to become a craftsman able to ceate great fortunes with that tool requires a good strategy."
--Stanley Kroll

In order to stay on course toward your destination, you should review the Ten Traits of a Self-Disciplined Person each day. The idea is that if you are not yet a self-disciplined trader, that you will eventually become one through the use of all the techniques I have outlined up until now and continual exposure to the ideal model presented through the Ten Traits.

TRAITS OF A SELF-DISCIPLINED PERSON	PLEASE RATE YOURSELF FROM 1(WEAK) TO 10 (STRONG)
1. Sense of purpose	1 2 3 4 5 6 7 8 9 10
2. Have positive role models in real world, history, and literature	1 2 3 4 5 6 7 8 9 10
3. Have a creative imagination that I use daily to visualize myself in possession of my goal	1 2 3 4 5 6 7 8 9 10
4. Have positive mental attitude that allows me to concentrate on	1 2 3 4 5 6 7 8 9 10

the positive, yet tackle solutions to the negatives	
5. Have unshakable belief in myself and complete confidence that I can and will achieve my goals and aspirations	1 2 3 4 5 6 7 8 9 10
6. Have ability to plan, organize, and subdivide large tasks into small easy steps along the way	1 2 3 4 5 6 7 8 9 10
7. Willing to acquire whatever skills are necessary to achieve goal	1 2 3 4 5 6 7 8 9 10
8. Am patient (in my trading)	1 2 3 4 5 6 7 8 9 10
9. Am persistent and persevere	1 2 3 4 5 6 7 8 9 10
10. Enjoy the work necessary to accomplish my goals (trading review and studying and consistent commitment to learning and growing)	1 2 3 4 5 6 7 8 9 10

Closing Remarks

Before this week, it may have crossed your mind that this guy Boucher was a natural born trader from the very beginning. To be quite frank, I went through the same struggles that every trader goes through when they open their first account. I got lucky while still in high school and caught the run-up in gold in 1979. But I lost a huge chunk of it trading Orange Juice a few months later because my early success caused me to become overconfident in my analytical abilities and money management skills; in reality I had very little skill in either department. This kind of story repeats itself over and over again in the lives of millions of traders and investors everyday. For most, particularly short-term traders, it is a life-to-death cycle. Typically, traders keep making the same mistakes repeatedly because they are in denial that a problem exists with them internally. The "blame-game" takes hold and they say to themselves:

- It's that damn system. But when I buy the right one, I'll be another Larry Connors or Jeff Cooper!
- It's that damn newsletter. I don't know what happened. This guy's been hot for past 10 years but now he's making my guts spill out! I'm gonna switch to this other guy and make back everything I lost. After that I'll be a millionaire within one year!
- Damn. I just don't have enough money in my account. Once I borrow some money off my wife's credit cards, I'll have $10,000 in my account. Then my ace-pro money management will kick in. Only 50% in open positions at any given time. From there, it'll be smooth sailing, yes baby!

In my early days as a trader, when I did not immediately achieve the wealth and success I had envisioned, I looked at myself as being a major part of the problem. I asked myself, "What do I have to do differently in order to become a successful trader?" I wound up not only testing hundreds of different methodologies in partnership with Tom Johnson, Ph.D. over a three year period in a relentless search for strategies the held the greatest promise for low risk/high reward opportunities, but I also focused a lot attention to re-engineering my own psyche. I studied successful traders, read hundreds of books, attended dozens of seminars in search of the tools and techniques that would enable me to think like a winning trader.

You cannot have sustained success as a trader without devoting serious attention to both the science of trading as well as the science of the human mind. I still go through this same process in an attempt to constantly expand, grow, and improve my trading and my life. One of the greatest things about trading is that it is so challenging that it constantly tests you and exposes weaknesses and problems. The trader that can take these reflections of reality and explore his inner self to learn how to grow from these experiences will be a master trader. Remember, "those that grow in the strongest wind will evolve into the best wood." Your trading and your life are nothing but a mirror of your consistent thoughts and focus. If you see the markets as a mirror of your inner self, the markets can become one of the most incredible tools for help you to improve, learn, and grow. If you blame the markets and don't take responsibility for your performance, your trading will eventually disintegrate and you will throw in the towel just as many thousands of people have over the years. I hope that this week, I have been successful in impressing this upon you.

Coming Next Week

It's hard to believe, but next week is the final week of our 10 Week Trading Course. I've enjoyed sharing my ideas with you and I look foward to tying it all together. **Be prepared--there will be a final exam!**

Best regard,

Mark Boucher

WEEK 10

One of the most time-worn but valid sayings that is applicable to many of life's different competitive arenas is:

Keep it Simple

This conclusion to the preceding 9 weeks of the Course is going to be no different. The markets are extremely complicated and by necessity, analyzing markets and searching for trading opportunities can be complex.

I know that much of what I've said may seem esoteric enough already to some. So this week I'm just going to talking about what comes to my mind as being most essential for you to focus on in order to get the most out of the Course.

To me, the best type of approach is interactive. It keeps people from falling asleep. So I'm going to summarize my main points by giving you a final exam. The big difference is that I'm not trying to judge your retention of the principles I've covered as much as I am just trying to reinforce what's important. Thus, you will see multiple choice or True/False questions followed immediately on the next page by the answer and a short explanation.

Let's get started, shall we?

Question 1

Question 1

What is the real Holy Grail?

   a. TBBLBG
   b. Breakouts from Flag patterns
   c. Runaway Markets
   d. Market Selection
   e. Money Management
   f. There is no Holy Grail

Answer

If you define a Holy Grail as a mechanical trading system which is able to produce huge returns with minimal drawdown for the entire span of your career as a trader, if its signals are followed religiously, I'd say that **IT NEVER HAS, DOES NOT CURRENTLY, AND NEVER WILL EXSIST**. Sorry I have to beat around the bush.

On the other hand, if you asked me what is most important to long-run success, I'd have to say that good Money Management is the Holy Grail. Stanley Kroll said it best:

> **"It is better to have a mediocre system and good money management than an excellent system and poor money management."**

The problem that traders face is that it is difficult psychologically to manage your trading in a way that limits risk because, by nature, that's also going to put a limit your hypothetical profit potential, although it will maximize your actual profits. The very reason that traders get attracted to this profession is that they get goo-goo eyed over the massive profits they can hypothetically garner in a short period of time. How ironic it is then, **that the very people who want to trade probably belong to the segment of population that is least suited for it psychologically.**

The good news is that it is possible to make a lot of money trading, but you have to focus on what successful traders focus on—and that's **money management** and not the promises of the latest trading system in some glossy full-page color ad.

Question 2

Of the following, which is the most key ingredient in long term trading success?

a. **Risk control**
b. Compounded Annual return
c. Annual return
d. The right methodology

Answer

The answer is a), risk control. Of course, risk control goes hand-in-hand with Money Management. When you trade, you are essentially walking a tight rope. While practically all traders realize that they can fall off the tight rope, most picture themselves getting up and walking away, bruised and bleeding, but still alive. The truth is that a fall from the tight rope without a safety net such as a protective stop can kill your ability to reenter the trading game, forever. **The reason is that when you suffer a heavy drawdown in a trading situation, you have substantially less capital to trade with--and your confidence can be ruined as well.** You have to work much harder to return to a break-even point than you would in order to make just a small profit with your original capital. Here is a graphic example: If your account drops 70 percent, you won't get back to break-even until you have made over 230 percent on your remaining money.

Whether you are thinking about becoming a trader or have already spent years doing it, you must consistently spend a large chunk of your time figuring out how not to lose money before you can make any money. If you mix your own experiences with a bit commonsense you'll realize that it is far, far easier to lose money in the markets than it is to make it. **Therefore, isn't it a no-brainer that you must focus defensive strategies first?**

Question 3

True or False:

The best way to maximize returns is to find the right system.

Answer

The correct answer is False. Ha, ha, I'm sure nobody had a problem with this one. I do not want to denigrate the importance of finding good tools because I have spent years identifying them for my own use. However, if you're going to place your emphasis anywhere, after acquiring good money management skills, it should be on market selection. That is, you must identify which markets are moving very fast either up or down and have a high probability of continuing; I call these Runaway Markets. Trading these types of markets, greatly reduces the burden of having to time the markets.

One trader came to office many years ago to evaluate his performance. He had very high profits, although his drawdowns were rather large. About that time another client came in for the same service--could we evaluate his trading and help him improve upon it? The second trader had mediocre profits and large drawdowns.

The first trader (Trader A) spent all of his time on vehicle selection and only traded the strongest Relative Strength markets on the long side and weakest Relative Strength markets on the short side. His system? Just a 21-day moving average (a system which, by the way, loses money in most stocks in the long run). We got Trader A to further improve and refine his selection techniques and improve his money management rules and skills to boost his performance.

The second trader (Trader B) had spent over a decade refining, testing, and playing with complex mechanical systems, which he applied to 100 S & P stocks. Selection wasn't a major component of his system. His system, while complex, did work well over the long run on almost any stock we could test it against. Yet, this trader with such an excellent system had done far worse than Trader A who had a simple system and good vehicle selection.

The moral of the story is this: Focus your energy and effort where it can make the greatest positive impact on your trading results: Market Selection.

Question 4

True or False:

If you find the right mechanical system, it doesn't matter if you understand the underlying causes of market behavior as long as you follow the system's signals religiously.

Answer

The correct answer is False. There are several reasons that you should step away from the crowd searching for easy answers and walk down the path of "seeking to understand." The most important reason is that I have never seen any mechanical system work for a very long period time. You might say, okay Mr. Boucher, I'll just trade the system until I it stops working; in the meantime, I'll still make a fortune doing so. My response is that that's probably the same thing as buying a stock without placing a stop order; you may catch a lucky streak. That lucky streak can last months, or even years. During that time, your confidence in the system will increase to the point where your money management discipline becomes lax. Then--the unthinkable happens and a crash of Biblical proportions hits the market. Will you survive? It's possible, but I have seen too many cases of people who thought they had the Holy Grail and actually made a lot of money over a fairly extended time--**only to be wiped out in the 1987 crash or other high magnitude move.**

The whole picture changes if you have a deep understanding the underlying causes of market behavior. If you use a system of some kind, you will know what circumstances, whether technical, fundamental, economic, or monetary made it work effectively in the past and be able to compare those circumstances with the ever-changing current market environment. You will know what kind of environment it makes sense to apply the system to and conversely, when you should ignore the system's signals.

A good pilot only flies under "autopilot" under the correct circumstances. Think of a mechanical system as an autopilot. It's helpful to an extent, but it doesn't take the place of a thinking participant.

Question 5

Statistically which type of correction pattern has a higher probability of yielding a profitable trade in a stock exhibiting Runaway Characteristics?

   a. Pullback from a new high followed by a TBBLBG
   b. **TBBLBG Breakout from a tight flag formation.**

Answer

In my own trading experience and historical research using data going back to the late 1800s, I found breakouts from flag formations to be more reliable to than pullback methodologies. This runs a little against the grain of the approach advocated by most short-term traders which is to trade pullbacks. In fact many traders try breakout strategies and get frustrated very quickly.

The thing you have to remember, however, is that I'm not telling to simply buy TBBLBG Breakouts from flags, but rather to only do so in a Runaway Market. When you do this, your chances of success are greatly increased.

Question 6

True or False:

It is better to become an expert in few markets and trade those exclusively using proven market timing tools rather than trying to follow many markets in search of those that are outperforming or underperforming the rest of the markets.

Answer

The answer is false. Those who focus on market timing most often teach the approach of focusing on a small static list of volatile markets. My major focus, however, is market selection because after testing, every method I could find, I never found any market timing methodology that I was confident enough in to use as anything more than a confirmation tool. Unless you are joining us for the first time in this course, you already know that my mantra is:

Go where the oil is.

Market selection consists of looking at the whole universe of markets and identifying those exhibiting extremely bullish or bearish behavior and then trade those exclusively in sync with their directional bias. I do this by using relative strength. Once I have narrowed down my top candidates, I look for 5 or more Runaway Characteristics to occur within a 21-day period. I go further down a checklist of criteria looking for Fuel and other properties in order to filter out the very best trading candidates.

By going through this process, I develop a list of trading candidates that is always changing and anything but static.

Question 7

True or False:

Like many older technical tools Relative Strength is so widely publicized and used by rank and file traders that it no longer works effectively.

Answer

False. Research that I did with Stanford Ph.D Tom Johnson covering the early 1900s to the mid-1980s shows that the single most reliable and robust trading tool is relative strength. I believe that remains true today. The fact that many professional hedge fund managers and traders beside myself rely heavily on this tool says something about it's robust staying power.

Question 8

1. The best part of the Liquidity Cycle to be a buyer of stocks occurs when:
    a. The Fed tries to stimulate a weak economy by lowering interest rates. The stock market reacts positively, but GDP, and various out economic indicators remain negative. Experts declare that the economy is still in a recession.
    b. The economy is booming, the stock market is a record levels. The Fed raises interest rates and still, he stock market drives relentlessly higher. The bond market, however, begins to head decisively lower.

Answer

The answer is a). The Liquidity Cycle leads economic statistics. When the Fed increases money supply by lowering interest rates, the first recipients of that money are the stock and bond markets. So what tends to happen is that the stock market will bottom out of bear and into a bull phase in response to Fed action while economic indicators are still strongly indicating that a recession is in full force. That is the most psychologically difficult time to be heavily biased toward the long side, but it is the time that offers the greatest potential profit.

Question 9

True or False:

As long as a stock qualifies as a Runaway Market and has TBBLBG Breakout, the underlying company's performance is irrelevant.

Answer

The answer is False. My own personal trading strategy dictates that a favorable technical indication has to also be accompanied by Fuel in order to qualify as a viable trading candidate. Fuel refers to the underlying business or commonsensical reasons that fuel a stock's rise. I know that there many purely technical traders who don't give a rip about a stock's earnings or business prospects. But if there is anything that is 99.99% reliable it is the fact that any stock's performance and valuation has a high correlation to its underlying company's business performance. Many traders think that this is significant only if you trade on a long-term time horizon. I totally disagree. Every moment in price, no matter how short term, is either going with or against the current. If you look at each trade with tunnel vision and see that all your technical indicators are pointing strongly in one direction, you're more likely to rationalize that Fuel is too insignificant worry about. But consider the cummulative effect of many trades which do not pay heed to the edge or lack thereof that Fuel yields. The more you trade without considering Fuel, the greater the likelihood that you'll run into a stock that makes a sudden explosive move against your position that is based upon some purely business-related factor. And similarly, <u>without fuel on your side the odds of hitting a home-run that just keeps running and running becomes much less.</u>

Question 10

1. What is the minimum number of Runaway Characteristics must you find within 21 days in order for a stock to be considered a Runaway Market

    a. 5
    b. 10
    c. 15
    d. 20

Answer

The answer is a) 5. But being as risk averse as I am, I like to see 10 or more runaway characteristics within a 21-day period in order to be fully satisfied with the upside or downside potential of a given trading candidate.

Question 11

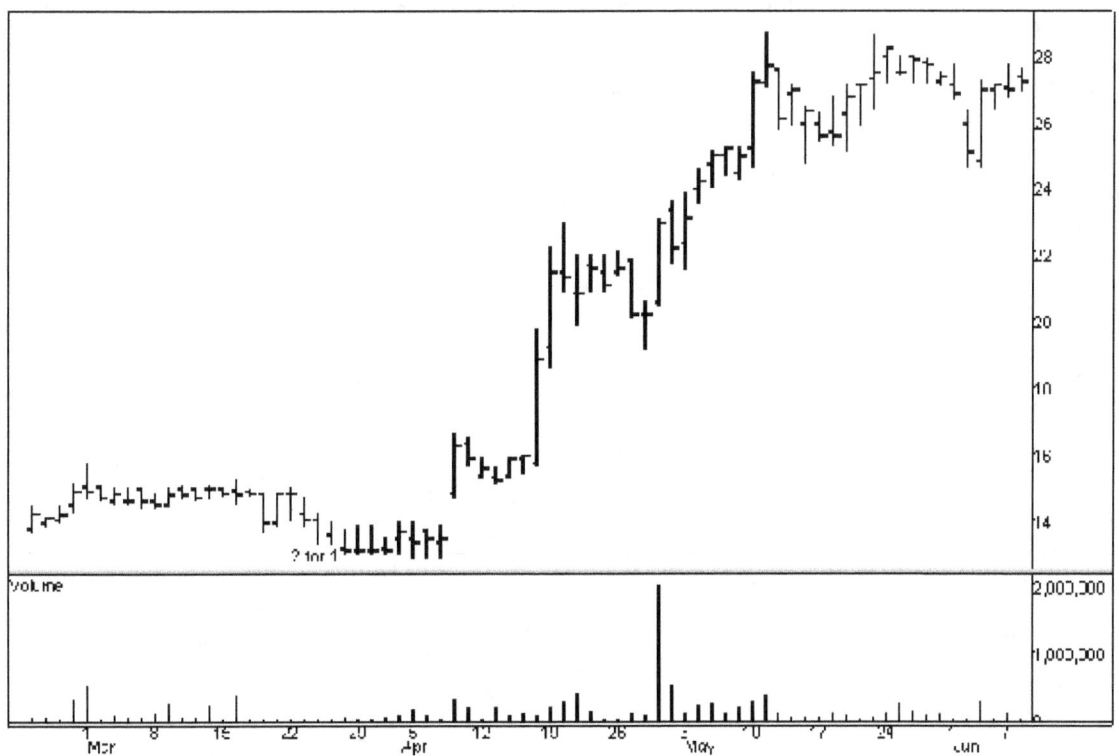

Find at least five Runaway Characteristics in the following chart of FWRD.

When a stock that has more than 5 Runaway Characteristics within 21 days, it may be a Runaway Market.

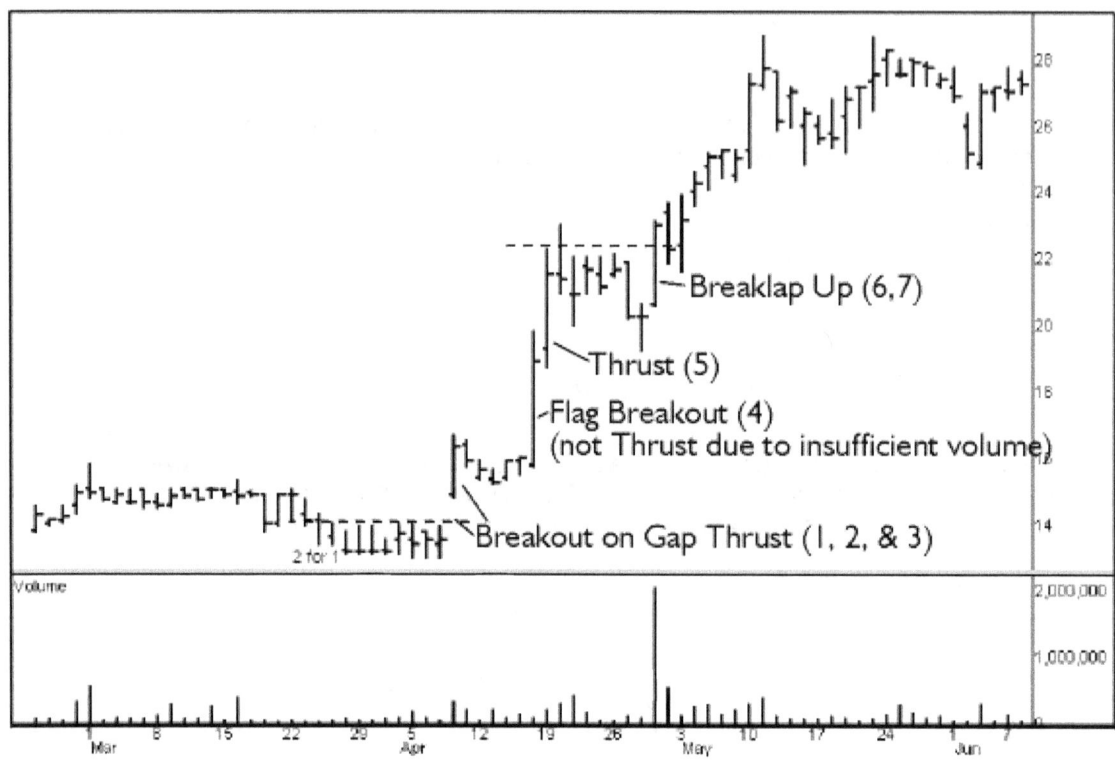

Find at least 5 Runaway Characteristics in this chart

MTW (Manitowoc Company)

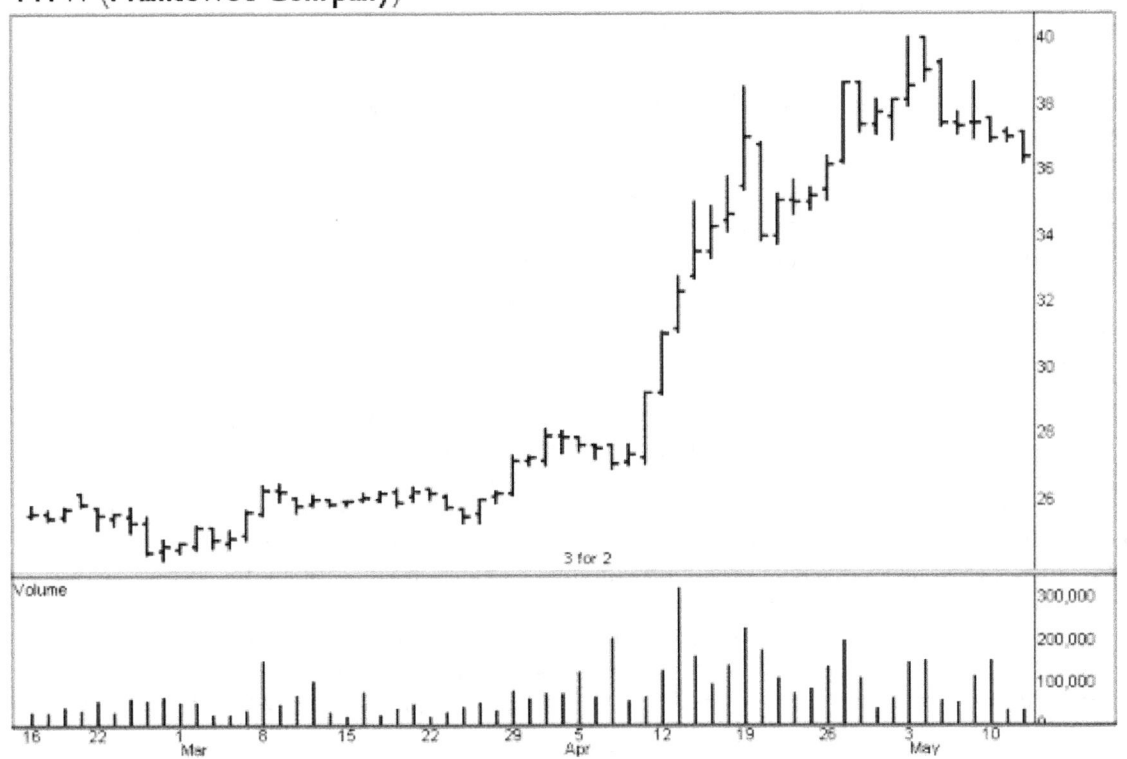

Here are the Runaway Characteristics in this chart. Both MTW and the previous stock shown, FWRD, have been among my recent winning positions. In the past ten weeks, I've given you the tools with which find these opportunities. The rest is up to you.

MTW (Manitowoc Company)

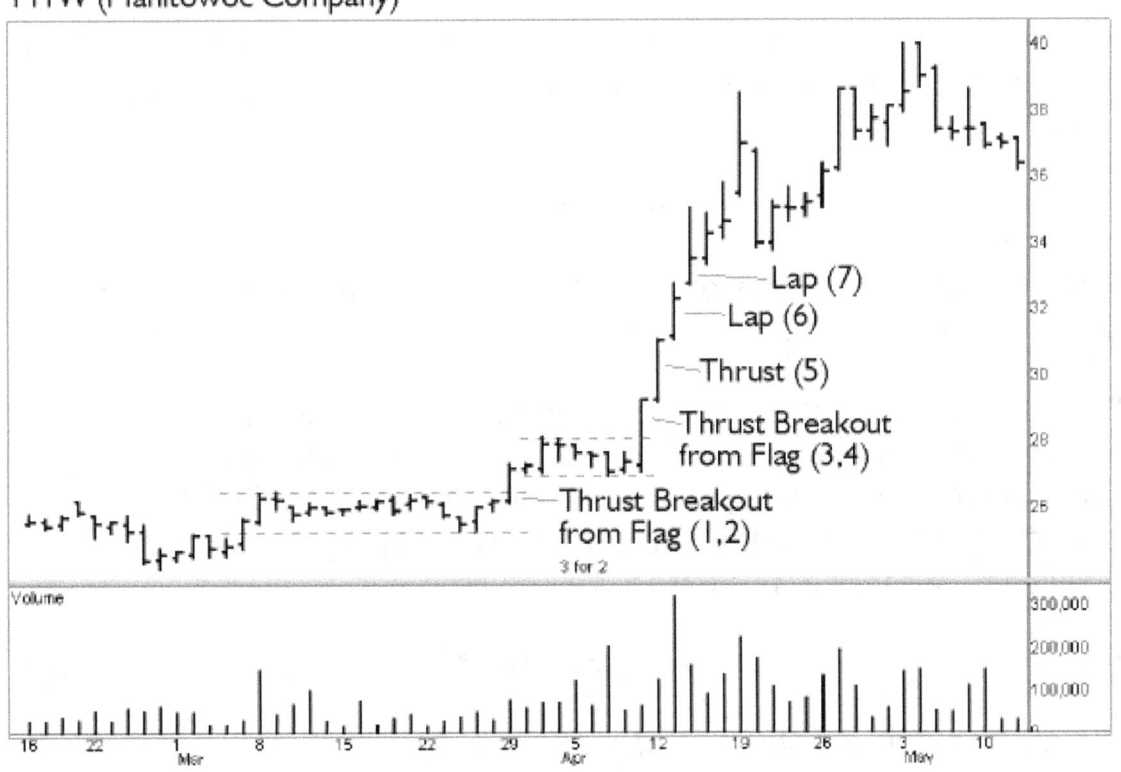

Foundations of Trading Success
Building Character: Some Key Principles and Processes

Success in trading comes from within. You can do a lot of shopping for the right book, seminar, or trading methodology, but all these are external factors that cannot make you a consistently profitable trader because trading tends to bring out the dark side in all of us. That dark side will cause you to shoot yourself in the foot no matter how good your tools are. In order to change your results, you must ultimately change "you." Remember that the results you get out of trading a really a mirror of your thoughts, beliefs, values, and focus.

Last week, I focused on trading psychology and discipline and gave you some techniques for reprogramming your behavior for success. But when we talk about the mental component of trading success, we also have to concern ourselves with the belief system that is at the root of our behavior. If your belief system is incongruent with that of successful traders, then any positive changes you make in your behavior will conflict with your deep-rooted beliefs. It would be like a career criminal who, after several years in prison, exhibits all the characteristics of a good citizen but then, upon release, goes out and commits his old crimes again. Even though his outer behaviors have changed, his inner belief system is locked into its old patterns. I don't want this to happen to you when it comes to the improvements you make in your trading habits.

In the following pages, I will pass along to you the beliefs and motivations of the successful traders that I've tried to emulate over the years. **In essence, to achieve the results of the top traders in the world, you have to think the way they think and believe what they believe.**

Key Concept #1

Concentrate on the process, not the result.

If you strive to trade at your top level every day and consistently improve your understanding, level of expertise, and skills, you will win big. Don't concentrate on winning; concentrate on the <u>process </u>that creates winning.

Key Concept #2

Make money and decisions from your skills, not your ability to see a crystal ball clearly.

Don't try to predict the markets; try to learn how to locate runaway trending instruments, and to exploit low-risk, high-reward opportunities for entering with those trends. Don't waste time predicting the environment; invest time developing the skills and abilities necessary to profit from any environment.

Key Concept #3

It's never the markets - it's always you.

Statistics and society may predict, but you alone determine whether you will succeed or fail. Remember, you alone are in control - take responsibility for your performance and your life. There are always tremendous opportunities in the markets. It's not what happens; it's what you do with what happens that makes the difference between profit and loss.

Key Concept #4

Every event holds the seed of a positive message or meaning.

Eventually every trader will face a larger-than-desired series of losses, or drawdown. How you react and what meaning and lessons you take from that challenge will determine how successful a trader you become. Man's greatest changes, ideas and improvements come from challenging adversity, and a <u>trader's greatest improvements usually come from drawdowns.</u> Seize each day and each loss and mistake as an opportunity to learn, and grow, not as evidence of your inadequacy

Key Concept #5

Seek to embody the true spirit of competition.

The Latin root for competition means "to conspire together." The idea isn't to try to beat your opponent. It's to pit yourself against a competitor so that you both improve faster and perform at a higher level than you would alone. Coach John Wooden said it best, "Never try to be better than someone else, but never cease to try to be the best you can be."

Key Concept #6

Farming versus cramming. Long-term trading success is like farming - there are no shortcuts.

Seek to study new methods and tools for farming your skills and understanding, not tips and predictions

Key Concept #7

Develop a love and respect for trading, free markets, and individual liberty and initiative so that profits are just the gravy.

Successful traders whose personalities are analyzed have in common an understanding of how trading and investing is a key component in the growth of the free enterprise system. Even day traders, who are often viewed as "bottom feeders," play an important role by providing liquidity that enables traders to hedge, companies to raise money, and small investors to hold stock with limited risk. The more you understand about how the financial markets ultimately contribute to progress for humankind by fueling new innovations and technologies, the more you feel that what you are doing is not purely self-serving, but part of a remarkable whole.

Key Concept #8

Become a voracious learner, reader, and knowledge seeker.

The more you learn, the more you earn. It's what you learn after you're sure you know everything that really makes you successful.

Key Concept #9

Don't seek money; seek "real wealth."

Real wealth, as I call it, isn't money or material goods, it is the creative and productive force, the indomitable spirit inside everyone. A person possessing real wealth has the ability to experience life with an unbridled capacity for joy regardless of his financial condition. <u>Real wealth is contained in the knowledge that what you have inside you is the source of your happiness and success, and that what life throws at you or takes away from you will only make you stronger. That feeling of certainty, confidence, abundance, and security is wealth.</u>

You can never get true feelings of security, happiness, abundance, success, or wealth from material goods, for these feelings come from within you. But if you develop the inner feelings and knowledge that security, happiness, abundance, success, and wealth come from within you, you can acquire all the riches you desire. It's not what you get in life, it's what you become that matters. A person who becomes happy, dynamic, enthusiastic, energetic, growing, producing, and contributing will create wealth and grow rich. A person who focuses on negative circumstances can win the lottery and he'll only experience his misery in style.

The person who is able to learn and grow because of the circumstances in his life is wealthy. He may be temporarily broke, but he can never be poor. The person who lets circumstances depress and control him is poor. He may temporarily acquire riches, but he will lose them or never enjoy them fully. The key to real wealth is not the circumstances we find ourselves in, but the meaning we take from them.

A person who gets his feelings of adequacy from the environment will only feel brief illusions of adequacy because we can't control the world we live in any more than we can control the markets we trade in. And who would want to anyway! How exciting and illuminating would trading really be if we knew in advance the high, low, and close, every day. It would be completely dull - virtually dead. Life itself is the process of growing and adapting as an organism to new input and situations, not trying to recreate only the situations we've already experienced.

Seeking money as a result of trying to improve the world by creating something of value, or by assisting others is a very noble pursuit that can lead to feelings of true abundance, happiness, confidence, and self-worth. Seeking money by trying to take advantage of or cheat others won't help produce anything but feelings of inadequacy.

And one doesn't get rich and the money suddenly changes his life. That's backwards. <u>Wealth is a result of successful living, not the source of it. Developing a character and value structure that is consistent with happy, productive living is the process that produces the result of real wealth and abundance.</u>

Key Concept #10

Understand and believe that investing and trading create and add real value to mankind.

Traders and investors are in the business of directing the force of the lifetime accumulation of our unconsumed productivity (savings, capital) to the areas that will most benefit mankind. Investing can entail assuming the risk of wheat price declines from a farmer; eliminating currency risk for a multi-national company; increasing the ease at which a company can acquire the capital to develop new factories, products, and innovations; helping to produce an efficient set of rewards and punishments for successful or unsuccessful management of a company, or simply increasing the liquidity of the structure that allows all of the above transactions to occur. In each case the result is the most efficient process for linking capital to its most productive uses, as indicated by demand, known to man.

Closing Remarks

The past ten weeks have provided as much information about how I approach trading as I could possibly stuff into them. My goal has been to pass along to you a way of thinking, being, and doing which will help you to produce dependable gains with low risk, whether you are a day trader or if you buy and sell stocks or futures on a long-term time frame. While the methods I have used with great success are mere tools and your performance is largely dependent on your own skills as a trader, one of the most important things you can get out of this Course is an awareness of what's really important.

What's really important is:

- **Controlling risk and minimizing drawdowns**
- **Understanding the markets**
- **Market Selection (Go where the oil is!)**
- **Continue learning and growing and educating yourself.**

One of the most important things I've emphasized is continuing education and consistent exploration of yourself and your trading performance. This is absolutely critical to your success and your enjoyment and fulfillment as a trader/investor.

There are many fine educational resources available and many market masters to whom I have been indebted over the years; I have recommended their books and courses quite highly at various points in this course.

One of my **own** great passions is educating other people. As I've mentioned before, the best expression of my gratitude towards the successful traders from whom I've learned my craft is to pass on this knowledge to others. Moreover, the very act of teaching helps me to attain deeper insights and understanding about my trading and myself.

So in answer to the many inquires I've gotten via email and phone calls about the books, courses, and investor services that this 10-Week Course on TRADEHARD.COM has been based on, I want to briefly explain what I have available.

Much of this 10-Week Course came from sections and parts of my book, "The Hedge Fund Edge." If what I've said in this course about money management, stock selection, the Liquidity

Cycle, relative strength, breakout patterns, and Runaway Markets was of use to you, then I'm sure you would benefit by spending a weekend or two with this book. In it, I explore these topics and others in far greater depth as well as discuss many models and methods that I wasn't able to include in the 10-Week Course. TRADEHARD.COM subscribers and those who've registered for this course will receive a 10% discount on the Hedge Fund Edge.

Another good chunk of this 10-Week Course was based on my 400 page, 20-hour audiocassette trading course called The Science of Trading. Its emphasis is on practical application and there are many examples and step-by-step instructions on how to apply methods I've found beneficial over the years. As a TRADEHARD MEMBER or subscriber to this course, you will receive a $50 discount on this item.

For more information on either the Hedge Fund Edge or the Science of Trading click here.

Speaking of courses, don't forget to take Kevin Haggerty's new 5-Week Day-Trading course. I certainly am. Learning how many traders with different approaches achieve substantial and consistent profits is critical if you want to understand how to do it yourself—even if their particular style doesn't necessarily match your own. For many of you very short-term traders, Kevin's techniques will be particularly enlightening.

Finally, I encourage all of you to remember that repetition is the mother of skill. This course is here for you to use it continuously. I would suggest that you review your notes on this course again and again every six months or so until you have integrated it fully into your own trading and performance. So many times I notice traders who have read great books or taken great courses get very excited with every intention of following through. Yet months later, their trading has changed very little and they have failed to integrate what they learned into their actual performance as traders. Certainly that's happened to all of us on some scale.

That's why it is critical for you to take action now. Remember that:

Knowledge is only potential power.
Knowledge + action based on that knowledge is power.

Please take a half hour or more to start your Mental Trading Account now if you haven't already done so—and I suggest you make a concrete plan of action for how you will actually integrate what you've learned into your actual trading process. What have you learned? How can you change your trading process to integrate what you've learned into action consistently? Write this down and then give yourself mental trading account points for taking these actions specifically and consistently.

I look forward to hearing from you about your continued growth and improved trading performance via the techniques I've outlined in this course. I only wish that such a course existed when I first started trading! Don't forget that I will be here at TRADEHARD.COM to help you improve, grow, and build capital through trading. Please use these resources. I would also appreciate your feedback on this course. I've tried to make it as concise and yet informative as I could given the format—but I need to know how to improve it and the services we provide you as traders at TRADEHARD.COM.

Let me finish by saying how much respect and appreciation I have for each and every one of you who have gone through the effort to take this course. I hope and trust that it will significantly enhance your trading and your life.

Yours for building profits and joy in life,